The Book of Crochet

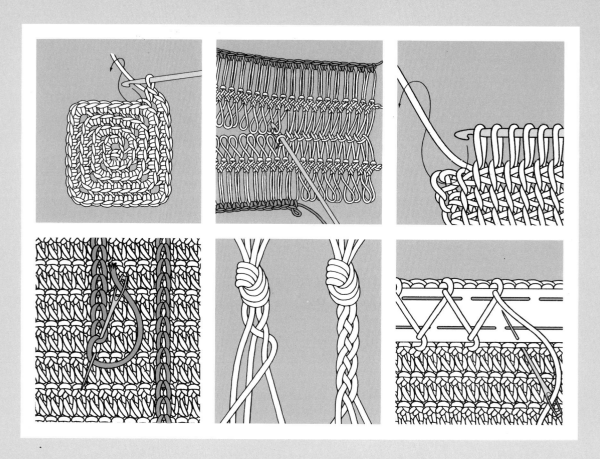

Marinella Nava

The Book of
Crochet

**From Beginner to Expert:
The Best Crochet Book for You**

*Drawings by Paola Francinetti and Roberto Maresca
Photographs by Roberto Circià and Giorgio Perego*

21 color photographs
Over 300 two-color photographs and illustrations

St Martin's Press
New York

Also by Marinella Nava
The Book of Knitting

The Book of Crochet

Copyright © 1984 Arnoldo Mondadori
Editore S.p.A., Milan
English translation copyright © 1985 Arnoldo
Mondadori Editore S.p.A., Milan

First published in Italy in 1984 by Arnoldo Mondadori
Editore S.p.A.

English translation by Sylvia Mulcahy

Library of Congress Cataloging in Publication Data

Nava, Marinella.
   The Book of Crochet.
   1. Crocheting. I. Title.
TT820.N387   1985   746.43′4   85-10686
ISBN 0-312-08832-9 (pbk.)

First U.S. Edition
Printed in Spain by Artes Graficas Toledo S.A.
D. L. TO:173-1986

10 9 8 7 6 5 4 3 2

Contents

The author wishes to thank Maria Luisa Artesani, Bruna Cortese and Aurelia Merli Savorani for their assistance.

Preface

The appeal of crochet is many-faceted. It is a craft which has been handed down from generation to generation for several thousand years, the earliest examples of crochet work having been found in ancient Egypt. It is almost certainly true that it developed in Europe as a humbler offshoot of the more intricate techniques of lace-making. Needlepoint and bobbin lace were used to adorn the altars of churches and the clothes of the aristocracy, but when these more elaborate crafts fell into decline as a result of historical and social events, there was a reversal of roles which allowed crochet to flourish at the expense of lace. Lace is now a collector's item and survives only in the limited, rapidly disappearing context of traditional regional handicrafts.

In contrast, because crochet is simpler and more versatile, it has kept pace with changing tastes and fashions. The exclusiveness of handmade lace now also applies to a great deal of crochet work.

Like knitting and embroidery, crochet enjoys widespread popularity and is perhaps the second-most common needlecraft after knitting. This is partly due to the fact that it is easy to learn to crochet. It is also a useful and relaxing pastime which requires no cumbersome equipment and allows you to make almost any type of garment and many useful and decorative items. With an imaginative approach on the part of the crocheter, most effective results can be achieved.

An important difference between crochet and knitting is that crochet remains an essentially handmade, exquisitely personal craft. There is no equivalent of the knitting machine which can produce perfectly even results with great speed. It is still the skill, patience, experience and taste of the crocheter that determine the final result.

The aim of this book is to enable the reader to undertake any piece of work from the simplest to the most complex. It has been structured with both the beginner and the more experienced crocheter in mind: it gives clear, step-by-step explanations of all the basic stitches for the benefit of the former and will be an invaluable reference book for the latter.

The book has been divided into four sections. The first part opens with a discussion of the accessories and yarns available for crochet and gives useful guidance on how to adapt an existing pattern or make up your own designs. This emphasis on encouraging readers to experiment with different yarns and effects and to use existing patterns as a springboard for their own ideas is a theme which runs throughout the book. There follows a detailed description of how to start and finish a piece of crochet and of how to work the basic stitches. In addition, less well-known types of crochet such as filet and Afghan crochet are discussed.

The second section illustrates how the basic stitches can be varied and combined to good effect. It includes patterns for fancy stitches, medallions, edgings, insertions and crochet lace edgings.

The third section consists of patterns for garments and household items using stitches explained earlier in the book. A novel feature of this section is the extensive use of charts to complement the written instructions for many items worked in filet and openwork crochet.

The fourth part gives useful information on making-up a crocheted garment and on the finishing touches which give a professional appearance to your work. There are also helpful tips on washing, ironing and caring for all types of crochet.

Finally, there is a glossary of the technical terms used in all crochet publications and throughout this book.

Introduction to crochet: hooks, yarns and basic stitches

Equipment

The main items of equipment used in crochet are illustrated in color on page 17. A key is given below.

1. yarn-winder
2. double-headed Afghan crochet hook
3. tapestry needles
4. Afghan crochet hooks
5. hairpin crochet loom
6. ordinary crochet hooks
7. tape-measure
8. fine hooks for crochet lace
9. bobbin-winder

No complicated equipment is necessary for crocheting; the only indispensable thing is the crochet hook itself, but there are various accessories that are especially useful in the preparatory and finishing stages of the work.

● *Crochet hook.* The hook at one end of the shaft picks up and guides the yarn. Crochet hooks are usually 13–20 cm (5–8 ins) long and may be made of stainless steel, coated aluminum, plastic, wood or even bone. Their size is given as a number or letter which corresponds to the diameter. In the case of very fine hooks used for lace the higher the number, the finer the hook. Most hooks are flattened in the middle of the shaft to give a better grip. The choice of hook is important since the size must be suitable for the thickness of the yarn being used and give the tension required.

● *Afghan crochet hook.* This has a hook at one end and a knob at the other end to prevent the stitches from slipping off and is 30–40 cm (12–16 ins) long. The length used is determined by the maximum number of stitches that will be on the hook at any one time. The shaft is of uniform diameter since any narrowing or widening would distort the stitches. Sizes are based on diameter and Afghan hooks are made of various materials.

● *Double-headed Afghan crochet hook.* This is a special type of crochet hook, with a hook at each end enabling several different threads to be worked in the course of a row.

● *Hairpin crochet loom.* This is used in conjunction with an ordinary crochet hook and consists of a U-shaped prong rather like a hairpin. The distance between the prongs of the loom determines the size of the loops formed by the stitches. The stitch that anchors each loop is usually made in the centre of the loom, but if loops of different lengths are required, a three-pronged "hairpin" can be used. The distance between the prongs of some looms can be adjusted. The size of the crochet hook used to make the stitches must correspond to the thickness of the thread, whereas the hairpin only affects the loop size. It should be fairly thick so that it is rigid, and may be of stainless steel, wood or plastic.

● *Yarn-winder.* This is a very useful accessory if you buy your yarn in skeins. It is generally made of wood and has four rotating arms. Unknot the skein and place it over the arms. Open these out so that they hold the skein and tighten the screw at the top of the central shaft. The yarn can then be wound off into a ball.

● *Bobbin-winder.* An accessory which is used mainly for winding large quantities of yarn, such as when machine-knitting. However, it can be very useful and is not expensive to buy. It consists of a bracket which is screwed on to a table-edge; a handle turns a shaft mounted vertically on the bracket and thus winds a bobbin placed on the shaft.

● *Tape measure.* Those made of coated ribbon should be re-coiled after use to prevent fraying or breaking. Remember that crochet must be placed on a flat surface to be measured.

● *Needle.* This is needed to sew the crocheted pieces of a garment together. Medallions may also be sewn together rather than joined by crochet. The needle should have a large enough eye to hold the yarn and a rounded point to avoid splitting the yarn.

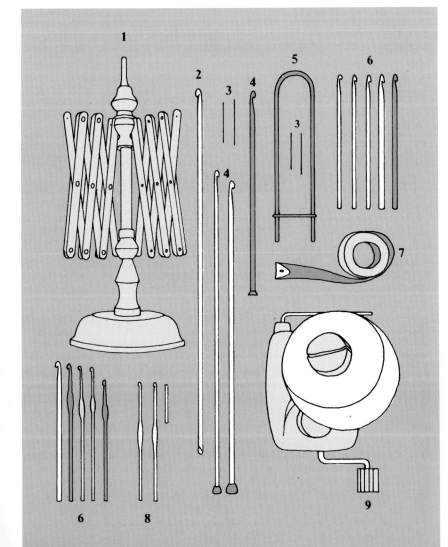

Yarns

Many types of yarns can be used for crocheting, although cotton tends to be used more than any other. An understanding of their different properties will allow you to use them to the best advantage and choose the most appropriate yarn for whatever you are making, whether it is a dress for yourself, a child's toy or a set of table mats.

This section aims to give a brief description of the main types of yarn, which will be helpful if you are new to crocheting or if you want to experiment with the wide range of commercially available yarns. Basically, yarns consist of textile fibers which have been processed for weaving or, more specifically, for knitting or crocheting.

The textile fibers from which crochet yarns are made can be divided into two groups: natural fibers and man-made fibers – that is to say, fibers produced artificially.

There are three main types of natural fibers: animal fibers, such as wool and silk, obtained from hair or substances of animal origin; vegetable fibers, which include cotton, linen, hemp, jute, raffia; mineral fibers, such as amianthus.

Man-made fibers include both organic and inorganic artificial and synthetic fibers – those produced from natural and synthetic polymers: nylon, terylene, acrylic, and metallic and fiberglass yarns.

Of course, yarns suitable for crochet cannot be produced from all of these fibers, notably amianthus. Nevertheless, there is a wider choice of yarns available than one might imagine.

Before studying the individual types of yarn, a little information about the commercial characteristics of yarns in general may be useful.

Yarns sold in balls or skeins are classified according to various characteristics: the type and quality of the fiber, the weight of the yarn, the extent to which it is twisted, its elasticity, ply and brand name. The main categories are:

- *Simple yarns*, consisting of a single strand.

- *Twisted yarns*, consisting of several strands.

Twisted yarns have a wide variety of trade names. One of the commonest descriptions indicates the number of strands, e.g. 2-ply, 4-ply, in conjunction with the names "crêpe", "sport yarn", etc.

Usually, the greater the number of ply, the thicker and heavier the yarn, but softness, strength, elasticity and bulk will depend on the thickness and nature of the basic thread.

Most twisted yarns are of one color and of uniform texture but there are now many fancy yarns on the market which are textured, shaded or flecked. The choice is endless but we will now go on to discuss the characteristics of some of the types of yarn most widely used for crochet work.

Vegetable fibers

Cotton. Cotton is the most widely used yarn for crocheting. This may be because the craft developed in imitation of the delicate effects of bobbin and needlepoint lace and nothing was more suited to this than the fine, strong yarns spun from cotton.

Cotton is a textile plant belonging to the Malvaceae family. Its precise place of origin is unknown as it has been grown throughout the world – in Asia, Africa and the Americas – since time immemorial. It is still cultivated today in every country which has a tropical or subtropical climate. The textile fiber is obtained from the fruit of the cotton plant – a green, oval pod. The seed produces very fine filaments – the cotton fibers – which continue to grow until the plant is fully mature.

Cotton is classified commercially on the basis of two main criteria: the type and country of origin of the cotton, or the physical characteristics of the fibers which determine their spinning qualities, i.e. length, fineness and strength.

The description "sea island cotton" means that the raw material, grown in the West Indies, consists of excellent, long fibers, while "maco" cotton comes from Egypt. These are the two best quality cottons. They are followed by Peruvian cotton, upland cotton from the southeastern United States, Indian cotton and the Asiatic, Australian and European varieties.

These names tend not to be given on manufacturers' labels, with the exception of maco cotton and sea island cotton.

The physical characteristics of cotton are strength and absorbency. It burns with a bright flame and may be white, yellow or reddish in color. The fibers vary in length from 10–50 mm ($\frac{3}{8}$–2 ins) and are sometimes classified on this basis: cotton with fibers of over 28 mm ($1\frac{1}{8}$ ins) is known as long-staple, with fibers from 18 to 28 mm ($\frac{3}{4}$–$1\frac{1}{8}$ ins) as medium-staple, and fibers under 18 mm ($\frac{3}{4}$ in) as short-staple. The thickness of the fiber varies from 15 to 30 microns. Other characteristics of cotton are its

The cotton plant. The textile fiber is obtained from the fruit, a green oval capsule.

luster, softness and elasticity. The softness and luster are improved by submitting the cotton to a process known as mercerization which consists of washing the fibers in a concentrated solution of caustic soda. Cotton treated in this way is known as "mercerized".

The international commodities market classifies the quality of the raw material with the terms "fine", "good", "fair", "middling", "inferior" and "ordinary". But yarn manufacturers use descriptions based on the appearance of the finished product, hence crochet cottons are described as "mercer-crochet", "perlé", "natural" and "coarse natural".

The thickness of the yarn is the most important factor affecting a finished piece of crochet work. A number indicates the diameter of the yarn: the higher the number the finer the thread; the lower the number, the thicker the thread. Hence crochet cottons no. 60 (very fine), 40 (fine) and 20 (fairly fine) are used mainly for delicate lace crochet such as edgings, table centers, etc. Crochet cottons no. 8 and no. 5 are of medium thickness and are mainly used for lightweight garments, swimsuits, table mats, etc. The "natural" and "coarse natural" cottons – also referred to as "dishcloth cotton" – are used to make thicker, hard-wearing items and clothes.

Linen. Linen originated in Asia and has been used as a textile fiber since the beginning of ancient Egyptian civilization.

It is obtained from flax, a herbaceous plant belonging to the Tiliaceae family which grows well in a cool, temperate climate. The raw textile fibers are extracted from the stem and are rough and coarse.

The best linens are produced by countries with a damp continental climate, notably those of Northern Europe, and country of origin is one of the main criteria in commercial classifications of linen. Russia produces excellent linen from Riga, Archangel and Leningrad; Belgian linen, especially that from Flanders, is regarded as the best in the world. Linen is also produced in Ireland, Bohemia, Holland, France and America.

Some of the physical characteristics of linen yarn are that it is a good conductor of heat, absorbent and very strong; it burns with a bright flame like cotton. Acid substances will eat into it but it can withstand fairly weak alkaline solutions. Its natural colour may be white, yellow, grey or greenish.

Hemp. Hemp was known and used as a textile fiber even earlier than cotton. It is obtained from the stem of an annual, *Cannabis sativa*, a member of the Cannabaceae family. It originated in Asia and the Far East and is now grown in regions which have a cool, temperate climate.

The hemp plant can grow quite tall and filaments 1.5–4 m (5–13 ft) long may be obtained from it. The fibers are very strong and have a distinctive, acrid, penetrating smell. Hemp burns easily, is eaten away by acid substances and is bleached by alkaline solutions.

Its natural color may be silvery-grey, greenish or yellowish. It can be put through a process of cottonization to produce a yarn that resembles a low-grade cotton.

There are numerous different commercial classifications of hemp. The terms common hemp, Chinese hemp and Italian hemp are commonly used. The latter is considered the best quality hemp.

Jute. Jute is obtained from a plant of the genus *Corchorus*, a member of the Tiliaceae family. It is grown chiefly in India, Indonesia and Burma. The textile fiber is obtained from the bark covering the stem of the plant.

Jute is very absorbent and may be white, yellowish or brown in color. The fibers are coarse and strong, producing a rough, stiff and very hard-wearing yarn.

Jute can be used for crochet either by itself or mixed with other types of yarn to make such items as bags, belts, hats and floor coverings.

Raffia. Raffia is obtained from the leaves of an African palm, *Raphia pedunculata*. It is shiny, fairly stiff, light and quite strong. It is a low-grade fiber suitable for bags, floor coverings, table mats, coasters, etc.

Animal fibers

Wool. Wool is the textile fiber obtained from the fleece of sheep, but the term is also applied to the yarn spun from the coat of various types of goat, including the Kashmir goat and the Angora goat. The hair of the camel, dromedary and other members of the Camelidae family such as the vicuña, llama, alpaca and guanaco is spun into yarns which are usually regarded as luxury wools.

There are eleven generally recognized breeds of sheep which are divided into three groups: merinos, domestic breeds and cross-breeds. The best quality sheep's wool comes from merino sheep.

The fleece of a merino sheep is curly, very soft and yellowish in color. The short, wavy fibers are very fine and are used to make good quality combed wools.

British domestic breeds are particularly well-known for the quality of their wool. Several of them have been crossed with merino sheep to produce the very highly regarded Dorset, Cheviot, Lincoln and Leicester, to mention only a few.

Crossbred sheep may be the result of crossing merinos with domestic sheep or of crossing different domestic breeds. The only ones whose wool is of commercial importance are crosses between British breeds or British breeds crossed with merinos.

Luxury wools are expensive and tend therefore to be available commercially mixed, in varying proportions, with sheep's wool. Brief descriptions of the most common luxury wools are given below.

● *Lambswool*. This is the wool shorn from a lamb less than one year old. When spun it is particularly soft and warm.

● *Cashmere*. This wool is obtained from the fleece of the goat that lives in Kashmir, a region of the Himalayas between India, China and Pakistan. The fibers are light, very soft and lustrous, and white or brown. Cashmere is delightfully warm to wear and is very expensive.

● *Mohair*. The wool obtained from the fleece of the Angora goat, which is raised mainly in Turkey and the United States. The hair is silvery, very lustrous, soft and fine. The fibers are long and almost straight.

● *Camel hair*. Exceptionally warm and very expensive, this wool is obtained from the undercoat of the Asian camel.

● *Alpaca*. This wool comes from the undercoat of the alpaca, a domestic member of the camel family, rather like a llama, found in Bolivia and Peru.

● *Llama*. The wool obtained from the undercoat of the llama, a member of the camel family that lives wild in Peru. The fibers are rather coarse and reddish white in color.

● *Vicuña*. The coat of the vicuña, the smallest of the South American members of the camel family, has lustrous, very fine, silky fibres which are reddish yellow or white. Vicuña is probably the most expensive wool in the world.

● *Angora*. Genuine angora comes from the fleece of the Angora rabbit. The fibres are very fine, soft and silky. It is very expensive but goes twice as far as ordinary wool.

Small amounts of wool from the yak, reindeer, chinchilla, mink and beaver are mixed with more common wools to produce very expensive, rare yarns.

The diameter of wool fibers varies from 15 to more than 80 microns and their length ranges from 3 to 40 cm ($1\frac{1}{4}$–16 ins). Wool is not a strong fiber but as a fabric it wears very well. It is stretchy, soft and absorbent. The color of raw wool varies from a yellowish white to grey or almost black. Wool is a poor conductor of heat and electricity. An important characteristic of wool is the tendency of its fibers to become matted or felted as a result of heat and pressure. Woolen fibers do not burn easily and leave a residue of blackish crumbly lumps. Wool withstands acid substances but is destroyed by alkaline reagents.

The quality of wool depends on both the breed of sheep and the part of the animal's body from which the wool is taken. Thus the wool from the back of an animal is of better quality than the fibers from the abdomen and legs because these are shorter and do not wear well.

The commercial descriptions "combed wool", "carded wool", "recycled wool" refer to these factors, but these terms do not appear on the labels of balls or skeins sold in the shop. The important distinctions to note when buying wool are the following:

● *pure virgin wool*: Indicated by the international Woolmark. This consists of 100% new wool.

● *pure wool*: This is 100% wool but recycled, i.e. obtained from unravelled woollen fabrics.

● *% virgin wool or wool*: The percentage of new or recycled wool that is mixed with other textile fibers.

The thickness or weight of yarn is often indicated only by the brand names of individual manufacturers. The terms 2-, 3-, or 4-ply strictly refer to the number of strands, but the also often give an indication of weight. The following names are commonly used:

- *Botany*: Fine wool usually used for machine knitting.

- *Fingering and worsted*: 2-, 3- or 4-ply classic wool which is soft and goes a long way. Suitable for light garments.

- *Baby-wool*: 3- or 4-ply wool which is strong and shrink-resistant although very soft. Suitable for baby clothes and other delicate garments.

- *Crêpe*: A high twist or braided yarn of various thicknesses which goes very far.

- *Sport yarn*: 4–8-ply wool which is twice as thick as worsted. It is popular because it knits up quickly and is hard-wearing; it is suitable for heavier crocheted garments.

- *Shetland*: Generally 2- and 3-ply wool, which is highly twisted and slightly fluffy. It comes from sheep bred in the Shetland Islands and is especially suitable for sweaters and other lightweight crocheted garments.

- *Bouclé*: A soft, slightly spongy wool with a fine, looped or very curly strand; when worked, it gives a lambskin effect.

- *Icelandic*: A very soft, loosely twisted thick wool.

- *Flecked or multicolored*: A yarn with different colored or random-dyed strands, which are sometimes of different textures.

- *Lurex*: Yarn spun with a fine silver, gold or copper metallic thread.

- *Natural wool*: Undyed yarn in natural colors; it tends to be thick and rough.

The international symbol for pure virgin wool; it denotes 100 per cent new wool.

Silk. Undoubtedly the aristocrat of yarns, for many centuries silk was only produced in China and very strict laws forbade the exportation of silkworms' eggs. In 550, however, two monks returning from Constantinople brought some eggs to Europe and the cultivation of the silkworm rapidly spread throughout Europe.

Silk is a very fine natural fiber, strong yet elastic, produced by a small caterpillar, *Bombyx mori*, belonging to the order of Lepidoptera. The silkworm transforms in-gested mulberry leaves into a thick liquid called fibroin which is secreted through two very narrow ducts extending from the silkworm's lower jaw. The two fine threads of fibroin are covered in a gummy substance called sericin. This viscous secretion solidifies on contact with the air, producing a silk filament, with which the silkworm builds a cocoon.

Because of the thin layer of sericin covering the two strands of fibroin, the raw silk is stiff and has almost no sheen. After being washed in hot water, part of the sericin is removed and the fibers soften and have more luster. The silk is now known as "semi-degummed". By repeated washing in hot water all the sericin is removed and the fibres become soft and lustrous.

The main physical characteristics of silk are the following: remarkable strength, exceptional fineness, good elasticity. Silk is a poor conductor of heat and electricity. It reacts to fire in the same way as wool: it does not burn easily and gives off an unpleasant smell.

Commercial classification of the various types of silk takes several factors into account: the type of silkworm, the country of origin of the raw silk, where the silk has been spun, the regularity of the thread and its physical characteristics.

A considerable amount of silk is now produced in European countries where the mulberry tree flourishes, but the very high costs of production keep the price of the fabric very high. Because of this, silk is often mixed with other fibres, such as wool.

Artificial and synthetic fibers

Artificial fibers include cellulose fibers and artificial protein fibers.

Cellulose fibers include various types of "rayon" or "artificial silk". They are classified according to the method of production used, into viscose rayon, cuprammonium rayon, or acetate.

The thread obtained by the first two methods is similar to silk and in the case of acetate, to cotton. It is soft, stretchy, hard-wearing and easy to dye.

The artificial protein fibers are known as azlons and are made from animal or natural substances such as groundnut and seed proteins. The most important is lanital which is obtained from casein, a protein present in milk.

The fiber that is produced is soft, nearly as warm as wool, shrink-resistant and moth-

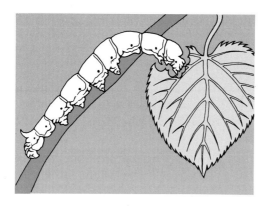

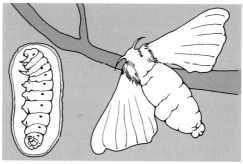

proof, but it pulls out of shape easily and is subject to stretching and creasing.

Synthetic fibers are the product of the chemical synthesis of two or more different elements, derived mainly from petro-chemicals. A great variety of synthetic fibers exists, suitable for all kinds of fabrics, and new ones are being created every day to meet new needs. The main groups, based on chemical composition, are listed below:

● *polyamide fibers*: obtained by the poly-condensation of petroleum derivatives, they include nylon, caprolactam and similar fibers.

● *polyester fibers*: also obtained by means of the condensation of components based on an ester (alcohol plus an acid). They include terylene and trevira and are mainly mixed with cotton or wool.

● *acrylic fibers*: very similar to polyamides. They include leacryl, orlon and dralon.

● *polypropylene fibers*: these include meraklon and other very strong fibers, which provide excellent insulation when worn next to the skin since they repel body moisture.

● *polyethylene fibers*: based on ethylene, they produce a very soft yarn which does not irritate the skin.

Opposite page: the main items of equipment used in crochet. A key is given on page 11.

1

2

3

4

5

6

7

8

9

10

11

12

13

18

Before starting

Before we enter into a detailed description of how to crochet, it is worth giving some consideration to the choice of yarn and crochet hook and to how this affects the finished result. Beginners will normally choose to follow a printed pattern where the amount and type of yarn will be given and the relationship between the yarn, the size of crochet hook and the size of garment will already be worked out. However if you already know how to crochet, you may wish to be more enterprising and start designing your own garments or adapt an existing pattern, in which case the following guidelines will be particularly useful.

Opposite page: some of the types of yarn most commonly used in crochet:

1. hemp
2. metallic thread
3. silk
4. wool and mohair mixture
5. camel-hair
6. raffia
7. Shetland wool
8. no. 5 crochet cotton
9. no. 8 crochet cotton
10. mohair
11. a skein of cotton yarn
12. synthetic ribbon
13. a skein of sport yarn

Choosing and buying the yarn

As the section on textile fibers makes clear, many different yarns may be used for crochet: cotton is the most commonly used, followed by wool and synthetic mixtures. Because the yarn manufacturers have their own brands and also make many novelty yarns, the range of yarns available in the shops is enormous and can be daunting for those without experience.

If you are working from a pattern which does not quote a brand name when giving the quantities, it is important to check that the yarn you buy is of the correct weight, so that the size of the finished garment and the amount of yarn required are not affected. The yarn you choose should also be of a texture which will give the desired effect.

If you are working without a pattern and are designing your own garment, the choice of yarn requires careful consideration. It must be in keeping with the type of garment you wish to make and the amount of wear it will be subjected to: choose a strong, hard-wearing yarn for items which will require frequent washing, but if you are making a garment that will be worn next to the skin, choose a soft yarn which will not irritate.

The yarn should also complement the stitch you intend to work the garment in. For example textured yarns are usually less suitable than smooth ones for fancy stitches. Also, complicated or relief patterns often show up to best effect when worked in lighter colors.

The best way to assess the most suitable type of yarn for your design is to experiment with odds and ends, working several small samples.

The amount of yarn you will need depends on several factors: the type of yarn, its thickness, the size of crochet hook you decide to use, the tension of your work and your chosen stitch. Some yarns go much further than others and there can be noticeable differences between similar yarns produced by different manufacturers. In general, fine yarns go further than thick ones, but do not underestimate the fact that some stitches take much more yarn than others. It is important to bear this in mind if you intend to modify a pattern by working it in a different stitch.

In order to calculate the amount of yarn you need accurately, you should work a sample square. This will be dealt with more fully on page 21.

The information printed on the label of some types of yarn gives a useful indication of the standard gauge and also gives the recommended sizes of crochet hook.

A final point to note when buying several

balls or skeins of the same shade is that it is important to check that they all have the same dye-lot number, since the tone of a particular shade can vary from one dye-lot to another. Although the difference may be almost imperceptible if you compare two balls, it often produces a much more obvious mark if they are worked consecutively in the same piece of crochet.

How to wind wool from a skein

Crochet cotton is usually sold in balls, but if you wish to make something from wool bought in skeins, the yarn must be wound into balls before you can begin to crochet.

The simplest and quickest method is to use two specially designed accessories: a skein-winder and a bobbin-winder. Place the skein on the skein-winder, extending the arms so that it is held taut but is not tightly stretched. Cut or undo the thread that keeps the skein together and slip one end of the wool into the groove on top of the bobbin-winder which

Right: a bobbin-winder clamped to a table being used in conjunction with a yarn-winder to wind a skein into a ball.

Far right: two ways of winding a ball of yarn by hand. Above, the working end is on the outside; below, the working end comes from the center of the ball. Winding the yarn over the tips of the fingers, as shown, insures that the yarn is not wound too tightly.

should be clamped to the edge of a table. By turning the handle of the bobbin-winder, the yarn will wind around the spool as the skein-winder rotates. This is the ideal way to wind balls of yarn since they will all be the same size, neither too tightly nor too loosely wound, with the working thread ready to use from the inside.

If, however, you do not have these two accessories, wool can be wound in the following way. Either ask someone to hold the skein over their outstretched hands or, if no one is available, place two chairs back to back, slip the skein over and move the chairs apart until the skein is taut.

It is easier to wind the yarn if you keep the skein towards the top of the chair backs. The balls must be wound by hand if you do not have a skein-winder, since a bobbin-winder can only be used in conjunction with a skein-winder.

Balls can be wound in two different ways, depending on whether you prefer to have the working end on the outside of the ball or coming from the inside.

To achieve the former, wind the yarn around three fingers; after several turns, remove your fingers and continue winding loosely, changing direction frequently.

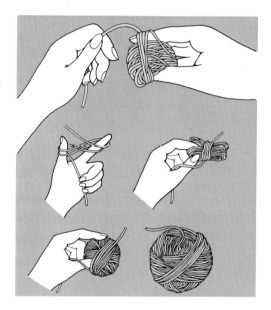

To make a ball that unwinds from the center, hold the working end in the palm of your hand and wind the yarn around the thumb and index finger in a figure-8. After a few turns, remove your fingers and wind the yarn around these threads, still keeping the working end in your palm. Continue in the same way, changing direction frequently and insuring that the yarn is not stretched tight.

Choosing a crochet hook

The size of crochet hook you use must allow you to work the stitches comfortably in your chosen yarn. It must also insure that the finished result resembles the pattern you are following in size and texture.

The general rule, of course, is that fine yarns are worked with fine hooks and vice versa, just as one would work a close fabric with small, delicate decorative motifs with a fine hook. The principal exception to this rule is when working with a stiff yarn such as string: one would use a much thicker hook than when using a softer yarn of the same thickness but with more "give," such as wool or cotton.

Working a gauge sample

The size of crochet hook, the thickness of the yarn and the type of stitch all affect the size of the finished article. However, the way in which each crocheter works varies, particularly in terms of how tightly the yarn is held as the stitches are worked; this is known as a crocheter's tension. The effect of these four factors on the size of an article can clearly be seen by working gauge samples, or squares with the same number of rows and stitches, such as those illustrated on this page.

The relationship between the yarn, crochet

The four main factors that determine the size of a crocheted sample.

Right, from top to bottom: the thickness of the yarn being used; the size of the crochet hook; the type of stitch. Far right, the difference in two people's tension due to how tightly the thread is held.

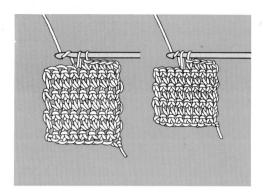

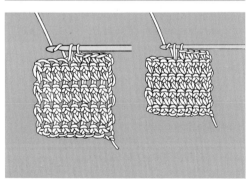

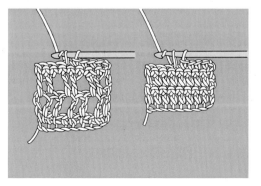

hook, stitch and tension varies in the following ways:

• If two samples are worked with different yarns but with the same crochet hook, stitch and tension, the thicker yarn will produce a larger sample.

• If two samples are worked with different sized hooks, the thicker hook will produce a larger sample.

• The size of two samples worked in different stitches but with the same yarn, hook and tension, will vary.

• If two identical samples are worked with a different tension, the one worked more tightly will be smaller than the other.

One of the pitfalls often encountered by beginners is that of crocheting a garment and then finding that it does not fit. This is often due to erratic tension which will become more even with experience.

This source of disappointment can be avoided to a large extent if sufficient care and time is spent first checking the measurements of the garment you wish to make against the body measurements of the person you are making it for, and secondly, checking that your gauge corresponds to that used in the pattern by working a sample square.

The sizes of crochet patterns tend to be based on standard bust/chest measurements. The table on page 22 gives the average sizes in centimeters and inches for a woman or child's classic sweater with set-in sleeves.

Since individual body measurements can vary considerably, it is always advisable to check whether you have to modify those of the pattern by measuring the person for whom the garment is intended. If this is not possible, measure a garment that you know fits the person concerned well.

Conversion table of sizes giving standard measurements for children and women.

	Years	2/3	4/5	6/7	8/9	10/11	12/13
CHILDREN		cm/ins	cm/ins	cm/ins	cm/ins	cm/ins	cm/ins
	Chest	50/20	56/22	61/24	66/26	71/28	76/30
	Width of front or back	28/11	30/12	33/13	35/14	38/15	41/16
	Length from shoulder to hips	$29/11\frac{1}{2}$	33/13	$37/14\frac{1}{2}$	41/16	45/18	$49/19\frac{1}{4}$
	Sleeve length	$26/10\frac{1}{4}$	30/12	$34/13\frac{1}{2}$	38/15	$42/16\frac{1}{2}$	46/18
	Width of neck opening (back)	$7/2\frac{3}{4}$	$8/3\frac{1}{4}$	$9/3\frac{1}{2}$	10/4	$11/4\frac{1}{4}$	12/5
	Armhole depth	12/5	$13/5\frac{1}{4}$	$14/5\frac{1}{2}$	15/6	$16/6\frac{1}{4}$	$17/6\frac{3}{4}$
WOMEN	British sizes	32	34	36	38	40	42
	USA sizes	30	32	34	36	38	40
	Continental sizes	38	40	42	44	46	48
	Bust	83/32	87/34	92/36	97/38	102/40	107/42
	Width of front or back	43/17	45/18	48/19	51/20	53/21	56/22
	Length from shoulder to hips	57/23	60/24	63/25	66/26	69/27	72/28
	Sleeve length	53/21	56/22	59/23	$62/24\frac{1}{2}$	$65/25\frac{1}{2}$	$68/26\frac{1}{2}$
	Width of neck opening (back)	$13/5\frac{1}{4}$	$14/5\frac{1}{2}$	15/6	$16/6\frac{1}{4}$	$17/6\frac{3}{4}$	18/7
	Armhole depth	$19/7\frac{1}{2}$	20/8	$21/8\frac{1}{4}$	$22/8\frac{1}{2}$	23/9	$24/9\frac{1}{2}$

A comprehensive list of body measurements for a variety of garments is given below.

If you want to make a *cardigan, pullover* or *jacket,* the following measurements should be taken:

1. *width across shoulders*

2. *neck*

3. *armhole (measured generously)*

4. *sleeve length (measured with arm slightly bent)*

5. *wrist*

6. *maximum circumference of the arm (measured about 4–5 cm ($1\frac{1}{2}$–2 ins) from the underarm*

7. *hips (measured across the broadest part)*

8. *waist (if the garment is shaped at the waist)*

9. *chest/bust (measure across the broadest part)*

10. *underarm length (from underarm to wrist)*

11. *total length (from shoulder to desired length)*

For *skirts* the following measurements are required:

1. *waist*

2. *hips*

3. *length*

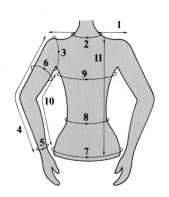

How to take measurements: below, for a cardigan or pullover; right, for a skirt.

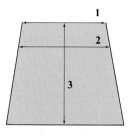

For *trousers* (usually only made for children):

1. *waist*

2. *hips*

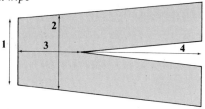

3. *crotch (measured from waist to crotch, sitting down)*

4. *inside leg*

For *socks* only the length of the foot is usually required. The length of a pair of knee socks tends to be three times the length of the foot. If, however, you wish to obtain the best possible fit, take the following measurements:

1. *calf*

2. *ankle*

3. *foot (measured at the broadest part)*

4. *length of sock (from heel to just below the knee for long socks and to just below the calf for short socks)*

Keeping to the measurements of a garment: the importance of a sample

If you are following a pattern, the correspondence between the finished size of the garment and the number of stitches and rows to be worked has already been established. Providing you use the yarn, crochet hook and stitch stipulated, and your tension is the same as that used in the pattern, the finished size of the garment you make should be identical to the pattern measurements. It is, however, very important to check your tension by working a sample square and comparing the number of stitches and rows per inch or centimeter with the gauge given in the pattern.

This is normally expressed as follows: 14 sts (stitches) and 14 rows to 10 cm (4 ins) or 14 sts × 14 rows = 10 × 10 cm (4 ins). This means that if you work a sample of 14 stitches and 14 rows, it should measure 10 × 10 cm (4 × 4 ins).

How to measure the sample. The sample must be measured very accurately, taking care not to

stretch it, since a small distortion here, when multiplied by the total number of stitches in the garment, would lead to an appreciable discrepancy in size and spoil the finished result.

Rather than working a sample with the number of stitches and rows given in the gauge, it is generally preferable to make a larger sample. Measure the size of square quoted in the pattern, mark this with pins, and count the number of stitches and rows it contains.

How to adjust the pattern instructions on the basis of your sample. If the gauge of your sample does not correspond exactly to that given in the pattern, the number of stitches and rows given in the pattern for each piece of the garment (front, back, etc) must be adjusted in order to ensure that the finished garment will be the right size. This is quite easy to work out on the basis of the following equation:

Width:

$$\frac{\text{no. of stitches in each piece} \times \text{no. of stitches in your sample}}{\text{no. of stitches in pattern sample}}$$

Height:

$$\frac{\text{no. of rows in each piece} \times \text{no. of rows in your sample}}{\text{no. of rows in pattern sample}}$$

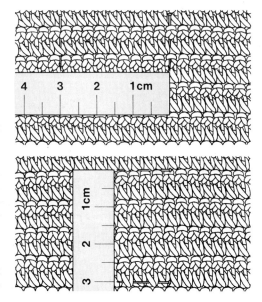

By repeating the calculation for the width every time stitches are increased or decreased in the pattern, it is possible to adjust the shaping correctly as well as the overall size.

How to modify the pattern or make a garment to your own design

It can happen that one wants to make a particular garment for which one has the pattern but it does not give the right size. In this case, the point of making a sample is not to check your tension but to find out how many stitches and rows will be needed for the desired size.

First of all, you must substitute the body measurements corresponding to the new size for the measurements given in the pattern. If the pattern only gives the bust/chest size, the other measurements can be inferred from the table on page 22.

You must now substitute the correct amount of stitches and rows corresponding to the width of each piece, sleeve length, depth of armhole etc. To do this, make a sample and measure the number of stitches and rows per centimeter or inch. Then work out the following equations for each piece of the garment:

$$\frac{\text{cm/ins of new size (length)} \times \text{no. of rows in your sample}}{\text{cm/ins of your sample}}$$

Or

$$\frac{\text{cm/ins of new size (width)} \times \text{no. of stitches in your sample}}{\text{cm/ins of your sample}}$$

These equations can also be used to calculate the amount of stitches and rows for each piece of a garment of your own design.

How to adjust the size of articles made up of repeated motifs

The above discussion of how to ensure that your finished piece of crochet is the desired size has concentrated on the problems relating to the fit of an article of clothing. When making other items, such as table centers, blankets, etc, the size of the finished result is not so important, but in the case of borders or items made up of repeated motifs, you should check your gauge on the basis of one motif. If there is a discrepancy between its size and the measurements given in the pattern, this will be multiplied by the number of motifs to be worked and may therefore make a considerable difference to the overall size of the finished article. Since it is usually impossible to alter the number of stitches in a motif, the only adjustment that can be made is to either alter the total number of motifs or to use a smaller or larger crochet hook.

Starting work and finishing off

This section describes the basic techniques for starting work and finishing off. The methods given are suitable for any type of crochet worked with an ordinary crochet hook.

The best conditions in which to work

One of the advantages of crochet is that it is less cumbersome and easier to carry around than other handicrafts such as knitting or embroidery. You can crochet wherever you are, whenever you have a spare moment, but especially when working complicated stitches or elaborate patterns with fine yarns, it is best to work in good light, sitting in a comfortable armchair so that you can rest your arms if you wish, with sufficient peace and quiet to allow you to concentrate. This will minimize the chance of making mistakes as well as contributing to the restfulness and enjoyment of crochet as a hobby.

Crochet techniques are not difficult and there are only a few basic stitches to be learnt. Once you have mastered these, with a little perseverance and practice, you will soon be able to make garments and other delightful items.

The first thing to learn is how to hold the crochet hook and yarn. This is important in achieving an even tension and a good result.

Holding the crochet hook and yarn

The secret to good crocheting is to work with a relaxed, even rhythm, which is only possible if you hold the hook and yarn in the correct way. The yarn is held and guided with the left hand. Pass it over the little finger – some people pass it once around this finger – under the third and second fingers and over the forefinger. As the work grows it is held taut between the thumb and the second finger. The third finger curves in towards the palm and controls the thread lightly so that it runs smoothly without slipping. There are two alternative ways of holding the thread. It can be passed over the forefinger, under the second, over the third and under the little finger, in which case the work is held between the thumb and forefinger. The second alternative method is to hold the thread in the closed palm of the hand, passing it over the forefinger but not over the little finger. The first method described above is the most common but which you adopt is a matter of personal preference.

The crochet hook is held with the right hand in one of two ways. Either it is held like a pen, between the thumb and forefinger, and rests on the middle finger which guides it, or it is

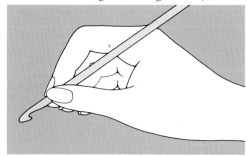

held between the thumb and forefinger and rests on the other three fingers which curl around it.

With the first method, the crochet hook is guided only by the tips of the fingers. It is by far the most common and is suitable for all types of stitches worked with most yarns.

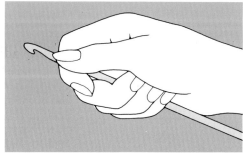

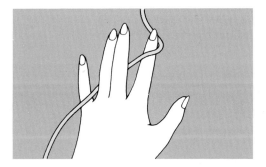

The first things to learn when starting to crochet. Right, how to hold the thread. Far right, how to hold the crochet hook: above, when working with fine or medium weight yarns; below, when working with thick, stiff yarns.

With the second method, the crochet hook is guided by the whole hand. This enables one to apply more force and is therefore used to work very thick, coarse materials that have little elasticity.

When crocheting, the aim is to develop a uniform and regular movement; speed will come with practice. The fingers should hardly move at all, except for those of the left hand which move slightly to allow the thread to run through. It is principally a swivelling action of the wrist of the right hand that moves the crochet hook when working.

The slip knot

The basis for all crochet stitches is a foundation chain, which is begun with a slip knot. This is made in the following way.

Hold the end of the yarn firmly in the palm of your left hand, pass the thread over the forefinger, under the next two fingers and over the little finger as described on page 25. Pass the hook under the yarn which is resting on the forefinger and make a complete counterclockwise turn with the crochet hook so that the thread is twisted and forms a loop.

Right: a slip knot, the first stitch worked at the beginning of every piece of crochet. Far right: making a length of chain. This is the basis for all crochet. It is important that the chain stitches should be even.

Hold the thread firmly between your thumb and forefinger where it overlaps, slip the hook under the thread (this movement is known as "yarn over", abbreviated to yo) and draw it through the loop (this movement is known as "draw yarn through"). You will now have made a slip knot which is the beginning of any foundation chain.

Chain stitch (ch)

Chain stitch is the simplest way to begin any piece of crochet and is also used in combination with other basic stitches when working more complicated, fancy stitches. It is easy to work, but it is important that your tension be even so that all the stitches in a foundation

chain are regular and the same size. If this is not the case, subsequent rows may be distorted.

Having made an initial slip knot, put the hook under the yarn on your forefinger (yo) and draw the yarn through the loop already on

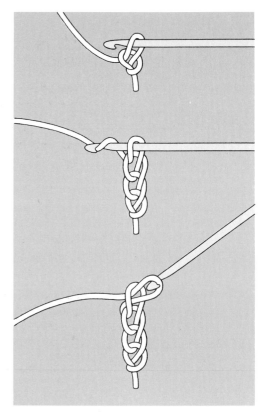

the hook. This corresponds to the instruction chain 1 (ch 1). Repeat until the chain is the length required. For circular work, or medallions that are worked continuously rather than back and forth, the length of the chain is joined into a circle by inserting the hook into the first slip knot, taking the yarn over the hook and drawing it through both loops on the hook.

Double chain stitch (dch)

Double chain stitch makes an firmer foundation for a piece of crochet than single chain stitch and is therefore suitable for articles such as gloves and hats which are constantly stretched. It can also be used as a decorative edging.

Work a slip knot and 2 chain stitches (ch 2), * insert hook into first chain, yarn over (yo) and draw a loop through, yo and draw

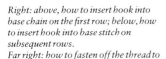

Right: making a length of double chain stitch, which is firmer than simple chain stitch, and is often used for edges of garments that are subjected to continual stretching.

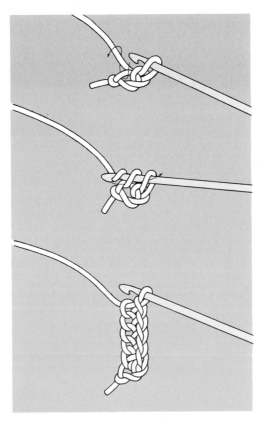

How to work into chain stitches

When working the first row of stitches on the foundation chain, insert the hook into the center of each chain stitch, between the upper and lower thread. Subsequent rows are usually worked by inserting the hook under both threads at the top of the stitches of the previous row, as illustrated in the diagram, unless the pattern gives instructions to the contrary.

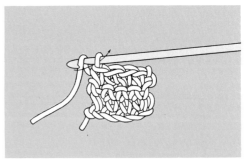

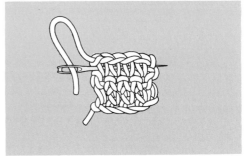

through both loops on hook *.

Repeat the stitch from * to *, inserting the hook into the left-hand loop of the stitch just completed until a chain of the required length is obtained.

Right: above, how to insert hook into base chain on the first row; below, how to insert hook into base stitch on subsequent rows.
Far right: how to fasten off the thread to finish the work.

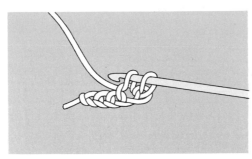

Finishing off

When you have finished a medallion or a piece of a garment, break or cut the thread from the ball and draw it through the loop on the hook to anchor the last stitch. When this has been done there is no risk of the work unravelling. Now finish off neatly by darning the loose end into the back of the work with a suitably-sized needle.

Basic stitches

The stitches described in this section are the basis of crochet. They can be used singly as stitches in their own right, or combined to make more complicated patterns.

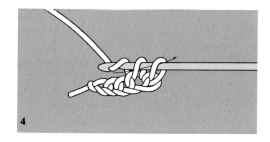

The basic crochet stitches are used either on their own or in combination to produce more complicated stitches.

1. 2. slip stitch
3. 4. single crochet
5. 6. and 7. half double crochet

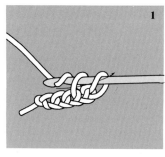

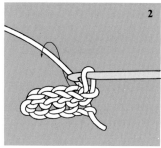

Slip stitch (sl st)

This is the simplest crochet stitch and is usually used as an edging or to close a round.

Work required length of chain. Working from right to left, * insert hook into top loop of second chain from hook, yarn over and draw the loop through both loops on hook.

Repeat from * to end of chain, inserting the hook into the stitch to the left of the slip stitch just worked.

Work 1 chain, turn. This is known as a turning chain and forms the first stitch of the next row.

Skip the first slip stitch and repeat from * to end of row.

Single crochet (sc)

This is the most widely used stitch, suited to almost all types of yarn, particularly cotton, wool and linen. It is a close-textured stitch that produces a fabric-like effect unless combined with other stitches. It is easy to work but it is important to keep it regular.

Work required length of chain. Working from right to left, * insert hook under the top loop of second chain from hook.

Yarn over and draw a loop through the chain. There are now 2 loops on hook. Yarn over and draw yarn through both loops on hook *. This completes one single crochet.

Repeat from * to *, working 1 single crochet into each chain to end of row. Work 1 chain.

Turn work, skip first single crochet of previous row and repeat from * to *, inserting hook under both loops of each stitch. Work 1 single crochet into each stitch.

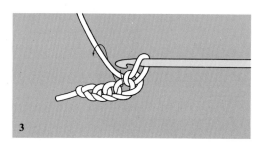

Half double crochet (hdc)

Work required length of chain plus 2 chains.

Skip first 2 turning chains, * yarn over (yo), insert hook under top loop of next chain, yo, draw yarn through. There are now 3 loops on hook. Yo, draw yarn through all 3 loops. This completes 1 half double crochet and 1 loop is left to start next stitch. Repeat from * to end of chain, chain 2, turn.

The last 2 chains form the first stitch of the next row.

On subsequent rows skip the first half double crochet from hook and insert hook under both loops at top of each stitch on previous row. The last half double crochet of each row is worked into the turning chain of previous row.

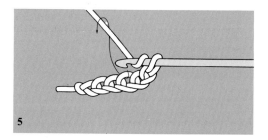

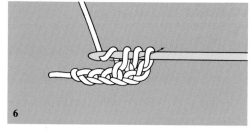

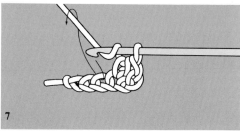

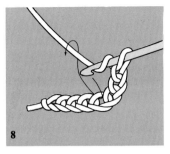

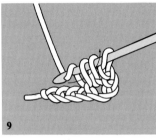

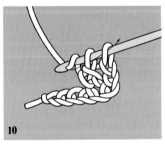

8. 9. and 10. double crochet
11. 12. and 13. treble
14. 15. and 16. double treble

Double Crochet (dc)

A very useful basic **stitch**, double crochet also forms the basis of filet **crochet** (see page 32).

Work required length of chain plus 3 chains.

Skip first 3 turning chains, ∗ yarn over (yo), insert hook under top loop of next chain, yo, draw yarn through (3 loops now on hook), yo, draw yarn through first 2 loops on hook (2 loops now on hook), yo, draw yarn through 2 remaining loops on hook. This completes 1 double crochet and one loop is left to start a new stitch.

Repeat from ∗ to end of chain, chain 3, turn.

On subsequent rows skip the first double crochet from hook and insert hook under both loops at top of each stitch on previous row. The last double crochet of each row is worked into the turning chain of previous row.

Treble (tr)

Work required length of chain plus 4 chains.

Skip first 4 turning chain, ∗ yarn over (yo) twice, insert hook under top loop of next chain, yo, draw yarn through (4 loops on hook), yo, draw yarn through first 2 loops on

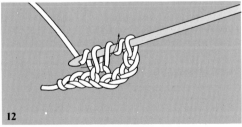

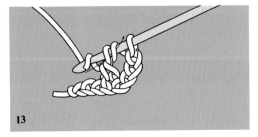

hook (3 loops on hook), yo, draw yarn through next 2 loops on hook (2 loops on hook), yo, draw yarn through 2 remaining loops on hook. This completes 1 treble and one loop is left to start a new stitch. Repeat from ∗ to end of chain, chain 4, turn.

On subsequent rows skip the first treble from hook and insert hook under both loops at top of each stitch on previous row. The last treble of each row is worked into the turning chain of previous row.

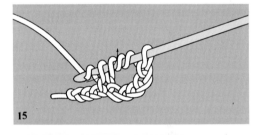

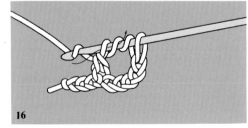

Double treble (dtr)

Work required length of chain plus 5 chains.

Skip first 5 turning chain, ∗ yarn over (yo) 3 times, insert hook under top loop of next chain, yo, draw yarn through (5 loops on hook), yo, draw yarn through first 2 loops on hook (4 loops on hook), yo, draw yarn through next 2 loops on hook (3 loops on hook), yo, draw yarn through next 2 loops on hook (2 loops on hook), yo, draw yarn through 2 remaining loops on hook. This completes 1 double treble and one loop is left to start new stitch.

Stitches	No. of turning chain at end of row	First stitch in which to insert hook on 1st row
Slip stitch	1	2nd
Single crochet	1	2nd
Half double crochet	2	3rd
Double crochet	3	4th
Treble	4	5th
Double treble	5	6th

Above: the table gives the number of turning the chain required to start a row worked in the various basic stitches. It also shows into which stitch the hook should be inserted at the beginning of the first row.

Below and right: examples of medallions worked in the round.

1. *joining foundation chain into a ring with a slip stitch*
2. *working a flat circle*
3. *working a square*
4. *working a hexagon*
5. *working a cylinder*
6. 7. *working an oval*

Rep from * to end of chain, chain 5, turn.

On subsequent rows skip the first double treble from hook and insert hook under both loops at top of each stitch on previous row. The last double treble of each row is worked into the turning chain of previous row.

Working back and forth with turning chain

With the exception of crab stitch, crochet is always worked from right to left. Unless the pattern indicates otherwise, the odd numbered rows form the right side of the work and the even, or return, rows form the wrong side.

When the work is turned at the end of a row, a number of turning chain are worked, as explained above for each of the basic stitches, and these constitute the first stitch of the new row.

Working in the round

Working in the round means that you work from right to left without turning the work. Hence you always work on the right side. Join the foundation chain into a ring with a slip

stitch (Fig 1) and work into the ring.

Different shapes can be obtained depending on where the increases are made during the rounds – increases are made by working two or more stitches into the same stitch.

To make a circle that lies flat, increase 1 stitch at regular intervals on each round (Fig 2).

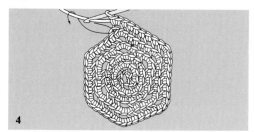

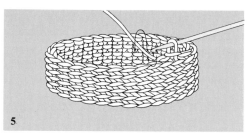

To make squares, hexagons or octagons you should increase 4, 6 or 8 times respectively at regular intervals on each round, the increases always being made over the increases in the previous round, to form the corners (Figs 3 and 4).

To make a tubular shape, for example when making socks, gloves, sleeves or hats, no increases are made except to shape the garment (Fig 5).

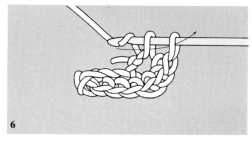

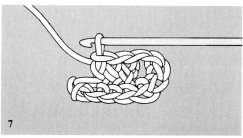

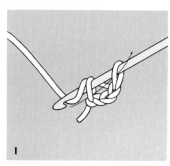

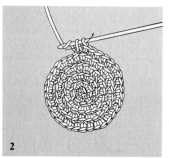

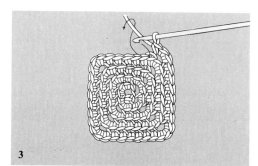

Making an oval

An oval is worked like a circle, on the right side, without turning the work. Having made a foundation chain, work in the stitch of your choice to the end of the chain, increase 2 or 3 stitches and work along the opposite edge of the chain, as shown in figures 6 and 7. Increase in the same way at both ends on all following rounds to keep the shape.

Variations on the basic stitches

All the basic stitches can be varied by inserting the hook into the stitches in a different way.

Some variations on the basic stitches:

8. 9. ribbed single crochet
10. reversed single crochet
11. elongated single crochet
12. spaced double crochet
13. forward raised double crochet

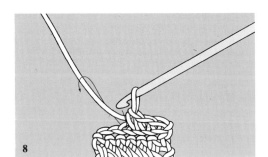

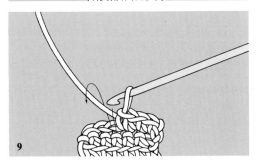

Ribbed basic stitches. By inserting the hook only into the front or back loop of each stitch in the previous row, rather than under both threads, a ribbed effect is achieved. Figure 8

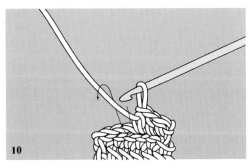

shows the hook being inserted into the back loop while in figure 9 it is inserted into the front loop.

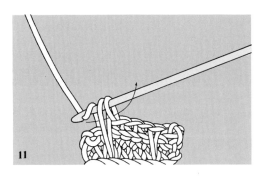

Reversed basic stitches. The hook is inserted from the back of the work under both loops of each stitch in the previous row, rather than from front to back (Fig 10).

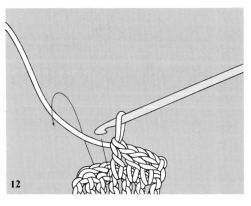

Elongated basic stitches. The hook is inserted into the space between two stitches two or more rows below (Fig 11).

Spaced basic stitches. The hook is inserted between the stitches of the previous row (Fig 12).

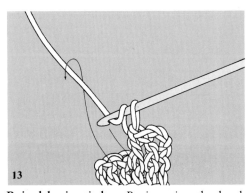

Raised basic stitches. By inserting the hook behind the vertical part of each stitch in the previous row, a raised effect will be achieved (Fig 15). If the hook is inserted from the back to the front and out to the back again, a recessed effect will result.

Special types of crochet

So far we have described the basic techniques of crochet using an ordinary crochet hook. This section will deal with the techniques of filet, Afghan and hairpin crochet. The special equipment required for Afghan and hairpin crochet has been described on page 11.

Filet crochet or mesh stitch

Filet crochet consists of geometrical designs worked in solid crochet which stand out against an openwork, mesh background. It is easy to work since the only stitches used are double crochet and chain. The patterns are usually in chart form and must be followed precisely if the result is to be successful.

Make a foundation chain in multiples of 3 plus 2.

Row 1: Skip 7 ch, 1 dc into next ch, * ch 2, skip 2 ch, 1 dc into next ch, repeat from * to end of row, ch 5, turn.

Row 2: Miss 1 dc and 2 ch, * 1 dc into next dc, ch 2, skip 2 ch. Repeat from * to last pattern, skip 2 ch, 1 dc into next ch, ch 5, turn.

Row 2 forms the pattern and is repeated as required.

A less open mesh can be obtained by working as follows. Make a foundation chain with an uneven number of stitches.

Row 1: Skip 5 ch, 1 dc into next ch, * ch 1, skip 1 ch, 1 dc into next ch. Repeat from * to end of row, ch 4, turn.

Row 2 and following rows: skip 1 dc and 1 ch, * 1 dc into next dc, ch 1, skip 1 ch. Repeat from * to last pattern, skip 1 ch, 1 dc into next ch, ch 4, turn.

Blocks and spaces in mesh stitch. Depending on the size of the spaces in the mesh, the blocks of solid crochet consist of 2 or 3 double crochets. If the block is to be worked above a space, insert the hook into the space below the chain stitches of the previous row and work the corresponding number of double crochets.

If it is to be worked above another block, work the double crochets normally into the top of each double crochet of the previous row.

How to make a chart for filet crochet. A chart for filet work consists of a design on squared paper. The white squares represent the open spaces in the mesh and the crosses or black squares the blocks. If you are working back

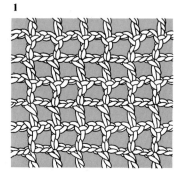
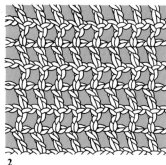

1

2
Filet crochet

1. a mesh consisting of 1 dc, ch 2
2. a mesh of 1 dc, ch 1
3. 4. working blocks and spaces in filet crochet
Chart for filet crochet:
5. 6. and 7. how to make a chart on graph paper

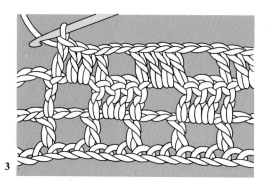

3

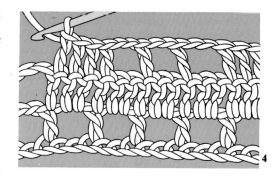

4

5

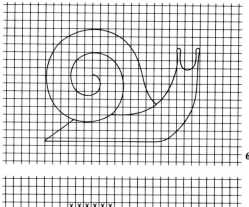

6

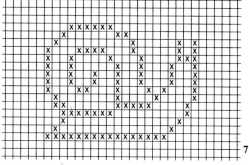

7

32

and forth, the chart is followed in this way: read the uneven-numbered rows from right to left and the even-numbered rows from left to right. If you are working in the round, read each row of the pattern from right to left.

It is not difficult to make up your own designs for filet crochet by drawing them on

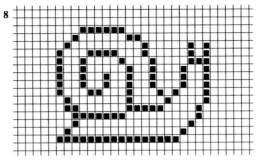

8

graph paper or by adapting an existing pattern or picture, as shown in figures 5–7.

Afghan stitch

An afghan hook is used for this type of crochet, which differs from ordinary crochet in that each row is worked in two stages, back and forth, and the work is never turned. During the first stage (A) all the stitches along the length of the row are worked onto the hook and are then worked off the hook during the second stage (B).

Work the required length of foundation chain.

Row 1 (A): Insert hook into second chain from hook, yo, draw yarn through. Leaving this loop on hook, repeat into each foundation chain.

Row 1 (B): Without turning the work and keeping the yarn at the back, yo, draw yarn through the first loop on hook, * yo, draw yarn through first 2 loops on hook. Repeat from * until only 1 loop remains on hook.

Row 2 (A): * Insert hook under the vertical thread of the second stitch of the previous row, yo, draw yarn through. Repeat from * to end, working into each vertical bar.

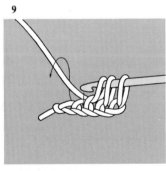

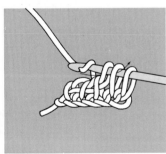

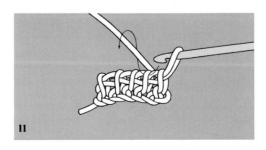

8. *alternative symbols used for a filet crochet chart*

Afghan crochet

9. *first row (A) worked from right to left*
10. *first row (B) worked from left to right*
11. 12. *Row 2 (A)*

Hairpin crochet

13. 14. *and 15. how to begin*

9

10

11

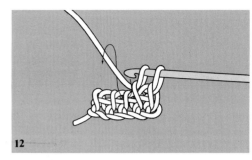

12

Row 2 (B): Work as Row 1 (B).

Row 2 forms the pattern and is repeated as required. To finish off neatly, work 1 sl st into each bar across work.

Hairpin crochet

Hairpin crochet is worked with a loom and an ordinary crochet hook. If cotton, linen or silk is used, the strips make attractive edgings, insertions or trimmings. Alternatively, strips worked in wool may be joined together to make very soft, light scarves or shawls.

Make a slip knot and a very loose chain

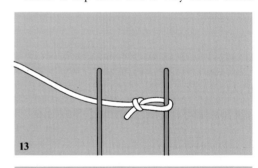

13

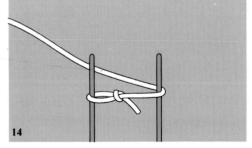

14

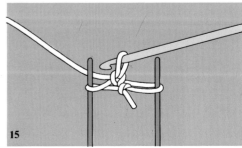

15

33

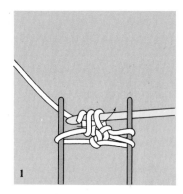

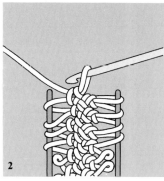

How to continue a strip of hairpin crochet

1. the first single crochet
2. working a strip longer than the loom

Finishing off strips of hairpin crochet

3. single crochet edging
4. bridge stitch edging
5. crossed loop edging

Joining hairpin-crochet strips:

6. interlacing

Opposite: six consecutive stages in the working of single crochet.

stitch, remove the crochet hook and, holding the loom firmly between your left thumb and forefinger, slip the right-hand prong through the loop, leaving the slip knot in the center between the two prongs.

Hold the thread normally over the fingers of your left hand and turn the hairpin from right to left so that the thread passes behind both prongs and the initial chain-loop is now on the left-hand prong (Fig 14). Holding the crochet hook in your right hand, pass the hook under the front thread of the chain-loop and work a single crochet loop (Fig 15). Turn the hairpin from right to left and make another single crochet in the new loop on the left prong (Fig 1).

Continue in this way until loops have been worked up the length of the loom. Then slip all the loops off the hairpin, thread the last 4 or 5 back onto the loom and continue for required length (Fig 2).

Finishing off strips of hairpin crochet. Here are some examples of how to finish off the strips to make a firm edge:

Single crochet edging
Working from right to left, make a single crochet in each loop, taking care not to twist the loops (Fig 3).

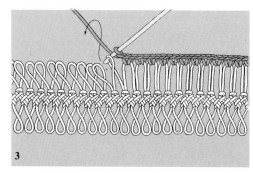

Bridge stitch edging
Working from right to left, join three loops

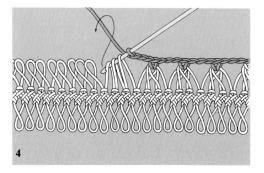

with a single crochet and make 3 chain. Continue to end of strip (Fig 4).

Crossed loop edging
Working from right to left, twist each loop one or more times before making a single crochet

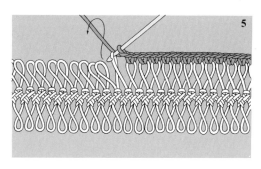

into it. Twisting all loops in the same direction and the same number of times, continue to end of strip (Fig 5).

Joining hairpin crochet strips. There are several ways in which hairpin-work strips can be joined together.

Interlacing
No extra yarn is used when joining hairpin crochet by this method. Place two strips so that the loops adjoin. Working from right to left,

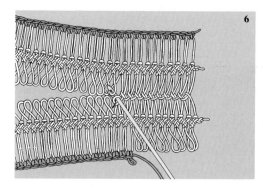

insert the crochet hook into the first loop of one strip and draw the first loop of the other strip through it to form a stitch. Pull the second loop from the first strip through this stitch and continue picking up alternate loops along the length of the strips (Fig 6).

Chain stitch
Place two strips of hairpin crochet together so that the loops adjoin. Thread the crochet hook, from right to left, through all the loops

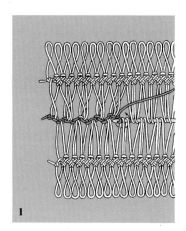

of both strips, picking up two at a time from alternate sides.

Now work back from left to right as follows: yo and make a chain stitch through the first two loops from one side; yo and make a chain stitch through first two loops from the other side. Continue in this way along the length of the strips (Fig 1).

Slip stitch
Place two strips of hairpin crochet together so that the loops adjoin. With a slip knot on the crochet hook, make one chain and, working from right to left, insert hook into first loop of

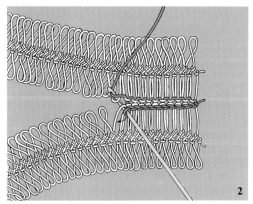

both strips, yo and draw a loop through all three loops on hook, making a stitch. Continue in this way, inserting the hook alternately into the strips until they have been joined (Fig 2).

Other ways of joining strips of hairpin crochet:

1. chain stitch
2. slip stitch

Elongated crochet:

3. working loops over the strip of card
4. anchoring the loops
5. working a second row of loops over the strip of card
6. decreasing and increasing over several strips

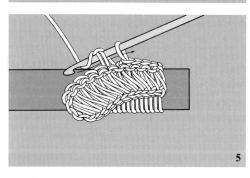

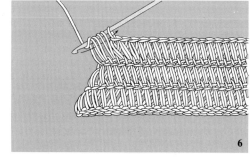

Elongated crochet

A strip of cardboard or wood can be used to make regular, elongated stitches which are then anchored with an ordinary crochet hook. This is a useful method for making fringes, insertions, open-work lace or shawls.

Make the required length of foundation chain, hold cardboard in your left hand or under your left arm and work from right to left as follows:

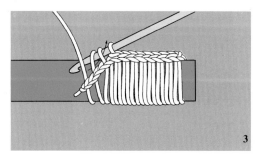

Insert hook into second chain, wind yarn twice around cardboard from back to front; pass hook through both threads on cardboard and anchor the stitch with a slip stitch, single crochet, half double crochet or double crochet. Continue in the same way to end of chain (Fig 3).

If you want to make a braid rather than a looped edging, after working as above, slip all the loops off the cardboard and, working from right to left, pick up and work the loops in pairs as shown in figure 4.

To make subsequent rows of elongated stitches, work as above, substituting the upper edge of the braid for the foundation chain (Fig 5).

To decrease when working several rows of elongated stitches, work four loops together instead of two at the end of a row (Fig 6).

To increase, wind the yarn around the cardboard four times but secure the loops two at a time.

Opposite: six consecutive stages in working Afghan crochet. The first two relate to the first stage (A) and the other four to the second stage (B) of a row.

Shaping

A common problem when first learning to crochet is that of keeping the same number of stitches on each row when working a straight-sided, rectangular piece. This problem can be overcome by carefully following the instructions for making turning chain given on page 30. It is important to remember to work the last stitch of one row into the turning chain of the previous row to avoid decreasing the number of stitches in a row.

However when crocheting a garment or a triangular or diamond-shaped motif, you must be able to work sloping or curved shaping, by means of regular increases or decreases.

Increases and decreases may be termed internal if stitches are increased or reduced within the rows, or external if the increases or decreases are made at the end of a row, at the edge of the work.

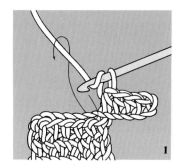

Shaping crochet:

1. increasing at the edge of the work
2. increasing 1 stitch at the beginning of a row
3. increasing 2 stitches within a row
4. decreasing 1 stitch at the beginning of a row
5. decreasing 1 stitch at the end of a row

Increasing at the edge of the work

At the end of each row where an increase is required, work as many additional chain stitches as necessary, plus the number of turning chains required by the stitch you are using. Then work over the extra chain stitches in your chosen stitch as part of the following row.

If a smooth increase is required to give a sloping edge without steps, make the first increase by working two stitches into the last base stitch before working the other extra chain stitches and the turning chain.

Increasing within rows or rounds

To insure that internal increases are worked above one another, mark the point where the increases are to be made with a contrasting thread. If the fullness is to be to the right of this point, work 2 stitches in the stitch preceding the thread. If the shaping is to be to the left of

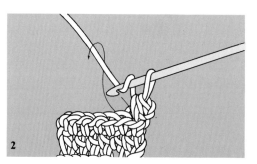

it, work 2 stitches in the stitch after the thread (Fig 2). On subsequent rows, continue to increase immediately before or after the thread.

A double increase can be made by working 3 stitches into one instead of 2 stitches into one (Fig 3).

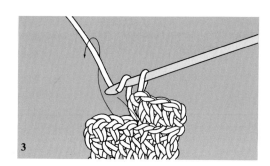

Decreasing at the edge of the work

Rapid decreases are made by leaving the required number of stitches unworked at the end of a row and slip-stitching to the required point at the beginning of a row. For a more gradual decrease, work the turning chain at the beginning of the row, skip the second stitch of the row below and work into the third stitch. At the end of the row, skip the second to last stitch.

When working in single crochet an even sloping edge is obtained in this way:

If you wish to decrease 2 stitches, work to within the last 2 stitches; work 1 slip stitch into next stitch, skip last stitch, work turning chain, turn, skip slip stitch just worked and

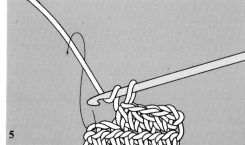

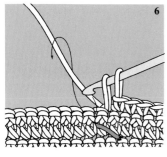

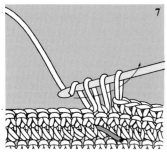

6.7. decreasing within rows
8.9. increasing 1 space at the beginning
and end of a row of filet crochet
10.11. increasing 1 block at the
beginning and end of a row of filet
crochet

work 1 single crochet into following stitch. Continue as required.

Decreasing within rows or rounds

As with increasing, internal decreases must be worked above one another to avoid spoiling the pattern. Again, it helps to mark the exact points where the decreases are to be made with a contrasting thread. When working in single crochet, a single decrease is made in this way: insert the hook into the stitch preceding the thread, yo, draw a loop through, insert hook into stitch immediately after the thread, draw a loop through all 3 loops on hook.

Increasing and decreasing filet crochet

Filet crochet can only be shaped by increasing or decreasing stitches at the edges of the work.

Increasing the number of spaces. To increase the number of spaces at the beginning of a row, make a chain consisting of three times as many stitches as the number of spaces you wish to add, plus 5 chains. Work the first double crochet on the eighth chain from hook and continue in mesh stitch.

To increase one space at the end of a row, work 2 chains and a double treble (dtr) as follows: yo 3 times, insert hook into base of last double crochet worked, draw yarn through, * yo, draw yarn through 2 loops. Repeat from * until all loops have been worked off the hook. Repeat for each additional space required.

Increasing the number of blocks. To increase at the beginning of a row, work three times as many chains as the number of blocks you wish to increase, plus 3 turning chains. Work 1 double crochet into each chain, starting from

the 4th chain from hook. At the end of a row, work as many trebles (tr) as are required, inserting the hook into the base of the previous stitch.

Decreasing the number of spaces. To decrease at the end of a row, simply skip the number of spaces required, work 3 turning chains and begin the following row.

To decrease at the beginning of a row, work slip stitches into the top of the previous row until the required point is reached, work 3 turning chains and continue.

Decreasing the number of blocks. Proceed exactly as described for decreasing spaces.

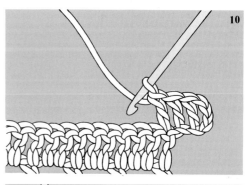

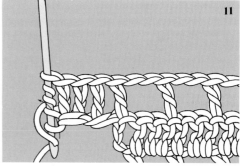

Increasing and decreasing on Afghan crochet

Increases and decreases can be made both internally and externally in Afghan crochet.

Increasing at the edge of Afghan crochet. To increase one stitch at the beginning of a row, insert hook into the vertical bar of the stitch at the beginning of the previous row, yo, draw yarn through and pick up the rest of the stitches as normal.

To increase one stitch at the end of a row, make 2 chains at the end of the A row. At the end of the following A row, pick up an extra

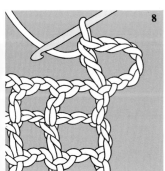

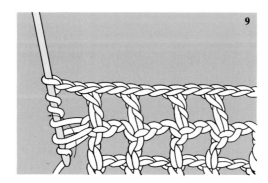

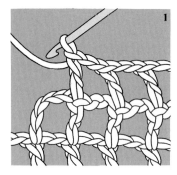

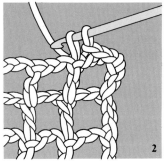

1. 2. *decreasing 1 space at the end and beginning of a row of filet crochet*
3. *increasing 1 stitch at the beginning of a row of Afghan crochet*
4. *increasing several stitches at the beginning of a row of Afghan crochet*
5. 6. *decreasing one stitch at the beginning and end of a row of Afghan crochet*

stitch by working into the second chain, before working the last stitch.

To increase more than one stitch at the beginning of a row, make the required number of extra chain at the end of the previous row, then work back, making a stitch in each chain.

To increase more than one stitch at the end of a row, join a spare piece of yarn to the work and make the required number of extra chain, then work into these chain with the working thread. The return row is worked normally.

Increasing within rows of Afghan crochet. Mark the exact point where you wish to increase with contrasting thread.

If the shaping is to be to the left, make a stitch in the chain between the stitch you have

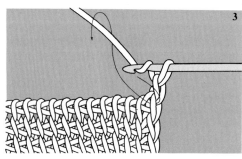

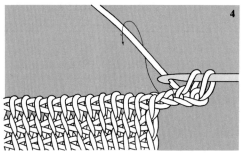

marked and the following stitch.

If it is to be to the right, make a stitch in the chain between the stitch you have marked and the preceding stitch.

Decreasing at the edge of Afghan crochet. To decrease one stitch at the beginning and end of a row, simply leave the last stitch of the previous row unworked when working the A row; at the end of the B row, draw the yarn through the last 3 stitches together (Figs 5 and 6).

To decrease more than one stitch at the

beginning of a row, slip stitch to the point required.

Decreasing within rows of Afghan crochet. Mark the exact point where you wish to have the decrease with contrasting thread.

If the shaping is to be to the right, pick up the vertical bars of the 2 stitches which precede the marking, yo, and draw yarn through to make

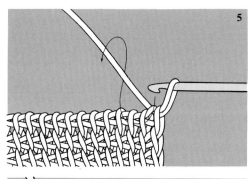

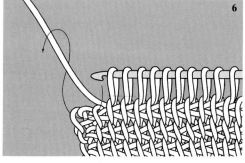

one loop. If the shaping is to be to the left, work 2 stitches together immediately after the thread.

To make more progress

Decorative stitches

The stitches described in this section can all be worked in more than one colour, and can give different effects depending on the type of yarn used and how closely they are worked. A general distinction can be made between close-textured and openwork stitches. Thicker wools are most suitable for the former and cotton, silk, fingering or mohair are suitable for the latter.

Crossed single crochet. Make foundation chain with an even number of stitches.

Row 1: Insert hook into 4th ch from hook, yo, draw loop through, skip 1 ch, insert hook into next ch, yo, draw loop through (3 loops on hook), yo and draw loop through all 3 loops on hook, ch 1, * insert hook into stitch just worked, yo, draw loop through, skip 1 ch, insert hook into next ch, yo, draw loop through, yo and draw loop through all 3 loops on hook, ch 1 *. Rep from * to * ending with 1 sc into last stitch worked, ch 2, turn.

Row 2: Insert hook under first ch of previous

row, yo, draw loop through, insert hook under next ch-1, yo, draw loop through, yo and draw loop through all 3 loops on hook, ch 1, * insert hook into stitch just worked, yo, draw loop through, insert hook under next ch-1, yo and draw loop through all 3 loops on hook, ch 1 *. Rep from * to * ending with 1 sc, ch 2, turn.

Row 2 forms the pattern and is repeated as required.

Elongated single crochet. Make foundation chain with an odd number of stitches.

Row 1: Starting in 2nd ch from hook, * 1 sc, ch 1, skip 1 ch *. Rep from * to * ending with ch 1, turn.

Row 2: * Insert hook under ch-1 of previous row and work 1 sc into back loop of founda-

tion ch skipped on Row 1, ch 1 *.Rep from * to *, ch 1, turn.

Row 3: * Insert hook under ch-1 and work 1 sc into back loop of sc worked 2 rows below, ch 1 *. Rep from * to *, ch 1, turn.

Row 3 forms the pattern and is repeated as required.

Fancy single crochet. Make foundation chain in multiples of 3 plus 1.

Right: Crossed single crochet

Far right, above: Elongated single crochet

Far right, below: Fancy single crochet

43

Row 1: Starting in 3rd ch from hook, * work 3 sc into next ch, skip 2 ch *. Rep from * to * ending with 3 sc into last ch, ch 1, turn.

Row 2: * 3 sc into 2nd sc of 3-sc group of previous row *. Rep from * to *, ch 1, turn.

Row 2 forms the pattern and is repeated as required.

Alternating stitch. Make foundation chain

with an odd number of stitches plus 3.

Row 1: 1 sc into 4th ch from hook, * 1 dc, 1 sc *. Rep from * to *, ch 3, turn.

Row 2: Work 1 dc into each sc of previous row and 1 sc into each dc.

Row 2 forms the pattern and is repeated as required. Ch 1 at end of row when first stitch of next row will be sc; ch 3 when first stitch is dc.

Basketweave stitch. Make foundation chain in multiples of 8 plus 2.

Row 1: 1 dc into 4th ch from hook, 1 dc into each ch to end, 2 turning ch, turn.

Row 2: Skip first stitch, 3 back dc (1 back dc = yo, insert hook from back of work in front of vertical bar of next dc in previous row, draw yarn through and finish as for normal dc), * 4 forward dc (1 forward dc = yo, insert hook behind vertical bar of next dc in previous row, draw yarn through and finish as for normal dc), 4 back dc *. Repeat from * to * ending with 4 forward dc, ch 2, turn.

Row 3: Repeat Row 2.

Row 4: Repeat Row 2.

Row 5: Skip first stitch, 3 forward dc, * 4 back dc, 4 forward dc *. Repeat from * to * ending with 4 back dc, ch 2, turn.

Row 6: Repeat Row 5.

Row 7: Repeat Row 5.

Rows 2 to 7 form the pattern and are repeated as required.

Fancy stitch no. 1. Make foundation chain in multiples of 3 plus 1.

Row 1: 1 sc into 2nd ch from hook, 1 hdc, 1 dc, * 1 sc, 1 hdc, 1 dc *. Rep from * to *, ch 1, turn.

Row 2: * 1 sc, 1 dc, 1 hdc *. Rep from * to *, ch 3, turn.

Row 3: Skip first stitch, 1 sc, 1 hdc, * 1 dc, 1 sc, 1 hdc *. Rep from * to *, ch 3, turn.

Row 4: Skip first stitch, 1 hdc, 1 sc, * 1 dc, 1 hdc, 1 sc *. Rep from * to *, ch 2, turn.

Row 5: Skip first stitch, 1 dc, 1 sc, * 1 hdc, 1 dc, 1 sc *. Rep from * to *, ch 2, turn.

Right, above: Alternating stitch

Right, below: Basketweave stitch

Far right: Fancy stitch no. 1

Row 6: Skip first stitch, 1 sc, 1 dc, * 1 hdc, 1 sc, 1 dc *. Rep from * to *, ch 1, turn.

Rows 1 to 6 form the pattern and are repeated as required.

Fancy stitch no. 2. Make foundation chain with any number of stitches.

Row 1: 1 dc into 4th ch from hook, 1 dc into each ch to end, ch 2, turn.

Row 2 (right side): Skip first dc of previous row, * yo, insert hook under 2nd stitch of previous row (insert hook from front to back between first and 2nd stitches, bringing it out between 2nd and 3rd stitches from back to front); draw yarn through, elongating loop to

about 1 cm ($\frac{1}{2}$ in), yo and complete stitch as for dc *. Rep from * to *, ch 2, turn.

Row 3: Repeat Row 2 except that hook is inserted from the back to the front between first and 2nd dc of previous row, bringing it out towards the back between 2nd and 3rd stitches.

Rows 2 and 3 form the pattern and are repeated as required.

Crazy single crochet. Make foundation chain in multiples of 3 plus 2.

Row 1: Starting in 2nd ch from hook * (1 sc, ch 1, 1 sc), skip 2 ch *. Rep from * to * ending with (1 sc, ch 1, 1 sc) into last ch, ch 1, turn.

Row 2: * 1 sc, ch 1, 1 sc into ch-1 space of previous row *. Rep from * to *, ch 1, turn.

Row 2 forms the pattern and is repeated as required.

Bobble stitch. Make foundation chain in multiples of 3 plus 2.

Row 1: 1 sc into 2nd ch from hook, * ch 3, skip 2 ch, 1 sc *. Rep from * to *, ending with ch 2, turn.

Row 2: * 1 bobble in ch-3 space (=** yo, insert hook under ch-3 and draw yarn through. Rep from ** 3 times. There are now 9 loops on hook. Yo, draw yarn through 8 loops; 2 loops now on hook. Yo, draw yarn through both loops), ch 3, 1 sc into next sc of previous row, ch 1 *. Rep from * to * ending with ch 2, turn.

Row 3: *1 bobble into ch-3 space, ch 3, 1 sc into bobble of previous row, ch 1 *. Rep from * to * ending with ch 2, turn.

Row 3 forms the pattern and is repeated as required.

Right, above: Fancy stitch no. 2

Right, below: Crazy single crochet

Far right: Bobble stitch

Ridged basketweave stitch. Make foundation chain in multiples of 6 plus 3.

Row 1 (wrong side): 1 dc into 4th ch from hook, 1 dc into each ch to end, ch 2, turn.

Row 2: Counting turning ch as first forward dc, * 3 forward dc (= yo, insert hook behind vertical bar of first dc in previous row, draw loop through and finish as for normal dc), 3 back dc (= yo, insert hook from back of work in front of vertical bar of next dc in previous row, draw loop through and finish as

for normal dc) *. Rep from * to *, ch 2, turn.

Row 3: 2 forward dc (counting turning ch as first forward dc), * 3 back dc, 3 forward dc *. Rep from * to * ending with 3 back dc, 1 forward dc, ch 2, turn.

Row 4: 2 back dc (counting turning ch as first back dc), * 3 forward dc, 3 back dc *. Rep from * to * ending with 3 forward dc, 1 back dc, ch 2, turn.

Row 5: 3 back dc (counting turning ch as first back dc), * 3 forward dc, 3 back dc *. Rep from * to * ending with 3 forward dc, ch 2, turn.

Continue in this way, moving the rib one stitch to the right on right side of work and one stitch to the left on wrong side.

Shell stitch. A shell is made by working 5 dc into 1 ch or 1 sc. Make foundation chain in multiples of 6 plus 2.

Row 1: 2 dc into 4th ch from hook, * skip 2 ch, 1 sc into next ch, skip 2 ch, 5 dc (= 1 shell) into next ch *. Rep from * to * ending with 1 sc into last ch, ch 3, turn.

Row 2: 2 dc into sc, * 1 sc into center of shell, 1 shell into next sc *. Rep from * to * ending with 1 sc into top of turning chain, ch 3, turn.

Row 2 forms the pattern and is repeated as required.

Daisy stitch. Make foundation chain in multiples of 8 plus 2.

Row 1: Starting in 2nd ch from hook, * 1 sc, skip 3 ch, (3 dc, 1 tr, 3 dc) into next ch, skip 3 ch. Rep from * ending 1 sc into last ch, ch 3, turn.

Row 2: Without drawing yarn through last loop (unfin dc), work 1 unfin dc into each of next 3 dc, yo and draw through all 4 loops on hook, * ch 2, 1 sc in tr, ch 2, 1 unfin dc into each of next 3 dc, 1 unfin tr into sc, 1 unfin dc into each of next 3 dc, yo and draw through all 8 loops on hook *. Rep from * to * ending with ch 2, 1 sc into tr, ch 2, 1 unfin dc into each of next 3 dc, 1 unfin tr into last sc, yo and draw yarn through all 5 loops on hook, ch 3, turn.

Row 3: 3 dc into stitch at base of turning ch, * 1 sc into next sc, (3 dc, 1 tr, 3 dc) in closing stitch of unfinished stitches of previous row *. Rep from * to * ending with 1 sc into next sc, (3 dc, 1 tr) into turning chain, ch 3, turn.

Row 4: * 1 unfin dc into each of next 3 dc,

Row 2 forms the pattern and is repeated as required.

Fan stitch no. 1. Make foundation ch in multiples of 10 plus 4.

Row 1 (wrong side): Starting in 2nd ch from hook, work in sc, ending with ch 1, turn.

Row 2: * 3 sc, skip 3 sc, 7 tr into next sc, skip

Right: Crossed bar stitch

Far right, above: Fan stitch no. 1

Far right, below: Fan stitch no. 2

1 unfin tr into next sc, 1 unfin dc into each of next 3 dc, yo and draw through all 8 loops on hook, ch 2, 1 sc into tr, ch 2 *. Rep from * to * ending by working last dc of repeat into turning ch of previous row, ch 1, turn.

Row 5: 1 sc into first sc, * (3 dc, 1 tr, 3 dc) into closing stitch of unfinished stitches of previous row, 1 sc into sc *. Rep from * to *, working last sc of repeat into turning ch, ch 3, turn.

Rows 2 to 5 form the pattern and are repeated as required.

Crossed bar stitch. Make a loose foundation chain in multiples of 3 plus 1.

Row 1: 1 hdc into 2nd ch, ch 1, * 1 unfin hdc into same ch (= yo, insert hook into ch and draw up loop; 3 loops on hook), skip 1 ch, 1 unfin hdc in next ch (5 loops on hook), yo, draw yarn through all 5 loops, ch 1 *. Rep from * to * ending with 1 hdc, ch 2, turn.

Row 2: 1 hdc into ch-1 loop of previous row, ch 1, * 1 unfin hdc into same ch loop, 1 unfin hdc into next ch loop, yo, draw yarn through all 5 loops, ch 1. Rep from * ending with 1 hdc, ch 2, turn.

3 sc *. Rep from * to * ending with 3 sc, ch 1, turn.

Row 3: Work in sc, ending with ch 3, turn.

Row 4: Skip first sc, 4 tr into next stitch, * skip 3 stitches, 1 sc into each of next 3 stitches, skip 3 stitches, 7 tr into next stitch *. Rep from * to * ending with 5 tr, ch 1, turn.

Rows 1 to 4 form the pattern and are repeated as required.

Fan stitch no. 2. Make foundation chain in multiples of 7 plus 4.
Row 1: 1 dc into 4th ch from hook, * skip 2 ch, (3 dc, ch 1, 3 dc) into next ch, skip 2 ch, 2 dc *. Rep from * to * ending with ch 3, turn.
Row 2: 1 dc into 2nd dc of previous row, * (3 dc, ch 1, 3 dc) into ch-1 space in center of fan, 1 dc in each of next 2 dc of previous row *. Rep from * to * ending with ch 3, turn.
 Row 2 forms the pattern and is repeated as required.

Fan stitch no. 3. Make foundation chain in multiples of 5 plus 1.
Row 1: 2 dc into 4th ch from hook, skip 1 ch, 1 sc, * ch 3, skip 2 ch, 4 dc into next ch (= fan), skip 1 ch, 1 sc *. Rep from * to * ending with ch 3, turn.
Row 2: 2 dc into last sc worked in previous row, skip fan, 1 sc into ch-3 loop to left of fan, * ch 3, 4 dc into sc, 1 sc into ch-3 loop. Rep from * ending with 1 sc into turning ch of previous row, ch 3, turn.
 Row 2 forms the pattern and is repeated as required.

Knotted single crochet. Make foundation chain with any numbers of stitches.
Row 1: * 1 sc into 2nd ch from hook, insert hook into same ch, yo, draw yarn through, insert hook into next ch, yo, draw yarn through, yo, draw yarn through all 3 loops.

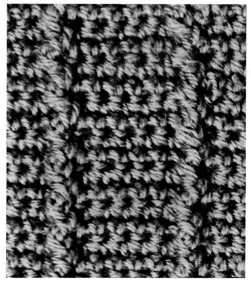

Rep from * ending with ch 1, turn.
Row 2: 1 sc, * insert hook into same stitch, yo, draw yarn through, insert hook into next stitch, yo, draw yarn through, yo, draw yarn through all 3 loops *. Rep from * to *, ch 1, turn.
 Row 2 forms the pattern and is repeated as required.

Rib stitch. Make foundation chain in multiples of 6.
Row 1 (wrong side): Starting in 2nd ch from hook, * 5 sc, 1 dc *. Rep from * to * ending with 5 sc, ch 1, turn.
Row 2: * 1 sc into each sc, 1 forward dc (= yo, insert hook from front to back under vertical bar of dc in previous row, draw yarn through and complete stitch as for normal dc) *. Rep from * to * ending with 5 sc, ch 1, turn.
Row 3: * 1 sc into each sc, 1 back dc (= yo, insert hook from back of work in front of vertical bar of dc, draw yarn through and complete as for normal dc) *. Rep from * to * ending with 5 sc, ch 1, turn.

Right, above: Fan stitch no. 3

Right, below: Knotted single crochet

Far right: Rib stitch

48

Rows 2 and 3 form the pattern and are repeated as required.

Transverse stitch. Make foundation chain in multiples of 3 plus 2.

This stitch is worked only on the *right side*, without turning the work.

Row 1: Starting in 2nd ch from hook, * 1 sc, ch 2, skip 2 ch *. Rep from * to * ending with 1 sc.

Row 2: Without turning work, ch 1, * 1 crab stitch into first sc (= insert hook between vertical bars of sc in previous row, yo, draw yarn through, yo, draw yarn through both loops), ch 2 *. Working from left to right, rep from * to * ending with 1 crab stitch.

Row 3: Without turning work, ch 2, * 1 sc into ch-2 loop, ch 2 *. Rep from * to * ending with 1 sc into ch-2 loop, ch 1, 1 sc into last crab stitch.

Row 4: Without turning work, ch 2, skip first sc in previous row, * 1 crab stitch into next sc, ch 2 *. Rep from * to * ending with 1 crab stitch into last sc, ch 2, turn.

Rows 1 to 4 form the pattern and are repeated as required.

Loop stitch. Make foundation chain with any number of stitches.

Row 1: 1 sc into 2nd ch from hook, 1 sc into each ch to end, ch 1, turn.

Row 2 (wrong side): * insert hook into back loop of first sc, wind yarn downwards around a piece of stiff cardboard, draw yarn through and finish with an ordinary sc *. Rep from * to * ending with ch 1, turn.

Row 3: 1 sc into each sc, ch 1, turn.

Rows 2 and 3 form the pattern and are repeated as required.

Four-leaf clover stitch. Make foundation ch in multiples of 8 plus 7.

On Rows 2 to 4, turning ch of one row counts as first dc of next row; last dc of row is always worked in turning ch of previous row.

Row 1: 1 dc into 4th ch from hook, 3 dc, *(ch 1, skip 1 ch, 1 dc into next ch) twice, 4 dc*. Rep from * to * ending with 4 dc, ch 3, turn.

Row 2: *5 dc, ch 1, 1 dc into dc, ch 1*. Rep from * to * ending with 5 dc, ch 4, turn.

Row 3: Skip 2 dc, 1 dc in next dc, ch 1, skip 1 dc, 1 dc in next dc, *(1 dc into ch-1 loop, 1 dc

Right, above: Transverse stitch

Right, below: Loop stitch

Far right: Four-leaf clover stitch

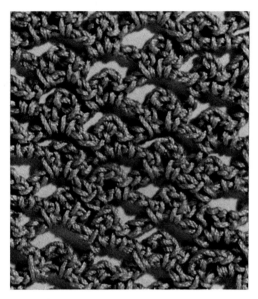

in next dc) twice, (ch 1, skip 1 dc, 1 dc into next dc) twice *. Rep from * to * ending with ch 4, turn.

Row 4: 1 dc into 2nd dc, ch 1, * 5 dc, ch 1, 1 dc into dc, ch 1 *. Rep from * to * ending with 1 dc into 3rd turning ch, ch 4, turn.

Rows 1 to 4 form the pattern and are repeated as required.

Irish loop lace stitch. Make foundation chain in multiples of 7 plus 1.

Row 1: 1 sc into 2nd ch from hook, ch 5, * skip 5 ch, 1 sc in next ch, ch 4, 1 sc in next ch, ch 5 *. Rep from * to * ending with 1 sc, ch 4, 1 sc into last ch, ch 7, turn.

Row 2: * (1 sc, ch 4, 1 sc) into ch-5 loop, ch 5 *.

Rep from * to * ending with ch 3, 1 dc into last sc, ch 5, turn.

Row 3: * (1 sc, ch 4, 1 sc) into ch-5 loop, ch 5 *. Rep from * to * ending with (1 sc, ch 4) into last ch-5 loop, 1 sc into 3rd turning ch, ch 7, turn.

Rows 2 and 3 form the pattern and are repeated as required.

Double mesh stitch. Make foundation chain in multiples of 8 plus 2.

Row 1: Skip 1 ch, * 1 sc, ch 3, skip 3 ch *. Rep from * to * ending with 1 sc, ch 1, turn.

Row 2: 1 sc into first sc, 1 sc into ch-3 loop, ch 4, skip 1 sc, 1 sc into ch-3 loop, 1 sc into sc, 1 sc into next ch-3 loop *. Rep from * to * ending with ch 4, 1 sc into ch-3 loop, 1 sc into sc, ch 1, turn.

Row 3: 1 sc into first sc, ch 3, * 1 sc into ch-4 loop, ch 3, 1 sc into 2nd of 3-sc group, ch 3 *. Rep from * to * ending with 1 sc into ch-4 loop, ch 3, 1 sc into last sc, ch 4, turn.

Row 4: * 1 sc into ch-3 loop, 1 sc into sc, 1 sc into next ch-3 loop, ch 4 *. Rep from * to * ending with 1 sc into ch-3 loop, 1 sc into sc, 1 sc into last ch-3 loop, ch 2, 1 dc into last sc, ch 1, turn.

Row 5: 1 sc into 1 dc, * ch 3, 1 sc into 2nd sc of 3-sc, ch 3, 1 sc into ch-4 loop *. Rep from * to * ending with ch 3, 1 sc into 2nd sc of 3-sc, ch 3, 1 sc into turning ch, ch 1, turn.

Rows 2 to 5 form the pattern and are repeated as required.

Broken mesh stitch. Make foundation chain in multiples of 9 plus 5.

Row 1: 1 sc into 2nd ch from hook, * ch 3, skip 2 ch, 1 sc, ch 2, skip 2 ch, 1 dc, ch 2, skip 2 ch,

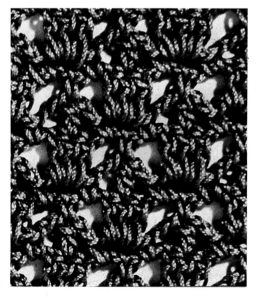

Right, above: Irish loop lace stitch

Right, below: Broken mesh stitch

Far right: Double mesh stitch

1 sc *. Rep from * to * ending with ch 3, skip 2 ch, 1 sc, ch 3, turn.

Row 2: * 3 dc into ch-3 loop, ch 2, 1 sc into dc, ch 2 *. Rep from * to * ending with 3 dc into last ch-3 loop, 1 dc into sc, ch 3, turn.

Row 3: * 1 dc into 2nd dc of 3-dc group, ch 2, 1 sc into ch-2 loop, ch 3, 1 sc into next ch-2 loop, ch 2 *. Rep from * to * ending with 1 dc into 2nd dc of last 3-dc group, 1 dc into turning ch, ch 1, turn.

Row 4: 1 sc into first dc, ch 2, 1 sc into next dc, ch 2, * 3 dc into ch-3 loop, ch 2, 1 sc into dc, ch 2 *. Rep from * to * ending with 1 sc into turning ch, ch 1, turn.

Row 5: 1 sc into first sc, * ch 3, skip 1 sc, 1 sc into ch-2 loop, ch 3, 1 sc into next ch-2 loop *. Rep from * to * ending with ch 3, 1 sc into last sc, ch 3, turn.

Rows 2 to 5 form the pattern and are repeated as required.

Bobbles on mesh stitch. Make foundation chain in multiples of 8 plus 2.

Row 1: Starting in 4th ch from hook, * 1 hdc, ch 1, skip 1 ch *. Rep from * to * ending with 1 hdc, ch 3, turn.

Row 2: Skip last hdc worked, * (1 hdc into next hdc, ch 1) 3 times, into next hdc work bobble (= ** yo, insert hook, draw yarn through to make a fairly long loop, rep from ** 3 times, yo, draw yarn through all 7 loops on hook), ch 1 *. Rep from * to * ending with (1 hdc into next hdc, ch 1) 3 times, 1 hdc into 2nd turning ch, ch 3, turn.

Row 3: Skip the last hdc worked, * 1 hdc into next hdc, ch 1 *. Rep from * to * counting each

bobble as a hdc and ending with 1 hdc into 2nd of the turning ch-3, ch 3, turn.

Row 4: Skip last hdc worked, 1 hdc into next hdc, * ch 1, 1 bobble into next hdc, (ch 1, 1 hdc into next hdc) 3 times *. Rep from * to * ending with ch 1, 1 bobble, ch 1, 1 hdc into next hdc, ch 1, 1 hdc into 2nd of the turning ch-3, ch 3, turn.

Row 5: As Row 3.

Rows 2 to 5 form the pattern and are repeated as required.

Open lacy stitch. Make foundation chain in multiples of 10 plus 3.

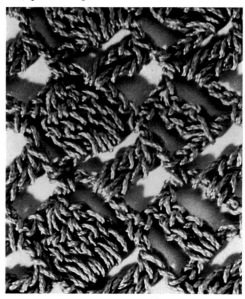

Row 1: Skip 6 ch, * 2 unfin tr into next 2 ch (= yo twice, insert hook into first ch, yo, draw yarn through, 4 loops on hook, ** yo, draw yarn through 2 loops on hook, rep from ** twice (2 loops on hook), yo twice, insert hook into 2nd ch, yo and draw yarn through (5 loops on hook), rep from ** to ** twice (3 loops on hook), yo, draw yarn through all 3 loops), ch 7, skip 2 ch, 1 sc into next ch, skip 5 ch *. Rep from * to * ending with 2 unfin tr, ch 7, skip 1 ch, 1 sc into last ch, ch 5, turn.

Row 2: * (5 unfin tr, yo, draw yarn through all 6 loops on hook, ch 7, 1 sc) into ch-7 loop, ch 1, (2 unfin tr finished together, ch 7, 1 sc) into ch-1 loop, ch 1 *. Rep from * to * ending with 1 sc into turning ch, ch 5, turn.

Row 3: * (2 unfin tr finished together, ch 7, 1 sc) into ch-7 loop, ch 1 *. Rep from * to * ending with 1 sc into turning ch, ch 5, turn.

Row 4: * (5 unfin tr finished together, ch 7, 1 sc) into first ch-7 loop, ch 1, (2 unfin tr finished together, ch 7, 1 sc) into next ch-7

loop, ch 1 *. Rep from * to * ending with 1 sc into turning ch, ch 5, turn.

Rows 3 and 4 form the pattern and are repeated as required.

Arabesque stitch. Make foundation chain in multiples of 4 plus 3.

Row 1: Starting in 3rd ch from hook, * work (1 dc, ch 1, 1 dc) into first stitch, skip 1 ch, 1 sc, skip 1 ch *. Rep from * to * ending with (1 dc, ch 1, 1 dc) into last stitch, ch 2, turn.

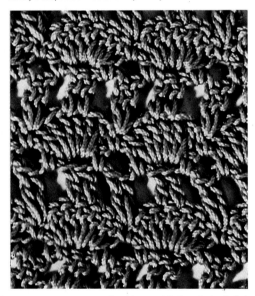

Row 2: * 1 sc into ch-1 loop, (1 dc, ch 1, 1 dc) into sc *. Rep from * to * ending with ch 2, turn.

Row 2 forms the pattern and is repeated as required.

Graziella's stitch. Make foundation chain in multiples of 6 plus 5.

Row 1: 2 dc into 4th ch from hook, * ch 2, skip 2 ch, 2 dc into next ch*. Rep from * to * ending with 1 dc into last stitch, ch 3, turn.

Row 2: * (1 sc, ch 2) into ch-2 loop *. Rep from * to * ending with 1 sc into turning ch, ch 3, turn.

Row 3: * 1 sc into first ch-2 loop of previous row, 6 dc into next ch-2 loop *. Rep from * to * ending with 1 sc into turning ch, ch 3, turn.

Row 4: 2 dc into first sc, * ch 2, 1 dc into 3rd dc, 1 dc into 4th dc of 6-dc group, ch 2, 2 dc into sc *. Rep from * to * ending with 1 dc into turning ch, ch 3, turn.

Rows 2 to 4 form the pattern and are repeated as required.

Smocking stitch. Make foundation chain in multiples of 4 plus 3.

Row 1: Skip 2 ch, * (1 dc, ch 2, 1 dc) into ch (= V-motif), skip 3 ch *. Rep from * to * ending with (1 dc, ch 2, 1 dc) into last ch, ch 2, turn.

Row 2: * 3 hdc into ch-2 loop, ch 1 *. Rep from * to * ending 1 hdc into turning ch, ch 2, turn.

Row 3: 1 dc into space before first V-motif 2 rows below, * skip 3 hdc, (1 dc, ch 2, 1 dc) into space between next 2 V-motifs 2 rows below *. Rep from * to * ending 3 hdc, 1 dc into turning ch 2 rows below, ch 1, turn.

Row 4: 1 hdc into first stitch, ch 1, * 3 hdc into ch-2 loop, ch 1 *. Rep from * to * ending with 1 hdc into turning ch, ch 2, turn.

Row 5: (1 dc, ch 2, 1 dc) into first stitch, * skip 3 hdc, (1 dc, ch 2, 1 dc) into space between next 2 V-motifs 2 rows below *. Rep from * to * ending with (1 dc, ch 2, 1 dc) into turning ch, ch 2, turn.

Rows 2 to 5 form the pattern and are repeated as required.

Eyelet stitch. Make foundation chain in multiples of 2.
Row 1: Starting in 2nd ch from hook, work across in sc, ch 1, turn.
Row 2: 1 sc into each stitch to end, ch 1, turn.
Row 3: As Row 2.

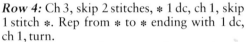

Row 4: Ch 3, skip 2 stitches, * 1 dc, ch 1, skip 1 stitch *. Rep from * to * ending with 1 dc, ch 1, turn.
Row 5: * 1 sc into dc, 1 sc into ch *. Rep from * to * ending with 1 sc into 2nd turning ch, ch 1, turn.

Rows 2 to 5 form the pattern and are repeated as required.

Sylvia's stitch. Make foundation ch in multiples of 6.

On Rows 2 to 5 the turning ch count as first dc of next row; the last dc is always worked into the 3rd turning ch.
Row 1: Starting in 4th ch from hook, 3 dc, * ch 2, skip 2 ch, 1 dc in each of next 4 ch *. Rep from * to * ending with ch 3, turn.
Row 2: 4 dc, * 4 dc in ch-2 loop, ch 2, 1 sc between 2nd and 3rd dc of 4-dc group, ch 2 *. Rep from * to * ending with 4 dc into ch-2 loop, 4 dc, ch 3, turn.
Row 3: 1 dc in each of next 4 dc, * 1 dc in each of next 4 dc, ch 2 *. Rep from * to * ending with 1 dc in each of last 8 dc, ch 3, turn.

Row 4: 1 dc in each of next 4 dc, * ch 2, 1 sc into space between 2nd and 3rd dc of 4-dc group of previous row, ch 2, 4 dc into ch-2 loop *. Rep from * to * ending with ch 2, 1 dc in each of last 4 dc, ch 3, turn.
Row 5: 1 dc in each of next 4 dc, * ch 2, 1 dc in each of next 4 dc *. Rep from * to * ending with ch 2, 1 dc in each of last 4 dc, ch 3, turn.

Rows 2 to 5 form the pattern and are repeated as required.

Openwork stitch no. 1. Make foundation chain in multiples of 6 plus 5.

Row 1: Starting in 2nd ch from hook, * 1 sc, ch 2, skip 2 ch *. Rep from * to * ending with 1 sc, ch 3, turn.

Row 2: * 1 dc into first ch-2 loop, ch 1, (2 dc, ch 1, 2 dc) into 2nd ch-2 loop (= 1 V-motif), ch 1 *. Rep from * to * ending with 1 dc into last ch-2 loop, 1 dc into sc, ch 1, turn.

Row 3: 1 sc between first 2 dc, * ch 2, 1 sc into

ch-1 loop after dc, ch 2, 1 sc into ch-1 loop of V-motif, ch 2, 1 sc into ch-1 loop before dc *. Rep from * to * ending with ch 2, 1 sc into turning ch, ch 3, turn.

Row 4: * (2 dc, ch 1, 2 dc) into ch-2 loop over dc, ch 1, 1 dc into sc over V-motif, ch 1 *. Rep from * to * ending with (2 dc, ch 1, 2 dc) into last ch-2 loop, 1 dc into turning ch, ch 2, turn.

Row 5: 1 sc into ch-1 loop of V-motif, * ch 2, 1 sc into ch-1 loop before dc, ch 2, 1 sc into ch-1 loop after dc *. Rep from * to * ending with ch 2, 1 sc into ch-1 loop of V-motif, ch 2, 1 sc into turning ch, ch 3, turn.

Row 6: 1 dc into sc over V-motif, * ch 1, (2 dc, ch 1, 2 dc) into ch-2 loop over dc, ch 1, 1 dc into sc over V-motif *. Rep from * to * ending with 1 dc into turning ch, ch 1, turn.

Rows 3 to 6 form the pattern and are repeated as required.

Openwork stitch no. 2. Make foundation chain in multiples of 6 plus 2.

Row 1: Starting in 2nd ch, * 1 sc, 1 dc, 4 tr. Rep from * ending with 1 sc, ch 3, turn.

Row 2: 1 dc into first sc, ch 3, * 1 sc between 2nd and 3rd tr, ch 6 *. Rep from * to * ending

with 1 sc between 2nd and 3rd tr, ch 3, 1 dc into last sc, ch 4, turn.

Row 3: 3 tr into ch-3 loop, * 1 sc into sc, (1 dc, 4 tr) into ch-6 loop *. Rep from * to * ending with 1 sc into sc, (1 dc, 2 tr) into ch-3 loop, 1 tr into last dc, ch 1, turn.

Row 4: 1 sc into first stitch, * ch 6, 1 sc between 2nd and 3rd tr, 1 sc into sc *. Rep from * to * ending with 1 sc into turning ch, ch 1, turn.

Row 5: * 1 sc into sc, (1 dc, 4 tr) into ch-6 loop. Rep from * ending with 1 sc into last sc, ch 2, turn.

Rows 2 to 5 form the pattern and are repeated as required.

Openwork stitch no. 3. Make foundation chain in multiples of 7 plus 2.

Row 1: 1 dc into 4th ch from hook, * ch 2, skip 1 ch, 1 sc into next ch, ch 2, skip 1 ch, 4 dc *. Rep from * to * ending with 2 dc (instead of 4) in last repeat, ch 5, turn.

Row 2: 1 sc into first ch-2 loop, * ch 3, 1 sc into 2nd ch-2 loop, ch 4, 1 sc into next ch-2 loop *. Rep from * to * ending with ch 3, 1 sc into last ch-2 loop, ch 2, 1 dc into ch at beginning of previous row, ch 1, turn.

Row 3: 1 sc into first ch-2 loop, ch 2, 1 fan (= 4 dc) into ch-3 loop, * ch 2, 1 sc into ch-4 loop, ch 2, 1 fan into ch-3 loop *. Rep from * to * ending with ch 2, 1 sc into 3rd ch of 5 turning ch, ch 4, turn.

Row 4: 1 sc into first ch-2 loop, * ch 4, 1 sc into next ch-2 loop, ch 3, 1 sc into next ch-2 loop *. Rep from * to * ending with ch 4, 1 sc into ch-2 loop, ch 2, 1 hdc into last stitch, ch 3, turn.

Row 5: 1 dc into first ch-2 loop, * ch 2, 1 sc into ch-4 loop, ch 2, 1 fan into ch-3 loop *. Rep from * to * ending with ch 2, 1 sc into ch-4 loop, ch 2, 1 dc into 2nd ch of 4 turning ch of previous row, ch 5, turn.

Rows 2 to 5 form the pattern and are repeated as required.

Two-color interweave. Make foundation chain in first color in multiples of 5.
Row 1 (first col): Starting in 5th ch from hook,

Right: Two-color interweave

Far right, above: Two-color double crochet

Far right, below: Two-color waves

previous row, ch 1 *. Rep from * to * ending with 1 sc into 3rd turning ch, ch 3, turn.

* 1 shell (= 2 dc, ch 1, 2 dc into same stitch), ch 2, skip 4 ch. Rep from * ending with 1 sc, ch 1, turn.
Row 2 (2nd col): 1 sc, * 5 ch, 1 sc into ch-4 loop in foundation ch, keeping shell in first col towards back of work *. Rep from * to * ending with 1 sc into 3rd turning ch of previous row, ch 4, turn.
Row 3 (2nd col): * 1 shell, inserting hook under ch-1 at top of first col shell and under the ch-5 loop in 2nd col, ch 2 *. Rep from * to * ending with 1 sc, ch 1, turn.
Row 4 (first col): 1 sc, * ch 5, 1 sc through ch-2 loop in first col (3 rows below), keeping shell of previous row towards back of work *. Rep from * to * ending with 1 sc into 3rd turning ch of previous row, ch 1, turn.

Rows 3 and 4 form the pattern and are repeated as required, working 2 rows in each color.

Two-color double crochets. Make foundation chain in first color in multiples of 3 plus 2.
Row 1 (first col): Starting in 2nd chain from hook, work in sc to end of row, ch 3, turn.
Row 2: 1 dc into last sc, * ch 1, skip 2 sc, 2 dc into next sc *. Rep from * to *, ch 2, turn.
Row 3: * 2 dc between 2 sc skipped on

Row 4 (second col): 1 dc between turning ch and dc of Row 2, * ch 1, 2 dc between 2 dc of Row 2 *. Rep from * to *, ch 2, turn.
Row 5: * 2 dc between 2 dc of Row 3, ch 1 *. Rep from * to * ending with 1 sc into 3rd turning ch of previous row, ch 3, turn.
Row 6 (first col): 1 dc between turning ch and dc at beginning of Row 4, * ch 1, 2 dc between 2 dc of Row 4 *. Rep from * to *, ch 2, turn.
Row 7: As Row 5, working between 2 dc of Row 5.

Rows 4 to 7 form the pattern and are repeated as required.

Two-color waves. Make foundation chain in first color in multiples of 14 plus 1.

Row 1 (wrong side, first col): Starting in 2nd ch from hook, * 1 sc, 2 hdc, 2 dc, 3 tr, 2 dc, 2 hdc, 2 sc *. Repeat from * to *, ch 1, turn.

Row 2: Starting in 2nd sc of previous row, work in sc to end. Work 4 ch in 2nd col, turn.

Row 3 (2nd col): Starting in 2nd sc, * 1 tr, 2 dc, 2 hdc, 3 sc, 2 hdc, 2 dc, 2 tr *. Repeat from * to *, ch 1, turn.

Row 4: As Row 2.

Rows 1 to 4 form the pattern and are repeated as required, changing color every 2 rows.

Star stitch. Make a foundation chain in first color in multiples of 6 plus 2.

Row 1: Starting in 2nd ch from hook, work in

sc ending with ch 1, turn.

Row 2: * 1 sc, skip 2 sc, 7 dc into next sc, skip 2 sc *. Rep from * to * ending with 2 sc, ch 3 in 2nd col (these 3 ch form first dc of first star in next row), turn.

Row 3 (2nd col): 1 unfin dc (= yo, insert hook, draw yarn through, yo, draw yarn through 2 loops) into each of next 3 dc, yo, draw yarn through all 4 loops, * ch 4, 1 sc into next dc, ch 3, 1 unfin dc into next 3 dc, 1 unfin dc into next sc, 1 unfin dc into next 3 dc, yo, draw yarn through all 8 loops *. Rep from * to * ending with a half star (= 1 unfin dc into last 3 dc and 1 unfin dc into last sc, yo, draw yarn through all 5 loops) ch 3, turn.

Row 4: 3 dc into stitch closing last 4-dc group

of previous row, * 1 sc into sc, 7 dc into stitch closing 7-dc group *. Rep from * to * ending with 4 dc into stitch closing last half star, ch 3 in first col, turn.

Row 5 (first col): 1 sc into first sc, ch 3, * 1 unfin dc into each of next 3 dc, 1 unfin dc into next sc, 1 unfin dc into each of next 3 dc, yo, draw yarn through all 8 loops, ch 4, 1 sc into next dc, ch 3 *. Rep from * to * ending with 1 sc into last dc, ch 1, turn.

Row 6: 1 sc into sc, * 7 dc into stitch closing

7-dc group, 1 sc into next sc *. Rep from * to * ending with 1 sc, ch 3 in 2nd col, turn.

Rows 3 to 6 form the pattern and are repeated as required, changing color every 2 rows.

Three-color stitch. Make foundation chain in first color in multiples of 4 plus 5.

Row 1 (first col): Starting from 4th ch from hook, work 2 dc, * ch 1, skip 1 ch, 3 dc *. Rep from * to *, ch 1, turn.

Row 2 (2nd col): Ch 2, * 3 dc into skipped foundation ch, ch 1 *. Rep from * to * ending with ch 1, 1 dc into turning ch, ch 1, turn.

Row 3 (3rd col): * 3 dc into 2nd dc of 3-dc group 2 rows below, ch 1 *. Rep from * to * ending with 1 dc into turning ch of Row 1, ch 1, turn.

Row 3 forms the pattern and is repeated as required, changing color on each row.

Fancy Afghan stitch. Make foundation chain with an odd number of stitches.

Row 1 (A) and (B): Work in Afghan stitch as explained on page 33, inserting hook below top loop of foundation chain.

Row 2 (A): * insert hook under two vertical

bars, yo, draw yarn through, insert hook into horizontal stitch between next two vertical

bars, yo, draw yarn through. Rep from * to *.
Row 2 (B): As Row 1 (B).

Row 2 forms the pattern and is repeated as required. To finish, work ch 1, then work 1 sl st into each vertical bar of previous row.

Afghan rib Make foundation chain in multiples of 6 plus 4.
Row 1 (A) and (B): Work in Afghan stitch.
Row 2 (A): Pick up 2 loops in normal way,

inserting hook under vertical bars, * skip next vertical bar, pick up 3 loops inserting hook into next 3 spaces between bars, pick up 3 loops in normal way *. Repeat from * to *.
Row 2 (B): As Row 1 (B)
Row 3 (A): Work 2 loops into vertical bars, * work 3 loops into next 3 spaces, skipping next vertical bar, work 3 loops into following bars *. Rep from * to *.
Row 3 (B): As Row 1 (B).

Rows 2 and 3 form the pattern and are repeated as required.

Kairomanta stitch Make foundation chain with an odd number of stitches.

Row 1 (A) and (B): Work in Afghan stitch, ch 1.
Row 2 (A): Skip first vertical bar, insert hook under next vertical bar, yo, draw yarn through, * place hook behind yarn, yo twice, insert hook under next 2 vertical bars in previous row, bring yarn forward under hook, yo, draw yarn through 2 vertical bars *. Rep from * to * ending with yo, insert hook under last vertical bar, draw through.
Row 2 (B): ch 1, * yo, draw yarn through 3 loops on hook *. Rep from * to *, ch 1.
Row 3 (A): Work from * to * of Row 2 (A) and rep to end.
Row 3 (B): As Row 2 (B).

Rows 2 and 3 form the pattern and are repeated as required.

Afghan check Make foundation chain in first color in multiples of 5.

Right, above: Afghan check

Right, below: Afghan houndstooth stitch

Far right: Broken Afghan stitch

Afghan houndstooth stitch. Make foundation chain in first color with an odd number of stitches.

Row 1 (A) and (B): (First col) work in Afghan stitch.

Row 2 (A): (2nd col) * work 1 stitch, skip 1 stitch *. Rep from * to *, ending with 1 stitch.

Row 2 (B): (First col) ch 1, * work 1 stitch off, ch 1 *. Rep from * to * until 1 stitch remains.

Row 3 (A): (First col) * skip 1 stitch, 1 unfin dc into single vertical bar of stitch (in first col) skipped in Row 2 (A) *. Rep from * to *, leaving last stitch unworked.

Row 3 (B): (2nd col) ch 1, * work 1 stitch off, ch 1 *. Rep from * to * until 1 stitch remains.

Row 4 (A): (2nd col) * 1 unfin dc into single vertical bar of stitch (in same col) skipped in Row 3 (A), skip 1 stitch *. Rep from * to *, ending with 1 unfin dc into last stitch.

Row 4 (B): (First col) ch 1, * work 1 stitch off, ch 1 *. Rep from * to * until 1 stitch remains.

Rows 3 and 4 form the pattern and are repeated as required.

Broken Afghan stitch Make foundation chain with an even number of stitches.

Row 1 (A) and (B): Work in Afghan stitch.

Row 1 (A) and (B): (First col) work in Afghan stitch.

Row 2 (A): (2nd col) * skip 2 stitches, work 3 stitches *. Rep from * to *.

Row 2 (B): * Work 3 stitches off hook, ch 2 *. Rep from * to * ending with ch 2, yo, draw yarn through remaining 2 loops on hook.

Row 3 (A) and (B): (2nd col) as Row 2.

Row 4 (A): (First col) * 1 unfin dc into each of 2 vertical bars (in first col) skipped in Row 2, work 3 stitches *. Rep from * to *.

Row 4 (B): Ch 1, work stitches off as usual.

Rows 2 to 4 form the pattern and are repeated as required.

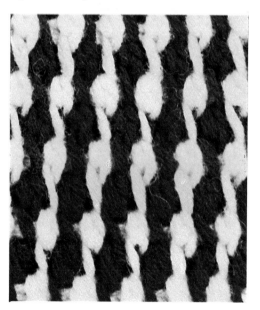

Row 2 (A): Skip 1 stitch, * insert hook under 1 vertical bar and 1 horizontal thread to left of vertical bar, yo, draw yarn through *. Rep from * to *.

Row 2 (B): Ch 1, work loops off in usual way.

Row 2 forms the pattern and is repeated as required.

Medallions

Medallions are crochet motifs, usually worked in the round, which can be joined together to make larger items. A variety of shapes are suitable: squares, circles, hexagons, diamonds etc. and different effects can be achieved depending on the yarn used. Simpler, brightly colored motifs worked in wool give an attractive patchwork effect suitable for rugs or shawls, while more elaborate or lacy medallions worked in cotton, linen or silk make elegant table mats.

Diamond in single crochet

Diamond in single crochet

Make 3 chains.

Row 1: 1 sc into 2nd ch from hook, 1 sc into next ch, ch 1, turn.

Row 2: 2 sc into first stitch, 1 sc into next stitch, ch 1, turn.

Row 3: 2 sc into first stitch, 1 sc into each of next 2 stitches, ch 1, turn.

Row 4: 2 sc into first stitch, 1 sc into each of next 3 stitches, ch 1, turn.

Continue in sc, increasing 1 stitch at beginning of every row until 15 rows have been worked (16 stitches).

Row 16: 1 decrease (= insert hook into first stitch, yo, draw yarn through, insert hook into 2nd stitch, yo, draw yarn through, yo, draw yarn through all 3 loops on hook), 1 sc into each of next 14 dc, ch 1, turn.

Row 17: 1 decrease, 1 sc into each of next 13 sc, ch 1, turn.

Continue in sc, decreasing 1 stitch at beginning of every row until 28 rows have been worked.

Row 29: 1 decrease, 1 sc; ch 1, turn.

Row 30: 1 decrease.

Do not cut off yarn but work a finishing row of single crochet around the edge of the diamond, working (1 sc, ch 1, 1 sc) at each corner and ending with a slip stitch into the first single crochet of the edging. Fasten off.

Granny square strip

Make 5 chains in first color and join with a slip stitch to form a ring.

Round 1: Ch 2, (3 hdc, ch 1) 4 times into ring. Close this round and all following rounds with a sl st into top of 2 starting ch. Cut off yarn. Start each round with 2 ch to replace first hdc.

Round 2 (2nd col): (3 hdc, ch 1, 3 hdc, ch 1) into each ch-1 loop (4 corners worked). Cut off yarn.

Round 3 (3rd col): ∗ (3 hdc, ch 1, 3 hdc) into corner ch, ch 1, (3 hdc, ch 1) into ch-1 loop between one corner and the next ∗. Rep from ∗ to ∗ 4 times altogether. Cut off yarn.

Round 4 (4th col): ∗ (3 hdc, ch 1, 3 hdc) into corner ch, (ch 1, 3 hdc, ch 1, 3 hdc, ch 1) on side between corners ∗. Rep from ∗ to ∗ 4 times altogether. Cut off yarn.

The medallions are joined together on Round 4. On subsequent medallions, work 3 rounds but work Round 4 as follows:

After working 3 hdc, ch 1 on the first corner, remove hook from work, insert it from back to front in one of the corner ch of previously

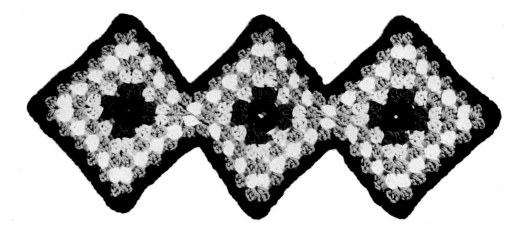

completed medallion, pick up dropped stitch from medallion being worked, yo, draw yarn through loop and stitch. This will result in a strip of medallions which can be varied according to the length or width of the article being made.

Rounds 5, 6 and 7 are worked around completed strip.

Round 5 (5th col): Starting at the top of the strip, work ✳ 1 corner (= 3 hdc, ch 1, 3 hdc), ✳✳ ch 1, 3 hdc ✳✳ 3 times, ch 1, 1 corner, rep from ✳✳ to ✳✳ 3 times, (3 hdc, ch 1) once into ch-1 joining corner of first medallion ✳. Rep from ✳✳ to ✳✳ 3 times along side of 2nd medallion. Rep from ✳ to ✳ around entire strip, ending the round with 1 sl st into starting chain. Cut off yarn.

Round 6 (6th col): As Round 5, working an extra 3-hdc group on each side of medallion.

Round 7 (7th col): As Round 5, working 2 extra 3-hdc groups on each side of medallion.

Two-color hexagon

Using first color, make 8 chains and join with a slip stitch to form a ring.

Round 1: 18 sc into ring, ending with 1 sl st into first stitch.

Round 2: Ch 1, 1 sc into first sc of previous round, ✳ ch 5, skip 2 stitches, 1 sc into next stitch ✳. Rep from ✳ to ✳ ending with 1 sl st into first sc (6 loops).

Round 3: 1 sl st into first loop, ch 5, 7 dtr into next loop, 8 dtr into each following loop, ending with 1 sl st into 5th ch, ch 1.

Round 4: 1 sc into 5th ch and into each of the 7 dtr of previous round, ✳ ch 3, 1 sc into each of the 8 dtr ✳. Rep from ✳ to ✳ ending with ch 3, 1 sl st into first sc. Fasten off first color.

Round 5: Join 2nd color in first ch-3 loop, ch 4, [2 unfin tr, yo, draw yarn through all 3 loops (= 2-tr cluster), ch 5, 3 unfin tr, yo, draw yarn through all 4 loops (= 3-tr cluster)] all into first ch-3 loop, ✳ (ch 3, one 3-tr cluster into 3rd sc) twice, ch 3, (one 3-tr cluster, ch 5, one 3-tr cluster) into next ch-3 loop ✳. Rep from ✳ to ✳ ending with (ch 3, one 3-tr cluster) twice into 3rd sc, ch 3, 1 sl st into closing stitch of first cluster. Fasten off 2nd col.

Round 6: Using first color, (3 sc, ch 3, 3 sc) into first ch-5 loop, ✳ 3 sc into each of next 3 loops, (3 sc, ch 3, 3 sc) into next space ✳. Rep from ✳ to ✳ ending with 3 sc into each of next 3 spaces, 1 sl st into first sc.

Round 7: 1 sl st into 2nd sc, ch 4, one 2-tr cluster into same st as sl st just worked, ✳ch 3,

(one 3-tr cluster, ch 5, one 3-tr cluster) into next loop, ch 3, one 3-tr cluster into 2nd sc, (ch 3, one 3-tr cluster) 3 times into 3rd sc *. Rep from * to * omitting 1 cluster at end of round and working 3 ch and 1 sl st into closing stitch of first cluster.

Round 8: 3 sc into next ch-3 loop, * (3 sc, ch 3, 3 sc) into next ch-5 loop, 3 sc into each of next five ch-3 loops *. Rep from * to * ending with 3 sc into each of last 4 ch-3 loops, 1 sl st into first sc. Fasten off first color.

Round 9: Using 2nd color, 3 sc into first ch-3 loop, * 1 sc into each of next 21 sc, 3 sc into next ch-3 loop *. Rep from * to * ending with 1 sc into each of next 21 sc, 1 sl st into first sc. Fasten off.

Multicolored zigzag strip

Multicolored zigzag strip

Make foundation chain with 20 stitches. Change color every 6 rows.

Row 1: Starting in 5th ch from hook, * 3 dc all into same stitch (= 1 cluster), skip 2 ch *. Rep from * to * 4 times altogether, 3 dc into next ch, skip 2 ch, 1 dc into last ch (5 clusters), ch 3, Turn.

Row 2: Skip the first dc and last cluster worked, * 1 cluster between 2 clusters of previous row *. Rep from * to * 4 times altogether, (1 cluster, ch 1, 1 dc) into ch-4 loop at beginning of Row 1, ch 4, turn.

Row 3: 1 cluster into the ch next to the dc, (1 cluster between 2 clusters) 4 times, 1 dc into 3rd ch at beginning of Row 2, ch 3, turn.

Rep Rows 2 and 3 until 11 rows have been worked.

Row 12: Skip the dc and last cluster worked, (1 cluster between 2 clusters) 4 times, 1 cluster into ch-4 loop at beginning of previous row, ch 3, turn.

Row 13: Skip last cluster worked, (1 cluster between 2 clusters) 4 times, (1 cluster, ch 1, 1 dc) into ch-3 loop at beginning of previous row, ch 4, turn.

Row 14: 1 cluster into ch next to dc of previous row, (1 cluster between 2 clusters) 4 times, 1 dc into 3rd ch at beginning of previous row, ch 3, turn.

Row 15: Skip the dc and last cluster worked, (1 cluster between 2 clusters) 4 times, (1 cluster, ch 1, 1 dc) into ch-4 loop at beginning of previous row, ch 3, turn.

Rep Rows 14 and 15 until 23 rows have been worked, ch 3, turn.

Row 24: 1 cluster into ch next to dc, (1 cluster between 2 clusters) 4 times, 1 dc into 3rd ch at beginning of previous row, ch 4, turn.

Row 25: 1 cluster into space between last dc worked and 5th cluster of previous row, (1 cluster between 2 clusters) 4 times, 1 dc into 3rd ch at beginning of previous row, ch 3, turn.

Rows 2 to 25 form the pattern and are repeated as required.

Multicolored strip of half-medallions

Make 13 ch in first color. Change color every 5 rows.

Row 1 (wrong side): 1 dc into 9th ch from hook, ch 4, 1 sc into last ch, ch 3, turn.

Row 2 (right side): 9 dc into first ch-4 loop, 1 dc into dc, 10 dc into 2nd ch-4 loop, ch 6, turn.

Multicolored strip of half-medallions

Row 3: 1 dc into 3rd stitch, * ch 2, skip 1 stitch, 1 dc in next stitch *. Rep from * to * ending with ch 2, 1 dc into 3rd ch of previous row, ch 3, turn. (There are now 10 spaces).

Row 4: * 3 dc into ch-2 loop, 1 dc into dc *. Rep from * to * ending with 3 dc into turning ch of previous row, ch 6, turn.

Row 5: Work as Row 3, making 20 spaces. This row completes the motif. Cut off yarn.

Row 6 (wrong side, i.e. working in same direction as Row 5): With 2nd color, 1 sc into 8th dc, ch 4, skip 1 dc, 1 dc into middle dc of first motif, ch 4, skip 1 dc, 1 sc into next dc.

To start each following row, work 2 ch and 1 sl st at the end of every row into the next dc of previous motif.

Row 7 (right side): 9 dc into first ch-4 loop, 1 dc into middle dc, 10 dc into 2nd ch-4 loop. End this row and all following rows with 1 sl st into next dc of previous motif.

Row 8: Skip 2 dc, * 1 dc, ch 2, skip 1 dc *. Rep from * to * ending with 1 sl st into next dc of first motif (10 spaces).

Row 9: * 3 dc into ch-2 loop, 1 dc into dc *. Rep from * to * ending with 1 sl st into next dc of previous motif.

Row 10: As Row 8 (20 spaces).

Rows 6 to 10 form the pattern and are repeated as required.

Medallion with star

Make 8 chains and join with a sl st to form ring.

Work beginning of each round as follows: replace 1 dtr by 5 ch, and 1 sc by 1 ch. Close each round with 1 sl st.

Round 1: 12 sc in ring.

Round 2: (2 sc, 2 sc in next stitch) 4 times.

Round 3: * 1 dtr, ch 2 *. Rep from * to * 15 times.

Round 4: 1 sc in each dtr and each ch (48 stitches).

Round 5: (7 sc, 2 sc in next stitch) 6 times (54 stitches).

Round 6: (8 sc, 2 sc in next stitch) 6 times (60 stitches).

Round 7: (9 sc, 2 sc in next stitch) 6 times (66 stitches).

Round 8: * 11 sc, turn; ch 3, skip 1 sc, 9 sc, turn; ch 3, skip 1 sc, 7 sc, turn. Continue in this way, decreasing 1 sc at each end of every row until 1 sc remains. Return to base of point by working sl sts along left side *. Rep from * to * 5 times, but omit sl sts after last point of star has been worked.

Round 9: * 1 sc in tip of point, ch 16 *. Rep from * to * 5 times.

Round 10: 1 sc in each ch, 3 sc in sc at each point. Fasten off.

Small circle

Make 14 chains and join with a sl st to form ring.

Round 1: ch 3 (= 1 dc), 31 dc into ring. Close this and following rounds with 1 sl st into 3rd starting ch (32 dc).

Round 2: ch 8 (= 1 dc plus 5 ch), skip 1 dc, (1 dc, ch 5, skip 1 dc) 15 times (16 loops).
Round 3: 1 sl st into each of first 3 ch of the ch-5 loop to reach center of loop, ch 3 (= 1 dc), (1 dc, ch 2, 2 dc) into same stitch. Work (2 dc, ch 2, 2 dc) into 3rd ch of each ch-5 loop to end of round (16 looped motifs worked).
Round 4: 2 sl sts into first 2 dc of previous round to reach the first ch-2 loop, ch 3 (= 1 dc), 2 dc, 1 picot (= ch 3, 1 sl st into 3rd ch from hook), 3 dc into ch-2 loop, (3 dc, 1 picot, 3 dc) into each ch-2 loop to end of round. Close round with 1 sl st into 3rd starting ch (16 motifs). Fasten off.

Small square medallion

Make 18 chains and join with a sl st to form ring.
Round 1: ch 1, 36 sc into ring, ending with 1 sl st into first stitch, ch 4.
Round 2: 1 unfin tr into each of next 2 stitches, yo, draw yarn through all 4 loops on hook (first petal), * ch 5, 1 petal (= 3 unfin tr into next 3 stitches, yo, draw yarn through all loops on hook) *. Rep from * to * ending round with ch 5 and 1 sl st into closing stitch of first petal, ch 1 (12 petals formed).

Right: Medallion with star

Below: Small circle

Round 3: 1 sc into next stitch, * ch 5, skip next ch-5 loop, ([1 dtr, ch 2] 9 times, 1 dtr) into following ch-5 loop, ch 5, skip next ch-5 loop, 1 sc into closing stitch of next petal *. Rep from * to * 3 more times, ending with ch 2 and 1 dc worked into first sc (instead of ch 5 and 1 sc).
Round 4: ch 3, * 1 dc into next ch-5 loop, (ch 5, skip next ch-2 space, 1 sc into next ch-2 space) twice, (5 ch, 1 sc into next space) twice, ch 5, skip next space, 1 sc into next space, ch 5, skip next ch-2 space, 1 dc into ch-5 loop *. Rep from * to * 3 more times, replacing last dc in final repeat with 1 sl st into 3rd starting ch, ch 1.
Round 5: 3 sc, ch 3, 3 sc (= 1 scallop) into each ch-5 loop of previous row ending with 1 sl st into first sc. Fasten off.

To join several squares, work 2nd square in the same way until Round 4 has been completed.
Round 5: 1 scallop into each of the first 3 loops, (3 sc, ch 1, 1 sc inserting hook into ch-3 loop of corresponding scallop of first square, ch 1, 3 sc) 6 times altogether, then continue as for first square.

Stylized flower

Make 16 chains and join with a sl st to form ring.
Work beginning of each round as follows: replace 1 dtr by ch 5, 1 tr by ch 4, 1 dc by ch 3, 1 sc by ch 1. Close each round with 1 sl st in top of starting chain.
Round 1: 34 dtr into ring.

Small square medallion

Hexagon with star design

Make 6 chains and join with a sl st to form ring.

Work beginning of each round as follows: replace 1 dc with ch 3 and 1 sc with ch 1. Close each round with 1 sl st into top of starting ch.

Round 1: (1 dc, ch 2) 6 times into ring.

Round 2: 3 sc into each ch-2 loop.

Round 3: * 1 bobble (= 5 dc into same stitch, remove hook from work, insert it into first of 5 stitches just worked, pick up working loop and draw it through), 1 ridged sc (= sc worked into back loop only of stitch below instead of through both loops), 3 ridged sc into next stitch *. Rep from * to * end of round.

Round 4: * 2 ridged sc, 3 ridged sc into same stitch, 2 ridged sc *. Rep from * to * to end of round.

Round 5: * 1 ridged sc, 1 bobble, 1 ridged sc, 3 ridged sc into next stitch (= 1 corner), 2 ridged sc, 1 bobble *. Rep from * to * to end of round.

Round 6: * 4 ridged sc, 1 corner, 4 ridged sc *. Rep from * to * to end of round.

Round 7: * 1 bobble, 1 ridged sc, 1 bobble, 2 ridged sc, 1 corner, 3 ridged sc, 1 bobble, 1 ridged sc *. Rep from * to * to end of round.

Round 8: * 6 ridged sc, 1 corner, 6 ridged sc *. Rep from * to * to end of round.

Round 9: * 1 ridged sc, 1 bobble, 5 ridged sc, 1 corner, 6 ridged sc, 1 bobble *. Rep from * to * to end of round.

Round 10: * 8 ridged sc, 1 corner, 8 ridged sc *. Rep from * to * to end of round.

Round 11: * 1 bobble, 8 ridged sc, 1 corner, 9 ridged sc *. Rep from * to * to end of round.

Round 12: * ** 1 ridged dc (= dc worked into back loop of stitch below), ch 1, skip 1 stitch **, rep from ** to ** 5 times, 1 ridged dc, ch 2, 1 dc into same stitch, ch 1, skip 2 stitches, rep from ** to ** 4 times *. Rep from * to * to end of round.

Round 13: 1 ridged sc into each stitch, working 3 sc into ch-2 loop at each corner.

Round 14: * ** 3 ridged sc, 1 bobble, 1 ridged sc **, rep from ** to ** twice, 2 ridged sc, 1 corner, rep from ** to ** twice *. Rep from * to * to end of round.

Round 15: * ** 2 ridged sc, 1 bobble, 1 ridged sc, 1 bobble **, rep from ** to ** twice, 3 ridged sc, 1 corner, 1 ridged sc, rep from ** to ** twice more *. Rep from * to * to end of round.

Round 16: * ** 1 ridged sc, 1 bobble, 3 ridged sc **, rep from ** to ** twice, 1 ridged sc, 1 bobble, 2 ridged sc, 1 corner, 2 ridged sc, rep

Round 2: 1 dc into each dtr.

Round 3: * 3 tr, ch 3, 1 picot (= ch 3, 1 sl st into 3rd ch from hook), ch 3, skip 1 stitch *. Rep from * to * 8 times. Close round with 1 sl st and work 6 sl st into first 6 stitches in order to reach first picot.

The 4 corners of the square are now worked separately, as follows:

Round 4: * (1 sc, ch 6, 1 tr, ch 7, 1 tr, ch 7, 1 tr, ch 6, 1 sc) into picot. Turn work and work 10 dc into each ch loop. Turn work again and work 1 dc into each stitch (40 dc). Turn work, ch 2, 1 sl st into ch following the 3-tr of Round 3, 1 dc into each dc ending with 1 sl st into ch loop of Round 3 *. Rep from * to * 3 times.

Having completed the 4 corners, finish the square by working all around it as follows:

Round 5: Turn work, sl st to 5th dc from beginning of corner, * 1 dc, ch 2, skip 1 stitch, (1 dc, ch 2, skip 1 stitch) until 5th dc from end of corner is reached *. Rep from * to * 3 times. Close round.

Round 6: (1 sc, 1 picot, 1 sc) into each ch-2 space of previous row. Fasten off.

Stylized flower

Hexagon with star design

from ** to ** twice more *. Rep from * to * to end of round.

Round 17: * 1 ridged dc, ch 1, skip 1 stitch *, rep from * to * along each side, working (1 dc, ch 3, 1 dc) at each corner.

Round 18: 1 ridged sc into each stitch, 3 ridged sc into same stitch at each corner. Fasten off.

Medallion with central flower

In starting from the middle of the flower, care must be taken always to work with the right side facing you, without ever turning the work. The petals of the flower should always be towards you.

Where a very small center is required, an alternative method of beginning a ring is to wind the yarn 2 or 3 times round a pencil leaving a short end free. Slip this ring off the pencil and hold it firmly between thumb and forefinger of left hand, keeping yarn away from you. Insert crochet hook through ring from front to back and draw loop through. Work 1 ch. Continue working as many sc as required in ring, joining last sc to beginning ch-1 with a sl st. When a few rounds of pattern have been worked, the free end of yarn may be drawn up tightly and fastened off.

Make 6 ch and join with a sl st to form ring.

Round 1: Ch 6 (= 1 dc plus 3 ch), (1 dc, ch 3) 7 times in ring. Complete round with 1 sl st into 3rd of starting ch-6 (8 loops).

Round 2: Ch 1, (1 sc, 3 dc, 1 sc) into each ch-3 loop of previous round. (First round of 8 petals.)

Round 3: Ch 1, 1 sc in sl st of Round 1 (between 2 petals), ch 4, (1 sc in next dc of Round 1, between 2 petals, ch 4) 7 times. Complete round with 1 sl st in sc of previous round (8 loops).

Round 4: Ch 1, (1 sc, 1 dc, 3 tr, 1 dc, 1 sc) in each ch-4 loop of previous round. (2nd round of 8 petals.)

Round 5: Ch 1, 1 sc in sl st of Round 3 (between 2 petals), ch 5, (1 sc in next sc of Round 3, between 2 petals, ch 5) 7 times. Complete round with 1 sc in first sc of previous round (8 loops).

Round 6: Ch 1, (1 sc, 1 dc, 5 tr, 1 dc, 1 sc) in each ch-5 loop of previous round. (3rd round of 8 petals.)

Round 7: Ch 1, 1 sc in sl st of Round 5 (between 2 petals), ch 6, (1 sc in next sc of Round 5, between 2 petals, ch 6) 7 times. Complete round with 1 sl st in first sc of previous round (8 loops).

Round 8: Ch 1, (1 sc, 1 dc, 3 tr, ch 1, 3 tr, 1 dc, 1 sc) in each ch-4 loop of previous round. (4th round of 8 petals.) The flower is now complete.

Round 9: 1 sl st in first 5 stitches of first petal in order to reach central ch-1 of petal, ch 4 (= 1 tr), (3 tr, ch 2, 4 tr, ch 2) in ch-1 loop, 2 dc between 2 petals, ch 3, 1 sc in central ch-1 loop of next petal, ch 3, 2 dc between next 2 petals, ch 2, (4 tr, ch 2, 4 tr, ch 2) in central ch-1 loop of next petal, 2 dc between the 2 petals, ch 3, 1 sc in central ch-1 loop of next petal, ch 3, 2 dc between the 2 petals, ch 2. Complete round with 1 sl st in 4th starting ch.

Round 10: 1 sl st in 4 tr in order to reach corner ch-2 loop, (ch 4 [= 1 tr], 4 tr, ch 2, 5 tr, ch 2) in corner ch-2 loop, ✳ (2 dc, ch 2) in ch-2 loop of previous round, (2 dc, ch 2) in next ch-3 loop, (2 dc, ch 2) in central sc of petal, (2 dc, ch 2) in ch-3 loop, (2 dc, ch 2) in next ch-2 loop, ch 2, (5 tr, ch 2, 5 tr, ch 2) in corner ch-2 loop ✳. Rep from ✳ to ✳. Complete round with 1 sl st in 4th starting ch.

Round 11: 1 sl st in 5 tr in order to reach corner ch-2 loop, (ch 4 [= 1 tr], 4 tr, ch 2, 5 tr, ch 2) in corner ch-2 loop, ✳ (2 dc, ch 2) in next two ch-2 loops of previous round, skip next 2 ch, (2 dc, ch 2) between 2-dc of previous round, skip next 2 ch, (2 dc, ch 2) in next two ch-2 loops, (5 tr, ch 2, 5 tr, ch 2) in corner ch-2 loop ✳. Rep from ✳ to ✳. Complete round with 1 sl st in 4th starting ch.

Round 12: Rep Round 11.

Round 13: Rep Round 11, working ch 3 (instead of ch 2) between the 2-dc groups.

Round 14: Ch 3 (= 1 dc), 1 dc in every ch, dc and tr of previous round, except on the corners. In each ch-2 loop at corner work 2 dc, ch 2, 2 dc. Complete round with 1 sl st in 3rd starting ch. Fasten off.

Medallion with interwoven centre

Make 18 chains and join with a sl st to form ring.

Work starting chain of each round as follows: Replace 1 tr by ch 4, 1 dc by ch 3, 1 sc by ch 1. Close each round with a sl st.

Round 1: 36 dc into ring. Cut off yarn.

Work 7 more identical rings, interweaving them before closing the foundation chain into a ring: slip the length of ch through the previous ring and join with a sl st into first ch. Then work the 36 dc into new ring, turning it as you work. When making the 8th ring, slip the length of foundation chain into the last ring worked and into the first, thus linking all

Medallion with central flower

the rings into a circle, and complete as before.

Rejoin yarn to point where 2 rings overlap, inserting hook through dc of front and back rings simultaneously, ∗ 1 sc, ch 9, skip 6 stitches of 2nd ring, 1 sc into next stitch of 2nd ring, ch 9, insert hook through dc of 2nd and 3rd ring, at point where they overlap ∗. Rep from ∗ to ∗ 7 times.

Round 1: 14 sc into each ch-6 loop.

Round 2: ∗ (2-dc cluster = 2 unfin dc, yo, draw yarn through all 3 loops, ch 2) 7 times, skip 5 stitches, 3 dc, ch 2, skip 6 stitches ∗. Rep from ∗ to ∗.

Round 3: ∗ (2-dc cluster, ch 2) 6 times into ch-2 loops between 2-dc clusters of previous round, 1 dc into ch-2 loop to right of the 3 dc of previous round (= 1 right increase), 1 dc into each dc of 3-dc, 1 dc into ch-2 loop to left of the same 3 dc (= 1 left increase), ch 2 ∗. Rep from ∗ to ∗.

Round 4: ∗ (2-dc cluster, ch 2) 5 times into ch-2 loops between 2-dc clusters of previous round, 1 right increase, 5 dc, 1 left increase, ch 2 ∗. Rep from ∗ to ∗.

Round 5: ∗ (2-dc cluster, ch 2) 4 times into ch-2 loops between 2-dc clusters in previous round, 1 right increase, 7 dc, 1 left increase, ch 2 ∗. Rep from ∗ to ∗.

Round 6: ∗ (2-dc cluster, ch 2) 3 times into ch-2 loops between 2-dc clusters in previous round, ch 1, 1 right increase, 9 dc, 1 left increase, ch 3 ∗. Rep from ∗ to ∗.

Round 7: ∗ (2-dc cluster, ch 2) twice into ch-2 loops between 2-dc clusters in previous round, ch 2, 1 right increase, 11 dc, 1 left increase, ch 4 ∗. Rep from ∗ to ∗.

Round 8: ∗ 2-dc cluster in ch-2 loop between 2-dc clusters in previous round, ch 5, 1 right increase, 11 dc, 1 left increase, ch 5 ∗. Rep from ∗ to ∗.

Round 9: ∗ 7 sc into first ch-5 loop, 1 sc into each of the 15 dc, 7 sc into next ch-5 loop ∗. Rep from ∗ to ∗.

Round 10: ∗ 1 sc into sc over 2-dc cluster of Round 8, ch 5, 1 sc into first of 15 sc, ch 14, 1 sc into last of 15 sc, ch 5, (1 dc, ch 3, 1 dc) into sc over 2-dc cluster of Round 8 (corner), ch 5, 1 sc into first of next 15 sc, ch 14, 1 sc into last of 15 sc, ch 5 ∗. Rep from ∗ to ∗.

Round 11: ∗ 7 sc into ch-5 loop, 15 sc into ch-14 loop, 7 sc into ch-5 loop (2 dc, ch 2, 2 dc) into ch-3 loop (corner), 7 sc into ch-5 loop, 15 sc into ch-14 loop, 7 sc into ch-5 loop ∗. Rep from ∗ to ∗.

Round 12: 1 dc into each stitch but on the 4 stitches at each corner work (1 dc, ch 2) twice, (1 dc, ch 3, 1 dc) into ch-2 loop, (ch 2, 1 dc) twice.

Medallion with interwoven center

Round 13: ✳ 1 dc, ch 2, skip 2 stitches ✳. Rep from ✳ to ✳ along each side, working each corner as follows: (1 dc, ch 2 into each dc) 3 times, 1 dc, ch 3, 1 dc into ch-3 corner loop, (1 dc, ch 2 into each dc) 3 times, ch 2.
Round 14: As Round 13. Fasten off.

Medallion with star design

Make 10 chains and join with a sl st to form ring.
Round 1: Ch 1, ✳ 1 sc, 1 hdc, 3 dc, 1 hdc (= 1 petal) ✳. Rep from ✳ to ✳ 4 times. Complete this and every following round with 1 sl st in first stitch.
Round 2: Ch 1, ✳ insert hook from *back to front* in sc of petal and work 1 sc, ch 4 ✳. Rep from ✳ to ✳ 4 times. (Petals will lie forward with ch loops behind.)
Round 3: Ch 1, ✳ (1 sc, 1 hdc, 5 dc, 1 hdc, 1 sc) in ch-4 loop ✳. Rep from ✳ to ✳ 4 times (5 petals).
Round 4: Ch 1, ✳ 1 sc in first sc of Round 2, ch 6, 1 sc between 2 sc ✳. Rep from ✳ to ✳ 3 times, ch 6.
    Replace the first dc of Rounds 5 to 13 by 3 starting ch.
Round 5: ✳ 1 dc in sc, ch 2, (1 dc, ch 2) twice in ch-6 loop ✳. Rep from ✳ to ✳ 4 times.
Round 6: ✳ 1 dc in dc, ch 2, 1 bobble (= ✳✳ yo, insert hook in next stitch, yo, draw yarn through ✳✳ 5 times, yo, draw yarn through all 11 loops on hook, ch 1), ch 1, 1 dc in dc, ch 2 ✳. Rep from ✳ to ✳ 6 times, 1 dc in dc, ch 2, 1 bobble, ch 1, 1 dc in base of ch-3, ch 2, sl st in top of ch-3.
Round 7: ✳ 1 dc in dc, ch 2, 1 bobble to the right and 1 bobble to the left of bobble in previous row, ch 1, 1 dc in dc, ch 1 ✳. Rep from ✳ to ✳ 7 times.
Round 8: 1 dc in dc, ch 2, 3 bobbles (1 to the right, 1 in between and 1 to the left of bobbles in previous row), ch 1, 1 dc in dc, ch 2 ✳. Rep from ✳ to ✳ 7 times.
Round 9: ✳ 1 dc in dc, ch 2, 1 bobble in ch-2 loop, 1 bobble between each of next 2 bobbles, 1 bobble in ch-2 loop, ch 1, 1 dc in dc, ch 2 ✳. Rep from ✳ to ✳ 7 times.
Round 10: ✳ 1 dc in dc, ch 2, 1 dc in closing stitch of next bobble, ch 2, 3 bobbles, ch 1, 1 dc in closing stitch of 4th bobble, ch 2, 1 dc in dc, ch 2 ✳. Rep from ✳ to ✳ 7 times.
Round 11: ✳ 1 dc in dc, ch 2, 1 dc, ch 2, 1 dc in closing stitch of next bobble, ch 2, 2 bobbles, ch 1, 1 dc in closing stitch of 3rd bobble, (ch 2, 1 dc in dc) twice, ch 2 ✳. Rep from ✳ to ✳ 7 times.
Round 12: ✳ (1 dc in dc, ch 2) 3 times, 1 dc in closing stitch of next bobble, ch 2, 1 bobble, ch 1, 1 dc in closing stitch of 2nd bobble, ch 2 (1 dc in dc, ch 2) 3 times ✳. Rep from ✳ to ✳ 7 times.
Round 13: ✳ (1 dc in dc, ch 2) 4 times, 1 dc in closing stitch of bobble, ch 2, (1 dc in dc, ch 2

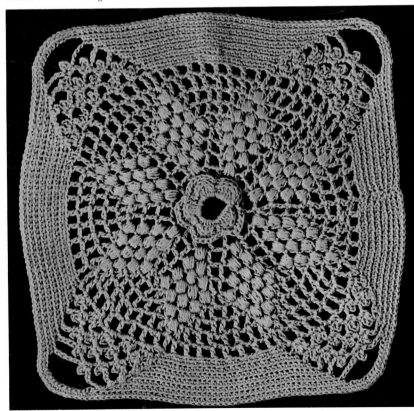

Medallion with star design

68

4 times *. Rep from * to * 7 times.

Round 14: Ch 1, * (1 ridged sc in dc [= insert hook in back loop only instead of through both loops], 2 ridged sc in ch-2 loop) 4 times, ch 4, skip one ch-2 loop, ** (1 sc, 1 picot [= ch 3 and 1 sl st in 3rd ch from hook], 1 sc, 4 ch) in next ch loop **, rep from ** to ** 5 times, skip one ch-2 loop, (2 sc in next ch-2 loop, 1 sc in dc) twice, 2 sc in ch-2 loop *. Rep from * to * 3 times.

Round 15: Ch 1, 12 ridged sc in ridged sc of previous round, * 2 ridged sc in next 2 ch, ch 5, (1 sc, 1 picot, 1 sc, ch 4) in each of next four ch-4 loops, ch 1, 2 ridged sc in last 2 ch, 20 ridged sc *. Rep from * to * 3 times, ending last repeat with 8 ridged sc.

Round 16: Ch 1, 14 ridged sc in ridged sc, * 2 ridged sc in next 2 ch, ch 6, (1 sc, 1 picot, 1 sc, ch 4) 3 times, ch 2, 2 ridged sc in next 2 ch, 24 ridged sc *. Rep from * to * 3 times ending last repeat with 10 ridged sc.

Round 17: Ch 1, 16 ridged sc in ridged sc, * 2 ridged sc in next 2 ch, ch 6, (1 sc, 1 picot, 1 sc, ch 4) twice, ch 2, 2 ridged sc in next 2 ch, 28 ridged sc *. Rep from * to * 3 times ending last repeat with 12 ridged sc.

Round 18: Ch 1, 18 ridged sc in ridged sc, * 2 ridged sc in next 2 ch, ch 7, 1 sc, 1 picot, 1 sc, ch 7, 2 ridged sc in next 2 ch, 32 ridged sc *. Rep from * to * 3 times, ending last repeat with 14 ridged sc.

Round 19: Ch 1, 20 ridged sc in ridged sc, * 2 ridged sc in next 2 ch, ch 15 (corner), 2 ridged sc in last 2 ch of ch-7 loop worked after picot, 36 ridged sc *. Rep from * to * 3 times, ending last repeat with 16 ridged sc.

Round 20: 1 ridged sc in every stitch to end of round. Fasten off.

Trimmings

Edgings

Crocheted edgings are quick and simple to make since they are crocheted directly on the work. They make an attractive finish for knitted as well as crocheted articles and if a sufficiently fine thread and hook is used, they can also be worked directly on to woven fabrics to trim handkerchiefs, tablecloths, hand towels, etc.

Crab-stitch edging. This is a very popular finish which reinforces an edge and helps to prevent stretching. It may also be used to finish off a knitted garment.

Work 1 row in sc along the edge of the main fabric on the right side, insuring that the stitches are evenly spaced. *Do not turn.*

Ch 1, * insert hook under both loops of last stitch of previous row, yo and complete sc in usual manner. Repeat from * across row, continuing to work from left to right.

Scalloped edging. This is a very simple but attractive finish.

Working into the edge of the main fabric on the right side, work 1 sc, * ch 3, skip 2 stitches, 1 sc into next stitch. Repeat from * to end. Fasten off.

Shell edging. There are several variations on this edging, but this is the simplest version.

Work 1 sl st into first stitch, * ch 3, 3 dc into next stitch, skip 2 stitches. Repeat from * to end. Fasten off.

Twisted cord edging. This edging gives an elastic but firm finish.
Row 1: Work 1 sc into each stitch to end, ch 1, turn.
Row 2: * Insert hook into first sc of previous row, yo, draw loop through keeping it fairly loose, turn the hook round so that the 2 loops on it are twisted, yo, complete stitch like a normal sc. Repeat from * to end. Fasten off.

Crab-stitch edging

Shell edging

Scalloped edging

Twisted cord edging

Borders

Crocheted borders are generally used to finish such articles as tablecloths, placemats, bedspreads or handkerchiefs. They tend to be worked in fairly complicated stitches in cotton or another smooth, fine yarn, to give a lacy effect. They can either be crocheted directly on to the main fabric or worked separately and neatly stitched on by hand.

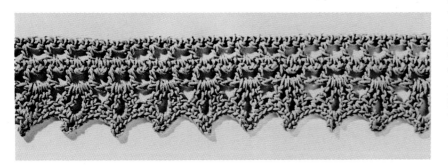

Border no. 1

Border no. 2

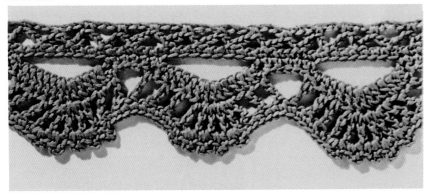

Border no. 1

Make a foundation chain in multiples of 4 plus 3.

Row 1: 1 sc in 2nd ch from hook, 1 sc in each ch, ending with ch 3, turn.

Row 2: Skip 2 stitches, * 1 dc in next stitch, ch 1, skip 1 stitch *. Rep from * to * ending with 1 dc, ch 1, turn.

Row 3: *1 sc in dc, 1 dc in ch-1 space *. Rep from * to * ending with 1 sc, ch 3, turn.

Row 4: Skip 2 stitches, * 1 dc in next stitch, ch 1, skip 1 stitch *. Rep from * to * ending with 1 dc.

Row 5: 1 sl st in first ch-1 space, ch 4 (1 tr, ch 2, 2 tr) in same ch-1 space, * skip one ch-1 space, (2 tr, ch 2, 2 tr) in next space *. Rep from * to * ending with ch 1, turn.

Row 6: 1 sc in each of first 2 tr, * (2 sc, ch 4, 2 sc) in ch-2 space, 1 sc in each of next 4 tr *. Rep from * to * ending with 2 sc. Fasten off.

Border no. 2

Make a foundation chain in multiples of 42 plus 29.

Row 1: 1 sc into 2nd ch from hook, * ch 5, skip 2 ch, 1 sc into next ch *. Rep from * to *, ch 3, turn.

Row 2: Sl st into 3rd ch of ch-5 loop, * ch 3, sl st into 3rd ch of next ch-5 loop *. Rep from * to * ending with ch 1, 1 dc into last sc, ch 1, turn.

Row 3: 1 sc into dc, 1 sc into ch-1 loop, * 3 sc into ch-3 loop *. Rep from * to * ending with 2 sc into last ch-3 loop, ch 1, turn.

Row 4: * 3 sc, ch 12, skip 8 stitches, 3 sc *. Rep from * to * to end.

Row 5: * Sl st over 3 sc, 1 dc into each of next 5 ch, (2 dc into next ch) twice, 1 dc into each of next 5 ch, sl st over 3 sc *. Rep from * to *, ch 4, turn.

Row 6: * 1 tr into dc, ch 1, skip 2 stitches, 1 tr, ch 1, skip 1 stitch, 1 tr, (ch 1, 2 tr into next stitch) twice, ch 1, 1 tr, ch 1, skip 1 stitch, 1 tr, ch 1, skip 2 stitches, 1 tr *. Rep from * to * ending with 1 tr into 3rd sl st, ch 1, turn.

Row 7: 1 sc into first dc, * (1 sc into dc, 1 sc into ch-1 loop) twice, 1 sc into dc, (ch 3, 1 sc into ch-1 loop, ch 3, 1 sc between 2 dc) twice, ch 3, 1 sc into ch-1 loop, skip 1 dc, 1 sc into ch-1 loop, 1 sc into dc *. Rep from * to * ending with 1 sc into turning chain. Fasten off.

Border no. 3

Make a foundation chain in multiples of 22 plus 6.

Row 1: 1 sc in 2nd ch from hook, 1 sc in each ch to end, ch 3, turn.

Row 2: Skip 1 stitch, * 1 dc, ch 1, skip 1 stitch *. Rep from * to * ending with 2 dc, ch 3, turn.

Row 3: Skip 2 dc, (1 dc in ch-1 loop, ch 1) 4 times, * 1 dc in ch-1 loop, ch 5, skip two ch-1 loops, (1 dc in ch-1 loop, ch 1) 8 times *. Rep from * to * ending with (1 dc in ch-1 loop, ch 1) 5 times, 1 dc in turning ch, ch 3, turn.

Row 4: (1 dc in ch-1 loop, ch 1) 5 times, * (2 dc, ch 1, 2 dc, ch 1, 2 dc, ch 1) in ch-5 loop,

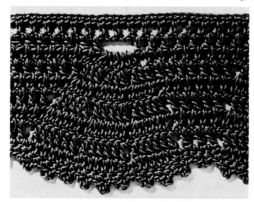

(1 dc in ch-1 loop, ch 1) 8 times *. Rep from * to * ending with (1 dc in ch-1 loop, ch 1) 4 times, 1 dc in turning ch, ch 3, turn.

Row 5: (1 dc in ch-1 loop, ch 1) 4 times, * 1 dc in ch-1 loop, ch 1, 1 dc in each of next 2 dc, ch 1, 1 dc in dc, 2 dc in next dc, ch 1, 1 dc in each of next 2 dc, 1 dc in ch-1 loop, ch 1, (1 dc in ch-1 loop, ch 1) 7 times *. Rep from * to * ending with (1 dc in ch-1 loop, ch 1) 4 times, 1 dc in turning ch, ch 3, turn.

Row 6: (1 dc in ch-1 loop, ch 1) 4 times, * (1 dc in each of next 2 dc, 2 dc in 3rd dc, ch 1) 3 times, (1 dc in ch-1 loop, ch 1) 6 times *. Rep from * to * ending with (1 dc in ch-1 loop, ch 1) 3 times, 1 dc in turning ch, ch 3, turn.

Row 7: (1 dc in ch-1 loop, ch 1) 3 times, * (1 dc in each of next 3 dc, 2 dc in 4th dc, ch 1) 3 times, (1 dc in ch-1 loop, ch 1) 5 times *. Rep from * to * ending with (1 dc in ch-1 loop, ch 1) 3 times, 1 dc in turning ch, ch 3, turn.

Row 8: (1 dc in ch-1 loop, ch 1) 3 times, * (1 dc in each of next 4 dc, 2 dc in 5th dc, ch 1) 3 times, (1 dc in ch-1 loop, ch 1) 4 times *. Rep from * to * ending with (1 dc in ch-1 loop, ch 1) twice, 1 dc in turning ch, ch 3, turn.

Row 9: (1 dc in ch-1 loop, ch 1) twice, * (1 dc in each of next 6 dc, ch 1) 3 times, (1 dc in ch-1

loop, ch 1) 3 times *. Rep from * to * ending with (1 dc in ch-1 loop, ch 1) twice, 1 dc in turning ch, ch 1, turn.

Row 10: * (1 sc in dc, 1 sc in ch-1 loop) twice, 1 sc in dc, skip 1 ch, (1 dc in each of next 6 dc, 1 dc in ch-1 loop) twice, 1 dc in each of next 6 dc, skip 1 ch *. Rep from * to * ending with 1 sc in dc, 1 sc in ch-1 loop, 1 sc in dc, 1 sc in each of next 2 ch (of turning ch), ch 1, turn.

Row 11: * 1 sc in each of next 2 sc, ch 4, skip 1 sc, 1 sc in each of next 2 sc, 1 sc in dc, (1 sc in dc, ch 4, skip 1 dc) 9 times, 1 sc in last dc of group *. Rep from * to * ending with 1 sc in next 2 sc, ch 4, skip 1 sc, 1 sc in next 2 sc. Fasten off.

Border no. 4

Make a foundation chain in multiples of 12 plus 10.

Row 1: 1 sc in 2nd ch from hook, 1 sc into each ch, ending with ch 3, turn.

Row 2: 2 dc, * ch 3, skip 3 stitches, 3 dc *. Rep from * to * ending with ch 5, turn.

Row 3: Skip 3 dc, * 1 sc in first ch-3 loop, ch 3, (3 dc, ch 2, 3 dc) in 2nd ch-3 loop, ch 3 *. Rep from * to * ending with 1 sc in last ch-3 loop, ch 3, 1 dc in turning ch, ch 4, turn.

Row 4: * 1 sc in sc, ch 4, (3 dc, ch 2, 3 dc) in ch-2 loop, ch 4 *. Rep from * to * ending with 1 sc in sc, 1 sc in 2nd ch, 4 ch, turn.

Row 5: * (2 dc, ch 2, 2 dc) in sc, ch 3, (1 dc, ch 1) 6 times in ch-2 loop, ch 2, *. Rep from * to * ending with 1 dc, ch 4, turn.

Row 6: * (1 dc, ch 2, 1 dc) in ch-2 loop of

previous row, ch 1, (1 dc in dc, 1 dc in ch) 5 times, 1 dc in dc, ch 1 *. Rep from * to * ending with 1 dc in 2nd ch, ch 3, turn.

Row 7: * 1 sc in ch-2 loop, 1 sc in each of 10 dc *. Rep from * to * ending with 1 sc in ch-2 loop, ch 2, 1 sc in turning ch. Fasten off.

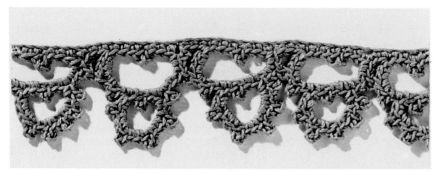

Above: Border no. 5

Right: Border no. 1 with corner

Border no. 1 with corner

Make a foundation chain in multiples of 16 plus 4 for each side, 1 ch for each corner and 1 turning ch.

Row 1: 1 sc in 2nd ch from hook, 1 sc in each remaining ch, working 3 sc in each ch where corners are to be made and ending with ch 4, turn.

Row 2: Skip 1 sc, * 1 dc, ch 3, skip 1 sc *. Rep from * to * ending with 1 dc in turning ch, ch 2, turn.

Row 3: * 1 sc in ch-3 loop of previous row, ch 2, skip next ch-3 loop, 7 tr in next ch-3 loop, ch 2, skip next ch-3 loop *. Rep from * to * working 9 tr in corner ch-3 loop and ending with 1 sc in first turning ch, ch 1, 1 sc in 3rd turning ch, ch 3, turn.

Row 4: * 1 sc in sc of previous row, ch 3, (1 tr,

Border no. 5

Make a foundation chain in multiples of 9 plus 6.

Row 1: Starting in 2nd ch from hook, work 3 sc, 1 picot (= ch 3, 1 sl st in 3rd ch from hook), 3 sc, ch 12. Remove hook from work, insert it in the 3rd stitch to the right of picot, replace working stitch (of 12th ch) on hook and work 1 sl st, (3 sc 1 picot, 3 sc, 1 picot, 4 sc, 1 picot, 2 sc) into the loop thus formed. Work 10 ch, remove hook and insert it in the middle of 4 sc just worked, replace working stitch (of 10th ch) on hook and work 1 sl st, (3 sc, 1 picot) 5 times in the new loop. This will bring work back to the 12-ch loop below. Work (2 sc, 1 picot, 3 sc, 1 picot, 3 sc) into this 12-ch loop. This will bring work back to the foundation ch. In this, work * 1 sc in each of next 6 ch, 1 picot, 3 sc, ch 12, insert hook in 3rd stitch to the right of the picot, 1 sl st, (3 sc, ch 2). In the new loop formed make a link with the picot on nearby loop, ch 1, 3 sc, 1 picot, 4 sc, 1 picot, 2 sc. Work 10 ch, insert hook in the middle of 4 sc just worked, 1 sl st, (3 sc, 1 picot) 5 times into the new loop formed. Work (2 sc, 1 picot, 3 sc, 1 picot, 3 sc) into the 12-ch loop below. This brings the work back to the foundation ch *. Rep from * to * until entire length of foundation chain has been worked. Fasten off.

Borders with corners

When working a border to edge a square item such as a placemat, tablecloth or handkerchief, extra stitches have to be worked, in keeping with the pattern, to form the corners. The examples described below show how a straight border can be adapted in this way.

ch 1) in 7 tr of previous row, ch 2 *. Rep from * to * along sides, working (1 tr, ch 1) into 9 tr in each corner and ending with 1 sc in sc, ch 1, 1 sc in turning ch, ch 4, turn.

Row 5: * 1 sc in ch-3 loop, ** 1 picot (= ch 3, 1 sc in 3rd ch from hook), (1 sc in ch-1 loop) twice **, rep from ** to ** twice, 1 picot, 1 sc in ch-3 loop *. Rep from * to * along sides, working from ** to ** four times altogether in corners and ending with 1 ch, 1 sc into 2nd turning ch. Fasten off.

Border no. 2 with corner

Make a foundation chain in multiples of 4 plus 3 for each side, 1 ch for each corner and 1 turning ch.

Row 1: 1 sc into 2nd ch from hook, 1 sc into

each remaining ch, ch 1, turn.

Row 2: 1 sc into each stitch, working 3 sc into stitch where corners are to be made.

Row 3: 1 sc, * ch 5, skip 3 sc, 1 sc into next sc *. Rep from * to * along sides, working (1 sc, ch 5, skip 2 spaces, 1 sc into central sc on corner, ch 5, skip 2 stitches, 1 sc) on each corner.

Row 4: (3 sc, 1 picot, 3 sc) into each ch-5 loop (picot = ch 3, 1 sl st into 3rd ch from hook). Fasten off.

Border no. 3 with corner

Make a foundation chain in multiples of 5 plus 1 for each side, 1 ch for each corner and

1 turning ch.

Row 1: 1 sc into 2nd ch from hook, 1 sc into each remaining ch, ch 1, turn.

Row 2: 1 sc into each stitch, working 3 sc into stitch where corners are to be made.

Row 3: Ch 7, * skip 3 stitches, 1 tr, ch 4, (3 unfin tr, yo, draw yarn through all 4 loops on hook) into next stitch *. Rep from * to * along sides but on central stitch of each corner work (1 tr, ch 4, 3 unfin tr, yo, draw yarn through all 4 loops on hook).

Row 4: * (1 sc, ch 3, 1 sc, ch 3) into each ch-4 loop, 1 sl st between tr and tr cluster *. Rep from * to *. Fasten off.

Border no. 4 with corner

Make a foundation chain in multiples of 4 plus 3 for each side, 1 ch for each corner and 1 turning ch.

Row 1: 1 sc into 2nd ch from hook, 1 sc into each remaining ch, ch 1, turn.

Row 2: 1 sc into each stitch, working 3 sc into stitch where corners are to be made.

Row 3: Ch 3, * skip 2 stitches, 1 scallop (=

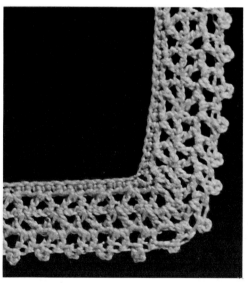

1 dc, ch 2, 1 dc) into next stitch *. Rep from * to * along the sides but work (1 scallop, ch 2, 1 scallop) on central sc at each corner.

Row 4: Ch 3, * 1 scallop between 1 scallop and the next of previous row *. Rep from * to * along the sides. At each corner work (ch 2, 1 scallop) twice into central ch-2 loop, ch 2.

Row 5: * 2 dc, 1 picot (= ch 3, 1 sl st into last dc worked) *. Rep from * to * in each ch-2 loop. Fasten off.

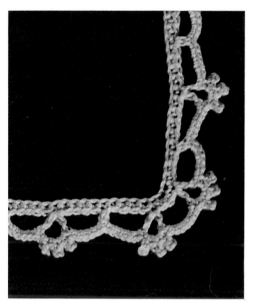

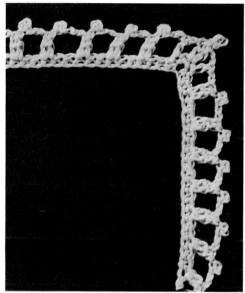

Border no. 5 with corner

Make a foundation chain in multiples of 9 plus 2 for each side, 1 for each corner and 1 turning ch.

Row 1: 1 sc into 2nd ch from hook, 1 sc into each remaining ch, ch 1, turn.

Row 2: 1 sc into each stitch, working 3 sc into stitch where corners are to be made.

Row 3: ∗ Ch 5, skip 4 stitches, 1 sc into next stitch, ch 5, skip 4 stitches, (1 dc, ch 3, 1 dc) into next stitch ∗. Rep from ∗ to ∗ along each side but work (1 dc, ch 3, 1 dc) on either side of 3-sc at each corner.

Row 4: ∗ 6 sc into ch-5 loop, 1 sl st into next sc, 6 sc into next ch-5 loop, (1 hdc, 1 picot, 1 hdc, 1 picot, 1 hdc, 1 picot, 1 hdc) into ch-3 loop ∗ (picot = ch 3, 1 sc into 3rd ch from hook). Rep from ∗ to ∗. Fasten off.

Border no. 6 with corner

Make a foundation chain in multiples of 4 plus 2 for each side, 1 ch for each corner and 1 turning ch.

Row 1: 1 sc in 2nd ch from hook, 1 sc in each remaining ch, ch 1, turn.

Row 2: 1 sc into each stitch, working 3 sc in stitch where corners are to be made, ending with ch 3, turn.

Row 3: 1 dc in second stitch, 1 picot (= ch 3, 1 sl st in 3rd ch from hook), ∗ ch 3, skip 2 stitches, 2 unfin dc, yo, draw yarn through all

3 loops on hook, 1 picot ∗. Rep from ∗ to ∗ along sides but turn corners as follows: On first of 3 sc work 1 dc, ch 2; on central sc work 2 unfin dc, yo, draw yarn through, 1 picot, ch 2; 1 dc on 3rd sc, then continue from ∗ to ∗. Fasten off.

Border no. 7 with corner

Make a foundation chain in multiples of 9 plus 7 for each side, 1 ch for each corner and 1 turning ch.

Row 1: 1 sc into 2nd ch from hook, 1 sc in each remaining ch, ch 1, turn.

Row 2: ∗ 9 sc, ch 3 ∗. Rep from ∗ to ∗ along sides to within 4 stitches of corner, 4 sc, (1 sc, ch 3, 1 sc) in corner, 4 sc, ch 3, then rep from ∗ to ∗. Fasten off.

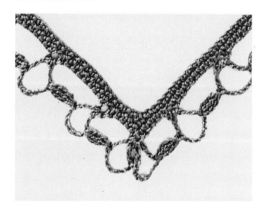

Lace edgings

If worked in very fine yarns, crocheted lace edgings can give a similar, although less delicate, effect to edgings worked in needlepoint or bobbin lace. The patterns tend to be more intricate and time consuming than those for other crochet edgings and therefore require patience and a certain amount of experience. If worked in a thicker yarn, a bolder effect is achieved.

Edging no. 1

Make 4 ch.
Row 1: 1 dc in 4th ch from hook, ch 2, 2 dc in same stitch, ch 5, turn.
Row 2: (2 dc, ch 2, 2 dc) into ch-2 loop of previous row, ch 5, turn.
Row 3: (2 dc, ch 2, 2 dc, ch 2) into ch-2 loop of previous row, 1 dc into last dc of previous row, 3 dc into ch-5 loop, ch 10.
Row 4: 1 dc into 4 dc of previous row, ch 2, 1 dc into next dc, ch 2, (2 dc, ch 2, 2 dc) into ch-2 loop, ch 5.
Row 5: (2 dc, ch 2, 2 dc) into ch-2 loop of previous row, ch 2, 1 dc into 2nd dc of next 2-dc, ch 2, 1 dc into next dc, ch 2, 3 dc into next ch-2 loop, 1 dc into first dc of 4-dc of previous row, ch 2, 16 dc into ch-10 loop (made at the end of Row 3), ch 5, 1 dc into ch-5 loop made in Row 1, ch 2.
Row 6: 1 dc into 3rd ch of ch-5, 1 dc into first dc of 16-dc, * 1 picot (= ch 5, 1 sc into 5th ch from hook), skip 1 stitch, 1 dc into next stitch *. Rep from * to * into the 16-dc, 4 dc into ch-2 loop, ch 2, 1 dc into next dc, ch 2, 1 dc into next dc, ch 2, 1 dc into next dc of previous row, ch 2, 2 dc, ch 2, 2 dc into next ch-2 loop, ch 5.
Row 7: As Row 2.

Rows 2 to 7 form the pattern and are repeated as required.

When the edging is complete, work 1 row on the side which will be attached to the fabric as follows: * 1 sc into center of ch-5 loop, ch 5 *. Rep from * to *. Fasten off.

Edging no. 1

Edging no. 2

Edging no. 2

Make 20 ch.
  Note: Replace first dc of each row with ch 3.
Row 1: 1 dc in 4th ch from hook, 1 dc in each ch to end.
Row 2: * 3 dc, ch 2, skip 2 stitches *. Rep from * to * twice more, 3 dc.
Row 3: As Row 1
Row 4: As Row 2
Row 5: As Row 1
Row 6: As Row 2
Row 7: As Row 1
Row 8: As Row 2, continuing with ch 14, 1 sl st into 3rd starting ch of Row 5, ch 2, 1 sc into first starting ch of Row 5, turn.
Row 9: 24 dc into ch-14 loop, 18 dc.

Row 10: (3 dc, ch 2, skip 2 stitches) 3 times, 3 dc, (ch 2, skip 1 dc, 1 dc into next stitch), ch 2, 1 sl st into 3rd starting-ch of Row 3, ch 1, 1 sc into first ch of Row 3, turn.

Row 11: 2 dc into each ch-2 loop and 1 dc into each dc.

Row 12: (3 dc, ch 2, skip 2 stitches) 3 times, 3 dc, (ch 2, skip 1 dc, 1 dc into next stitch) 19 times, ch 1, 1 sl st into 3rd starting ch of Row 1, turn.

Row 13: Ch 1, 1 sc into first ch-1 loop, * 1 picot (= ch 3, 1 sl st into first ch), 1 sc in ch-2 loop, 1 sc in dc, 1 sc in ch-2 loop *. Rep from * to * ending with 1 picot in last ch-2 loop.

Rows 2 to 13 form the pattern and are repeated as required.

Edging no. 3

Make 14 ch.

Row 1: 1 tr in 9th ch from hook, ch 8, 1 sc in last ch, ch 1, turn.

Row 2: 11 sc in ch-8 loop, 1 sc in tr, ch 1, 1 sc in 2nd ch, ch 4, turn.

Row 3: 1 dc in sc of previous row, (ch 2, skip 1 stitch, 1 sc in next stitch) 4 times, ch 4, skip 4 stitches, 1 sc in last stitch, ch 6, turn.

Row 4: 1 sc in ch-4 loop (ch 5, 1 sc) in each ch-2 loop, ch 1, 1 sc in dc of previous row, ch 1, 1 sc in 2nd ch, ch 6, turn.

Row 5: 1 tr in 2nd sc of previous row, ch 8, skip 1 loop, 1 sc in next ch-5 loop.

Rows 2 to 5 form the pattern and are repeated as required.

Edging no. 4

Make 20 ch.

Row 1: 1 dc into 8th ch from hook, 2 dc, ch 2, skip 2 ch, 3 dc, ch 5, turn.

Row 2: 3 dc into ch-2 loop, ch 2, skip 3 dc, 3 dc into turning ch of previous row, ch 5, turn.

Row 3: Skip 3 dc, 3 dc into ch-2 loop, ch 2, skip 3 dc, 3 dc into turning ch-5, ch 10, 1 sc into first of the 20 foundation ch, 2 turning ch, turn.

When working subsequent fans, link the ch 10 with a sc into the 4th picot of the previous fan.

Row 4: 14 dc into ch-10 loop, ch 2, skip 3 dc, 3 dc into ch-2 loop, ch 2, skip 3 dc, 3 dc into 5 turning ch, ch 5, turn.

Row 5: Skip 3 dc, 3 dc into ch-2 loop, ch 2, skip 3 dc, 3 dc into ch-2 loop, 14 dc worked between 14 dc of previous row, ch 2, turn.

When working subsequent fans, after the 14 dc work 1 sc into the 7th picot of previous fan.

Row 6: (1 dc, ch 1) 14 times, worked between 14 dc of previous row, ch 2, skip 3 dc, 3 dc into next ch-2 loop, ch 2, 3 dc into 5 turning ch, ch 5, turn.

Row 7: Skip 3 dc of previous row, 3 dc into ch-2 loop, ch 2, skip 3 dc, 3 dc into next ch-2 loop, ch 1, (1 tr into ch-1 loop, ch 1) 14 times, ch 2, turn.

When working subsequent fans, after the 14 dc work 1 sc into the 9th picot of previous fan.

Row 8: * Ch 4, 1 sc into ch-1 loop, 1 sc into next tr of previous row *. Rep from * to * 15 times, working picots on the last 3 stitches;

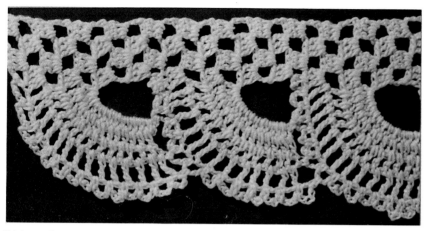

Edging no. 4

ch 2, 3 dc into ch-1 loop, ch 2, skip 3 dc, 3 dc into next 5 turning ch, ch-5, turn.

Row 9: Skip 3 dc, 3 dc into ch-2 loop, ch 2, skip 3 dc, 3 dc into ch-2 loop, ch 5, turn.

Rows 2 to 9 form the pattern and are repeated as required.

Edging no. 5

Make 23 ch.

Row 1 (right side): 1 dc in 7th ch from hook, 11 dc, ch 4, skip 4 ch, 1 sc, ch 6, turn.

Row 2: 1 sc into first ch loop, ch 4, skip 2 dc, 9 dc in between dc of previous row, skip 2 dc, ch 4, turn.

Row 3: Skip 2 dc, 6 dc between dc of previous row, ch 4, skip 2 dc, 1 sc into ch-4 loop, ch 4, 1 sc into turning ch loop, ch 6, turn.

Row 4: 1 sc into first ch-4 loop of previous row, ch 4, 1 sc into next ch-4 loop, ch 4, skip 2 dc, 3 dc in between dc of previous row, skip 2 dc, ch 6, turn.

Row 5: Skip 3 dc, 1 sc into first ch-4 loop of previous row, ch 4, 1 sc into next ch-4 loop, ch 4, 1 sc into turning ch, ch 6, turn.

Row 6: 1 sc into first ch-4 loop, ch 4, 1 sc into next ch-4 loop, ch 4, 3 dc into turning ch, turn.

Row 7: Ch 8, 1 dc into 7th ch from hook, 1 dc into next ch, 2 dc between dc of previous row, 2 dc into ch-4 loop, ch 4, 1 sc into next ch-4 loop, ch 6, turn.

Row 8: 1 sc into ch-4 loop, ch 4, 2 dc into next ch-4 loop, 5 dc between dc of previous row, 2 dc into turning ch of previous row, turn.

Row 9: Ch 8, 1 dc into 7th ch from hook, 1 dc into next ch, 8 dc in between dc of previous row, 2 dc into ch-4 loop, ch 4, 1 sc into turning ch, ch 6, turn.

Rows 2 to 9 form the pattern and are repeated as required.

To complete the scalloped edge, work as follows:

Row 1: ∗ (2 dc, ch 3, 2 dc, ch 3, 2 dc) into ch-6 loop at point of scallop; (2 dc, ch 3, 2 dc) into ch-4 loop at end of 6-dc row (Row 3); 1 sc into dc at end of 3-dc row (Row 6); (2 dc, ch 3, 2 dc) into ch-6 loop on 6-dc row (Row 7) ∗. Rep from ∗ to ∗ for entire length.

Row 2: (1 sc, ch 4) twice in each of next three ch-3 loops, ∗ 1 sc in ch-1 loop (ch 4, 1 sc) twice in next four ch-3 loops ∗. Rep from ∗ to ∗.

With right side facing, rejoin yarn to right-hand corner of straight edge and work 1 row of sc along entire length.

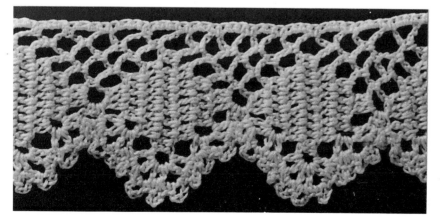

Edging no. 5

Insertions

Insertions are strips of crochet which, as the name implies, are inserted into a piece of fabric as a decorative band, rather than being attached to the edge. For example, one or more insertions could be used to enliven a plain fabric table runner. An insertion is worked separately and its width is determined by the number of stitches in the pattern.

Insertion no. 1

Make 12 ch.

Row 1: 1 dc in 4th ch from hook, 4 dc, ch 4, skip 4 ch, 1 dc in last ch, ch 3, turn.

Row 2: 4 dc in ch-4 loop, ch 4, skip 4 dc, 1 dc in turning ch, ch 3, turn.

Row 2 forms the pattern and is repeated as required.

Finish edges as follows: Join yarn to first foundation chain. Working along length of insertion, ch 3, (1 tr, ch 4, 1 tr) in each space formed by dc at ends of alternate rows, ending with 1 tr in last dc.

Fasten off and work the other edge in the same way.

Insertion no. 2

Make 30 ch.

Row 1: 1 sc in 6th ch from hook, * ch 5, skip 5 ch, 1 sc *. Rep from * to *, ending with 1 sc, ch 5, turn.

Row 2: * 1 sc into 3rd ch of ch-5 loop, ch 5 *. Rep from * to * ending with 1 sc in 3rd turning ch, ch 5, turn.

Rows 3 to 7: As Row 2.

Row 8: * 1 sc into 3rd ch of ch-5 loop, ch 5 *. Rep from * to * once, ch 3, 4 dc into next ch-5 loop, ch 3, 1 sc into next loop, ch 5, 1 sc in 3rd turning ch, ch 5, turn.

Row 9: 1 sc in ch-5 loop, ch 3, 4 dc in ch-3 loop, ch 3, skip 4 dc, 4 dc in ch-3 loop, ch 3, 1 sc in ch-5 loop, ch 5, 1 sc in 3rd turning ch, ch 5, turn.

Row 10: 1 sc in ch-5 loop, ch 5, 1 sc in ch-3 loop, ch 3, skip 4 dc, 4 dc in ch-3 loop, ch 3, skip 4 dc, 1 sc in ch-3 loop, ch 5, 1 sc in 3rd turning ch, ch 5, turn.

Row 11: 1 sc in ch-5 loop, ch 5, 1 sc in ch-3 loop, ch 5, skip 4 dc, 1 sc in ch-3 loop, ch 5, 1 sc in ch-5 loop, ch 5, 1 sc in 3rd turning ch, ch 5, turn.

Rows 2 to 11 form the pattern and are repeated as required.

Insertion no. 3

Make 31 ch.

Row 1: 1 dc in 6th ch from hook, ch 2, skip 2 ch, 8 dc, ch 2, skip 1 ch, 8 dc, ch 2, skip 2 ch, 1 dc, ch 2, skip 2 ch, 1 dc, ch 5, turn.

Insertion no. 1

Insertion no. 2

79

Insertion no. 3

Row 2: 1 dc in 2nd dc, ch 2, 4 dc, skip 4 dc, ch 5, 1 dc into ch-2 loop, ch 5, skip 4 dc, 4 dc, ch 2, 1 dc, ch 2, 1 dc in 3rd of 5 turning ch, ch 5, turn.

Row 3: 1 dc in 2nd dc, ch 2, 2 dc, ch 5, skip 2 dc, 1 sc into 3rd ch of ch-5 loop, ch 5, 1 sc in 3rd ch of next ch-5 loop, ch 5, skip 2 dc, 2 dc, ch 2, 1 dc, ch 2, 1 dc into 3rd of 5 turning ch, ch 5, turn.

Row 4: 1 dc in 2nd dc, ch 2, 2 dc, 2 dc in first 2 ch of ch-5 loop, ch 5, 1 dc into 3rd ch of 2nd ch-5 loop, ch 5, 2 dc in 4th and 5th ch of 3rd ch-5 loop, 2 dc in next 2 dc, ch 2, 1 dc, ch 2, 1 dc into 3rd of 5 turning ch of previous row.

Rows 1 to 4 form the pattern and are repeated as required.

Insertion no. 4

Make a chain of 12 stitches and join with a sl st to form a ring.

Row 1: Ch 1 (= 1 sc), 11 sc into ring, keeping these stitches on one half of ring, turn.

Row 2: Ch 4 (= 1 dc, ch 1), skip first sc, (1 dc, ch 1) into each sc, ending with 1 dc into starting ch of previous row, turn.

Row 3: Ch 5 (= 1 dc, ch 2), skip 1 dc, (1 dc, ch 2) into each dc, ending with 1 dc into 3rd starting ch.

Without breaking the yarn, continue as follows: * Make 12 ch and join with sl st into first ch to form another ring.

Row 1: Working into only half the ring, on the opposite side to previous ring, ch 1, 11 sc, turn.

Row 2: Ch 4, skip first sc, (1 dc, ch 1) into each sc, ending with 1 dc into starting ch. Work 1 sl st into last dc of Row 2 of previous motif, do not turn.

Row 3: 1 sl st into last sc of Row 1 of first motif, turn. (No turning ch is required as work is now level with top of dc.) (Ch 2, 1 dc) into each of following 12 dc *. Rep from * to * for length of insertion, making each motif on alternate sides of ch rings.

Complete both sides of insertion by working 9 sc into each unworked half-ring and 3 sc into each ch-2 loop. Fasten off.

Insertion no. 4

49 patterns for garments, toys and articles for the home

The following pages offer a choice of designs for men, women and children, as well as patterns for household items such as tablecloths and bedcovers. The patterns have been graded according to the degree of expertise required to make them, from one to three stars (✽ = beginner, ✽✽ = intermediate, ✽✽✽ = advanced).

In the case of garments, instructions for one or more alternative sizes are given in brackets after the first size. We recommend that the crocheter should underline in pencil the relevant size throughout the pattern before beginning work. Sizes for adult garments are based on chest measurements.

Where appropriate the patterns are accompanied by charts and diagrams with arrows indicating the direction of the work and where the yarn is rejoined.

The patterns

White curtains in filet crochet (1)
Color illustration on page 85

Standard: ☆☆

Gauge: 14 × 14 filet crochet squares = 10 × 10 cm (4 × 4 ins).

Size: The curtain measures 63 × 48 cm (25 × 19 ins).

Materials: 140 g (5 oz) crochet cotton no. 8 in white; size 4 steel crochet hook.

Stitches used: Filet crochet (see page 32); double treble (see page 29); single crochet (see page 28); slip stitch (see page 28).

The articles illustrated in color on page 85

Method

● Make 214 foundation chains and work first row in sc, starting in 2nd ch from hook.

Continue in filet crochet, working the mesh as follows: * 1 dc, ch 2, skip 2 foundation ch *, repeat from * to *. Work 4 cm (1½ ins).

Begin following the chart below, but to form a framework of filet crochet around the border of blocks at the edge of the chart, work the first and last 7 squares in open mesh stitch as above, i.e. repeat from * to * 7 times at the beginning and end of each row, working the intervening stitches in blocks and spaces according to the chart.

When the floral motif is complete, continue until curtain measures 63 cm (25 ins). Work the last row as follows: * 1 dtr, ch 2, skip 2 base stitches *. Rep from * to * ending with 1 dtr. When the curtain is complete, the curtain rod will be threaded through this row, under alternate dtr.

● *To finish:* Work a row of single crochet down one side of curtain, along lower edge and up the other side, making one stitch into each space, turn.

Next row: into each sc work one picot (= ch 3, 1 sl st into 3rd ch from hook) and 1 sl st. Finish off.

Now work a border along lower edge as follows:
Row 1: * 1 sl st into picot, ch 10, skip 1 picot *. Rep from * to * ending with 1 sl st.
Row 2: Ch 5, * 1 sc into center of ch-10 loop, ch 10 *. Rep from * to * ending with 1 sc.
Row 3: Ch 5, * 4 dc into 5th ch of ch-10 in previous row, ch 6, 4 dc into 6th ch of ch-10 in previous row, 1 sc into center of next ch-10 loop *. Rep from * to * to end of row.
Row 4: Ch 5, * (5 dc, 1 picot, 5 dc) into ch-6 loop, 1 sc into sc. Rep from * to * to end of row. Finish off.

Press curtain under a damp cloth with a hot iron.

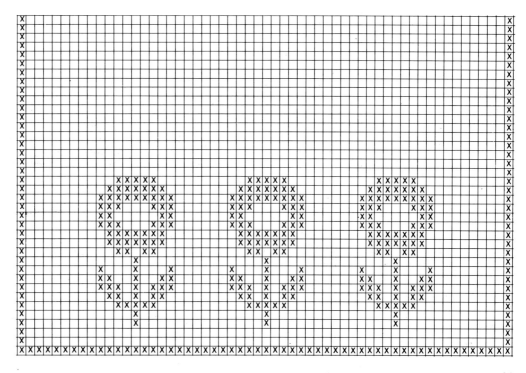

Chart for the flower motifs of the curtain in filet crochet

☐ space

☒ block

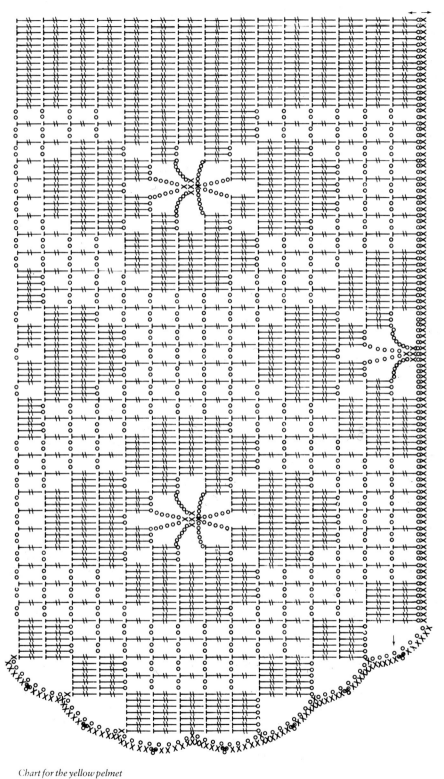

Chart for the yellow pelmet
○ chain stitch
⟊ treble
✕ single crochet
⊕ 1 picot − 3 chain stitches joined by 1 slip stitch

Yellow valence (2)
Color illustration on page 85

Standard: ☆☆

Gauge: 28 stitches × 10 rows = 10 × 10 cm (4 × 4 ins).

Size: The pelmet measures 53 × 37 cm (21 × 14½ ins).

Materials: 100 g (4 oz) crochet cotton no. 5 in yellow; size D aluminum or size 1 steel crochet hook.

Stitches used: Treble (see page 29); single crochet (see page 28); slip stitch (see page 28).

Method
● The valence is worked back and forth, following the chart, starting at top right. Even numbered rows are read from top to bottom of the page and odd numbered rows from bottom to top.

Unlike most examples of filet crochet, the valence is worked in blocks and spaces consisting of treble and chain rather than double crochet and chain. The centers of the flower motifs are worked in single crochet. The symbols for these stitches are given in the key to the chart but since this type of chart may be unfamiliar, the first 3 rows are written out in detail below.

Note that the chart does not show the turning chain required at the end of each row: the first treble of each row must be replaced by 4 turning ch.

Make 100 chains.

Row 1: Starting in 5th ch from hook, 6 tr, (ch 2, skip 2 foundation ch, 1 tr) 7 times, 9 tr, ch 10, skip 6 foundation ch, 3 sc, ch 10, skip 6 foundation ch, 10 tr, (ch 2, skip 2 foundation ch, 1 tr) 8 times, 14 tr, ch 4, turn.

Row 2: 14 tr, (ch 2, skip 2 stitches, 1 tr) 8 times, 12 tr, ch 8, 1 sc into 2nd sc of ch-3 in previous row, ch 8, 13 tr, (ch 2, skip 2 stitches, 1 tr) 7 times, 6 tr, ch 9, turn.

Row 3: Starting in 5th ch from hook, 5 tr into remaining ch-5, 1 tr into last tr of previous row, (ch 2, skip 2 stitches, 1 tr) 10 times, 6 tr, ch 2, skip 2 stitches, 1 tr in tr of previous row, 3 tr into first 3 ch of ch-8 loop, ch 2, 3 tr into last 3 ch of next ch-8 loop, 1 tr, ch 2, skip 2 stitches, 7 tr, (ch 2, skip 2 stitches, 1 tr) 9 times, 14 tr, ch 4, turn.

Continue according to chart.

● *To finish:* Fold the 14-tr border along the long, straight edge in half and hem; this is to take the curtain rod.

Now work around the other 3 sides as follows. With the right side towards you, starting below the hem just made, work in sc to the corner. Work (1 sc, ch 8) according to the chart to form the scalloped border along the bottom of the pelmet, and then work 1 sc into each foundation chain. Finish off. Rejoin thread to bottom left-hand corner and work * (5 sc, 1 picot [= ch 3, 1 sl st into 3rd ch from hook], 5 sc) into ch-8 loop, 1 sc into sc of previous row *. Repeat from * to * to end of row. Finish off and fasten ends.

Press the valence under a damp cloth with a hot iron, starching lightly if necessary.

Lace tablecloth
Color illustration on page 86

Standard: ☆☆☆

Gauge: The circle formed by the first round of trebles (Round 2) measures 2 cm (¾ in) in diameter.

Size: The tablecloth is 200 cm (approx. 78 ins) in diameter.

Materials: 400 g (14½oz) no. 12 crochet cotton in écru; size 9 steel crochet hook.

Stitches used: Slip stitch and single crochet (see

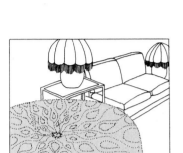

The lace tablecloth illustrated in color on page 86

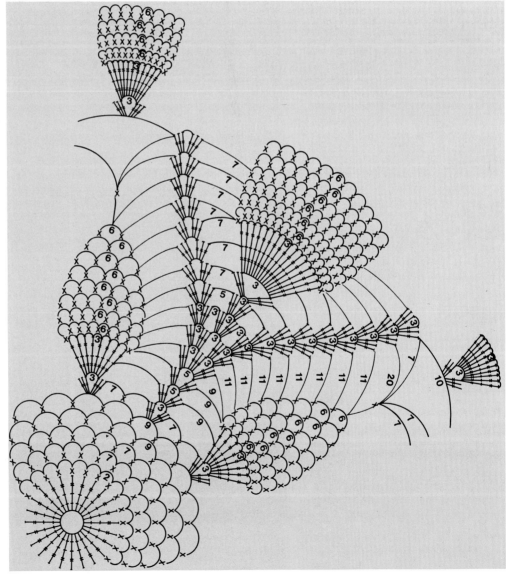

Chart for the first 21 rounds of the lace tablecloth

2⌢ chain loop (the figure indicates the number of chain stitches to be worked)

Ŧ   double crochet

Ŧ   treble

✕   single crochet

Chart for a segment of the complete lace tablecloth

◁ double group of trebles linked by a chain loop (the figure indicates how many trebles and chains are to be worked)

◑ base of pineapple motif (the figure indicates how many trebles are to be worked)

○ the number of chain stitches to be worked

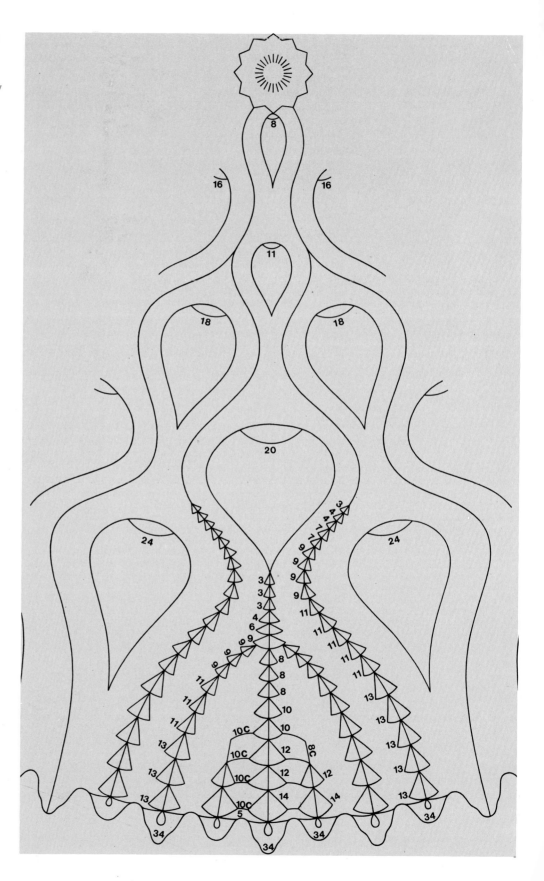

page 28); double crochet and treble (see page 29).

Method

● The tablecloth is worked in the round, as described on page 30, without turning the work.

Make 12 ch and join with a sl st to form a ring.

Round 1: 3 starting ch, 23 dc into ring; close round with 1 sl st.

Round 2: 4 starting ch, 23 tr; close round with 1 sl st.

Round 3: Ch 3, * 1 sc into tr, ch 2 * to end of round, closing with 1 sl st in first ch.

Round 4: 1 sl st into 2nd ch of previous round, (1 sc, ch 7) into each ch-2 loop to end of round, closing with 1 sl st into first sc.

Round 5: Sl st to 4th ch of previous round, (1 sc, ch 7) into each ch-7 loop to end of round, closing with 1 sl st into first sc.

Round 6: Sl st to 4th ch of previous round, (1 sc, ch 9) into each ch-7 loop to end of round, closing with 1 sl st into first sc.

Round 7: Sl st to 5th ch of previous round, (1 sc, ch 9) into each ch-9 loop to end of round, closing with 1 sl st into first sc.

Round 8: Sl st to 4th ch of previous round, * (3 tr, ch 3, 3 tr) into ch-9 loop, ch 7, 1 sc into next ch-9 loop, ch 7 *. Rep from * to * to end of round, closing with 1 sl st into first tr.

Round 9: 2 sl sts into 2 tr of previous round, * 8 tr (= base of pineapple motif) into the ch-3 loop between the two groups of tr, ch 9, (3 tr, ch 5, 3 tr) into ch-3 loop between next two groups of tr, ch 9 *. Rep from * to * to end of round, closing with 1 sl st into first tr.

Round 10: * (1 tr, ch 3 into tr of previous round) 7 times, 1 tr into last tr, ch 9, (3 tr, ch 5, 3 tr) into ch-5 loop between the two groups of tr, ch 9 *. Rep from * to * to end of round, closing with 1 sl st into top of starting ch.

Round 11: Ch 7, * (1 sc into ch-3 loop, ch 6) 7 times, 1 sc into last tr, ch 9, (3 tr, ch 3, 3 tr, ch 3, 3 tr) into ch-5 loop between the two groups of tr in previous round, ch 9, 1 sc into tr, ch 6 *. Rep from * to * to end of round, closing with 1 sl st into first ch.

Round 12: Sl st to 3rd ch of first ch-6 loop of previous round, * (1 sc into ch-6 loop, ch 6) 7 times, 1 sc into last ch-6 loop, ch 11, (3 tr, ch 3, 3 tr) into first ch-3 loop between two groups of tr in previous round, ch 3, (3 tr, ch 3, 3 tr) into 2nd ch-3 loop between two groups of tr, ch 11 *. Rep from * to * to end of round, closing with 1 sl st into first sc.

Round 13: Sl st to 3rd ch of first ch-6 loop of previous round, * (1 sc into ch-6 loop, ch 6) 6 times, 1 sc into last ch-6 loop, ch 11, (3 tr, ch 3, 3 tr) into first ch-3 loop between two groups of tr in previous round, ch 3, (3 tr, ch 3, 3 tr) into 2nd ch-3 loop between two groups of tr in previous round, ch 3, (3 tr, ch 3, 3 tr) into 3rd ch-3 loop between two groups of tr in previous round, ch 11 *. Rep from * to * to end of round, closing with 1 sl st into first sc.

Round 14: Sl st to 3rd ch of first ch-6 loop of previous round, * (1 sc into ch-6 loop, ch 6) 5 times, 1 sc into last ch-6 loop, ch 11, (3 tr, ch 3, 3 tr) into first ch-3 loop between two groups of tr in previous round, ch 5, skip next ch-3 loop, (3 tr, ch 3, 3 tr) into 3rd ch-3 loop of previous round, ch 5, skip next ch-3 loop, (3 tr, ch 3, 3 tr) into 5th ch-3 loop of previous round, ch 11 *. Rep from * to * to end of round, closing with 1 sl st into first sc.

Round 15: Sl st to 3rd ch of first ch-6 loop of previous round, * (1 sc into ch-6 loop, ch 6) 4 times, 1 sc into last ch-6 loop, ch 11, (3 tr, ch 3, 3 tr) into first ch-3 loop of previous round, ch 7, (3 tr, ch 3, 3 tr) into 2nd ch-3 loop of previous round, ch 7, (3 tr, ch 3, 3 tr) into 3rd ch-3 loop of previous round, ch 11 *. Rep from * to * to end of round, closing with 1 sl st into first sc.

Round 16: Sl st to 3rd ch of first ch-6 loop of previous round, * (1 sc into ch-6 loop, ch 6) 3 times, 1 sc into last ch-6 loop, ch 11, (3 tr, ch 3, 3 tr) into first ch-3 loop of previous round, ch 7, 16 tr (= base of pineapple motif) into 2nd ch-3 loop, ch 7, (3 tr, ch 3, 3 tr) into 3rd ch-3 loop of previous round, ch 11 *. Rep from * to * to end of round, closing with 1 sl st into first sc.

Round 17: Sl st to 3rd ch of first ch-6 loop of previous round, * (1 sc into ch-6 loop, ch 6) twice, 1 sc into last ch-6 loop, ch 11, ** (3 tr, ch 3, 3 tr) into ch-3 loop of previous round **, ch 7 (1 tr, ch 3) into each of the 16 tr of previous round, ch 4, repeat from ** to **, ch 11 *. Repeat from * to *, closing with 1 sl st into first sc.

Round 18: Sl st to 3rd ch of first ch-6 loop, * 1 sc into ch-6 loop, ch 6, 1 sc into next ch-6 loop, ch 11, ** (3 tr, ch 3, 3 tr) into ch-3 loop of previous round **, ch 7, 1 sc into first tr of 16 tr, (ch 6, 1 sc into ch-3 loop of previous round) 15 times, ch 6, 1 sc into last tr of previous round, ch 7, repeat from ** to **, ch 11 *. Repeat from * to *, closing with 1 sl st into first sc.

Round 19: As Round 18, working 1 sc into single ch-6 loop at tip of pineapple motif and (1 sc, ch 6) into each of 16 ch-6 loops.

Round 20: Sl st to 3rd ch of ch-6 loop, ch 20, * ** (3 tr, ch 3, 3 tr) into ch-3 loop of previous round **, ch 7, (1 sc, ch 6 into ch-6 loop) 14 times, 1 sc into last ch-6 loop, ch 7, repeat from ✹✹ to ✹✹, ch 20, 1 sc into ch-6 loop, sl st along 13 stitches of ch-20 just worked, ch 7 ✹. Repeat from ✹ to ✹, ending last repeat with ch 7, 1 sl st into 13th ch of 20 starting ch.

Round 21: As Round 20, reducing the number of ch-6 loops worked in the larger pineapple motifs by 1 and working (ch 7, 1 sc into 13th ch of previous row, ch 7) at tips of completed pineapple motifs.

Round 22: As Round 21, but working ch 10 above (ch 7, 1 sc, ch 7) of previous row.

On the following row, a (3 tr, ch 3, 3 tr) group worked into the ch-10 loop forms the base of a new pineapple motif. Proceed as described above. The size of each successive pineapple motif is determined by the number of trebles worked into the ch-3 base, as shown on the chart on page 90. The number of treble groups forming the border between the pineapple motifs corresponds to the number of rows of ch-6 loops worked for each motif.

● *To finish:* Press the tablecloth under a damp cloth with a hot iron or have the cloth professionally pressed.

The centerpieces illustrated in color on page 87

Flower motif centerpiece (1)
Color illustration on page 87

Standard: ☆☆☆

Gauge: At the end of the first round the ring measures 1 cm (⅜ in) in diameter.

Size: The centerpiece is 30 cm (12 ins) in diameter.

Materials: 30 g (1 oz) crochet cotton no. 12 in white; size 10 steel crochet hook.

Stitches used: Slip stitch and single crochet (see page 28); treble (see page 29).

Method
● The centerpiece is worked in the round (see page 30) without turning the work.

Make 8 ch and join with a sl st to form a ring.

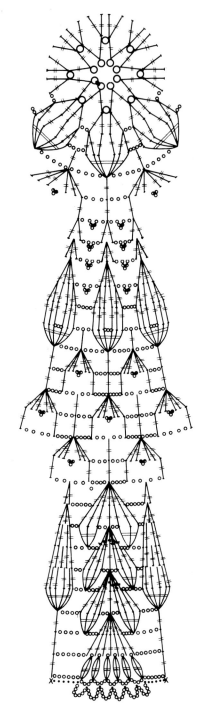

Chart for the flower motif centerpiece
- ○ chain stitch
- ⟊ treble
- ● slip stitch
- ✕ single crochet
- ⛬ 1 picot = 3 chain stiches joined together by 1 slip stitch
- ⚠ unfinished trebles closed together

Round 1: Ch 5, (2 tr, ch 1) 7 times into ring, 1 tr. Close round with 1 sl st into 4th starting ch.

Round 2: Ch 4, 1 tr into base of ch, (2 tr into next tr, ch 2, 2 tr into next tr) 7 times, 2 tr into next tr, ch 2. Close round with 1 sl st into 4th starting ch.

Round 3: Ch 4, 1 tr into base of ch, (1 tr into each of next 2 tr, 2 tr into next tr, ch 4, 2 tr into next tr) 7 times, 1 tr into each of next 2 tr, 2 tr into next tr, ch 4. Close round with 1 sl st into 4th starting ch.

Round 4: Ch 4, 5 unfinished tr, (yo, draw yarn through all 6 loops on hook, ch 5, 1 tr into ch-4 loop of previous round, ch 5, 6 unfinished tr) 7 times, yo, draw yarn through all 6 loops, ch 5, 1 tr into ch-4 loop, ch 5. Close round with 1 sl st into 4th starting ch.

Round 5: Ch 7, (3 tr into tr of previous round, 1 picot [= ch 3, 1 sl st into 3rd ch from hook], 3 tr into same tr, ch 3, 1 tr into closing stitch of 6-tr group, ch 3) 7 times, 3 tr into last tr, 1 picot, 3 tr into same tr, ch 3. Close round with 1 sl st into 4th starting ch.

Round 6: Ch 6, 1 picot, ch 2 (1 tr into first tr of 6-tr group, * ch 2, 1 picot, ch 2 *, 1 tr into last tr of 6-tr group, repeat from * to *, 1 tr into tr of previous row, repeat from * to *) 7 times, 1 tr into first tr of last 6-tr group, repeat from * to *, 1 tr into last tr, repeat from * to *. Close round with 1 sl st in 4th starting ch.

Round 7: As Round 6, working 2 tr into each tr of previous round.

Round 8: 1 sl st, as Round 6, working 3 tr between each pair of tr in previous round.

Round 9: 1 sl st, as Round 6, working 4 tr into the second tr of the 3-tr in previous round.

Round 10: As Round 3, working repeat 23 times.

Round 11: Ch 4, 2 tr, * ch 3, 3 tr *. Repeat from * to *, ending with ch 3. Close round with 1 sl st into 4th starting ch.

Round 12: As Round 4, but working 4 ch between tr instead of 5 ch. Work repeat 23 times.

Round 13: As Round 5, working repeat 23 times.

Round 14: Ch 8, * 1 tr into first tr of 6-tr group, ch 4, 1 tr into last tr of 6-tr group, ch 4, 1 tr into 1-tr of previous round, ch 4 *. Repeat from * to *. Close round with 1 sl st into 4th starting ch.

Round 15: As Round 5, beginning with 6-tr group and working 1 tr into ch loop above picot of Round 13. Work repeat 23 times.

Round 16: As Round 14.

Round 17: 2 sl sts, work as Round 13.

Round 18: As Round 14.

Round 19: Ch 4, 6 tr into base of ch, * ch 5, 2 tr into ch-4 loop above picot of Round 17, ch 5, skip 1 tr, 7 tr into next tr of previous round *. Repeat from * to * ending with ch 5, 2 tr into ch-4 loop above picot of Round 17, ch 5. Close round with 1 sl st into 4th starting ch.

Round 20: Ch 4, 2 tr, * ch 2, 1 tr, ch 2, 3 tr, ch 2, 3 tr between 2-tr of previous round, ch 2, 3 tr *. Repeat from * to * ending with 3 tr between last 2-tr of previous round, ch 2. Close round with 1 sl st into 4th starting ch.

Round 21: Ch 4, 2 unfinished tr, * yo, draw yarn through all 3 loops on hook, ch 3, 7 tr into tr of previous round, ch 3, 3 unfinished tr, yo, draw yarn through all 3 loops on hook, ch 2, 4 tr into 3 tr of previous round, ch 2, 3 unfinished tr *. Repeat from * to * ending with 4 tr into last 3-tr of previous round, ch 2. Close round with 1 sl st into 4th starting ch.

Round 22: 1 sl st, ch 4, * 3 tr, ch 2, 1 tr, ch 2, 3 tr, 1 tr into first ch of ch-3 loop, ch 2, 5 tr into 4-tr group, ch 2, 1 tr into last ch of next ch-3 loop *. Repeat from * to *, ending with 5 into last 4-tr group of previous round, ch 2. Close round with 1 sl st into 4th starting ch.

Round 23: As Round 21, working 4 unfinished tr instead of 3 unfinished tr and 6 tr into 5-tr group of previous round.

Round 24: 2 sl sts, as Round 22 but replacing 5-tr group by (6 unfinished tr worked into 6-tr of previous round, yo, draw yarn through all 6 loops on hook).

Round 25: Ch 4, 3 unfinished tr, * yo, draw yarn through all 4 loops on hook, ch 4, 7 tr, ch 4, 4 unfinished tr, yo, draw yarn through all 4 loops on hook, ch 4, 1 tr into closing stitch of 6 tr group of previous round, ch 4, 4 unfinished tr *. Repeat from * to * ending with 1 tr into last 6-tr group, ch 4. Close round with 1 sl st into 4th starting ch.

Round 26: 4 sl sts, ch 4, (1 tr, ch 1) into next 6 tr, * ch 6, 1 tr into tr of previous round, ch 6, (1 tr, ch 1) into 7-tr *. Repeat from * to *, ending with 1 tr, ch 6. Close round with 1 sl st into 4th starting ch.

Round 27: 1 sl st, ch 4 (= 1 unfinished tr), * (3 unfinished tr, yo, draw yarn through all 3 loops on hook, ch 4) into each ch-1 loop of previous round, ch 6, 1 tr into tr, ch 6 *. Repeat from * to *. Close round with 1 sl st into 4th starting ch.

Round 28: * (ch 7, 1 sl st into ch-4 loop, ch 7) 6 times, 1 sl st into ch-6 loop, 1 sc into tr, 6 sl sts *. Repeat from * to *. Close round with 1 sl st into first ch. Fasten off.

● *To finish:* Press the centerpiece under a damp cloth with a hot iron, starching lightly if necessary.

The centerpieces illustrated in color on page 87

Écru centerpiece (2)
Color illustration on page 87

Standard: ☆

Gauge: At the end of the first round the ring measures 1.1 cm ($\frac{7}{16}$ in) in diameter.

Size: The centerpiece is 15 cm (6 ins) in diameter.

Materials: 30 g (1 oz) crochet cotton no. 12 in écru; size 10 steel crochet hook.

Stitches used: Single crochet and slip stitch (see page 28); double crochet (see page 29).

Method
• The centerpiece is worked in the round (see page 30), without turning the work.
   Make 10 ch and join with a sl st to form a

Chart for the écru centerpiece

○ chain stitch
⊤ double crochet
● slip stitch
✕ single crochet
⊗ 1 picot = 3 chain stitches joined by
    1 slip stitch

ring. Work beginning of each round as follows: replace first dc by ch 3.

Round 1: Work 16 sc into ring.

Round 2: (1 dc, ch 4, skip 1 base stitch) 8 times. Close round with 1 sl st into 3rd starting ch.

Round 3: 2 sl sts, * (2 dc, ch 2, 2 dc) into ch-4 loop, ch 3 *. Rep from * to * to end of round, closing with 1 sl st into 3rd starting ch.

Round 4: 3 sl sts, * (2 dc, ch 2, 2 dc) into ch-2 loop, ch 5 *. Rep from * to * to end of round, closing with 1 sl st into 3rd starting ch.

Round 5: 3 sl sts, * (2 dc, ch 2, 2 dc) into ch-2 loop, ch 3, insert hook into the ch-5 and ch-3 loops of the two previous rounds and work 1 sc, ch 3 *. Rep from * to * to end of round, closing with 1 sl st into 3rd starting ch.

Round 6: 3 sl sts, * 1 sc into ch-2 loop, ch 14 *. Rep from * to * to end of round, closing with 1 sl st into first sc.

Round 7: * 1 dc into sc of previous round, ch 2, skip 2 ch, (1 dc, ch 2, skip 2 ch) 4 times *. Rep from * to * to end of round, closing with 1 sl st into 3rd starting ch.

Round 8: 1 sl st, * (2 dc, ch 2, 2 dc) into ch-2 loop, ch 4, skip one ch-2 loop *. Rep from * to * to end of round, closing with 1 sl st into 3rd starting ch.

Round 9: 2 sl sts, * (2 dc, ch 2, 2 dc) into ch-2 loop, ch 6, skip next ch-2 loop *. Rep from * to * to end of round, closing with 1 sl st into 3rd starting ch.

Round 10: 2 sl sts, * (2 dc, ch 2, 2 dc) into ch-2 loop, ch 4, insert hook into the ch-6 and ch-4 loops of the two previous rounds and work 1 sc, ch 4 *. Rep from * to * to end of round, closing with 1 sl st into 3rd starting ch.

Round 11: 2 sl sts, * 1 sc into ch-2 loop, ch 11 *. Rep from * to * to end of round, closing with 1 sl st in first sc.

Round 12: * 1 dc into sc of previous round, ch 2, skip 2 ch, (1 dc, ch 2, skip 2 ch) 3 times *. Rep from * to * to end of round, closing with 1 sl st into 3rd starting ch.

Round 13: 1 sl st, * (2 dc, ch 2, 2 dc) into ch-2 loop, ch 4, skip one ch-2 loop *. Rep from * to * to end of round, closing with 1 sl st into 3rd starting ch.

Round 14: 2 sl sts, * (2 dc, ch 2, 2 dc) into ch-2 loop, ch 6 *. Rep from * to * to end of round, closing with 1 sl st into 3rd starting ch.

Round 15: 2 sl sts, * (2 dc, ch 2, 2 dc) into ch-2 loop, ch 4, insert hook into ch-6 and ch-4 loops of previous two rounds and work 1 sc, ch 4 *. Rep from * to * to end of round, closing with 1 sl st into 3rd starting ch.

Round 16: 2 sl sts, * 1 picot (= ch 3, 1 sl st into 3rd ch from hook) above ch-2 loop, work 13 sl sts to reach next ch-2 loop *. Rep from * to * to

The centerpieces illustrated in color on page 87

end of round, closing with 1 sl st in first sl st. Finish off.

● *To finish:* Press the centerpiece under a damp cloth with a hot iron, starching lightly if necessary.

Leaf motif centerpiece (3)
Color illustration on page 87

Standard: ☆☆☆

Gauge: At the end of the first round the ring measures 2 cm (¾ in) in diameter.

Size: The centerpiece is 22 cm (8¾ ins) in diameter.

Materials: 20 g (1 oz) crochet cotton no. 12 in white; size 10 steel crochet hook.

Stitches used: Treble (see page 29); single crochet and slip stitch (see page 28).

Method
● The centerpiece is worked in the round (see page 30), without turning the work.

Make 16 ch and join with a sl st to form a ring. Work starting ch of each round as follows: replace 1 dc by ch 3, 1 tr by ch 4.

Round 1: Work 30 tr into ring, closing round with 1 sl st into 4th starting ch.

Round 2: (1 sc, ch 5, skip 2 tr) 10 times. Close round with 1 sl st into first sc.

Round 3: 2 sl sts, * 1 sc into 3rd ch of ch-5 loop, ch 8 *. Rep from * to * to end of round, closing with 1 sl st into first sc.

Round 4: 2 sl sts, * 5 tr into ch-8 loop of previous round, ch 3 *. Rep from * to * to end of round, closing with 1 sl st into 4th starting ch.

Round 5: 2 sl sts, * 1 sc into 3rd tr of previous round, ch 5, 1 sc into ch-3 loop, ch 5 *. Rep from * to * to end of round, closing with 1 sl st into first sc.

Round 6: As Round 3.

Round 7: 3 sl sts, * (1 tr, ch 1, 1 tr) into ch-8 loop of previous round, ch 4 *. Repeat from * to *, closing round with 1 sl st into 4th starting ch.

Round 8: 1 sl st, * (1 tr, ch 2, 1 tr) into ch-1 loop of previous round, ch 4, 1 tr into next ch-1 loop, ch 4 *. Repeat from * to *, closing round with 1 sl st into 4th starting ch.

Round 9: 1 sl st, * (1 tr, 1 ch, 1 tr) into ch-2 loop, ch 3, (5 unfinished tr, yo, draw yarn

Chart for the Leaf motif centerpiece

○   chain

$\overline{\overline{\mathsf{T}}}$ treble

●   slip stitch

✕   single crochet

⬮   unfinished trebles closed together

    1 picot = 3 chain stitches joined by

⋊⋉   1 slip stitch

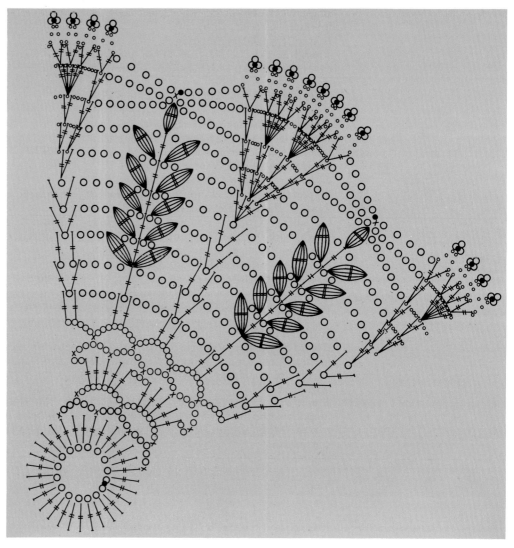

through all 5 loops on hook [= 1 closing stitch], ch 2, 1 tr, ch 2, 5 unfinished tr, 1 closing stitch) into tr of previous round, ch 3 *. Repeat from * to *, closing round with 1 sl st into 4th starting ch.

Round 10: 1 sl st, * (1 tr, ch 1, 1 tr) into ch-1 loop, ch 3, (5 unfinished tr, 1 closing stitch) into ch-2 loop after first 5-tr group of previous round, ch 2, 1 tr into tr of previous round, ch 2, (5 unfinished tr, 1 closing stitch) into ch-2 loop before second 5-tr group of previous round, ch 3 *. Repeat from * to *, closing round with 1 sl st into 4th starting ch.

Round 11: As Round 10.

Round 12: 1 sl st, * (1 tr, ch 1, 1 tr, ch 1, 1 tr, ch 1, 1 tr) into ch-1 loop, ch 4, (5 unfinished tr, 1 closing stitch) into first ch-2 loop, ch 2, 1 tr into tr, ch 2, (5 unfinished tr, 1 closing stitch) into 2nd ch-2 loop of previous round, ch 4 *. Repeat from * to *, closing round with 1 sl st into 4th starting ch.

Round 13: 1 sl st, * (1 tr, ch 1, 1 tr) into first ch-1 loop, ch 2, (1 tr, ch 1) 4 times into second ch-1 loop, ch 1, (1 tr, ch 1, 1 tr) into last ch-2 loop, ch 4, (5 unfinished tr, 1 closing stitch) into first ch-2 loop, ch 1, 1 tr into tr, ch 1, (5 unfinished tr, 1 closing stitch) into 2nd ch-2 loop of previous round, ch 4 *. Rep from * to * to end of round closing with 1 sl st into 4th starting ch.

Round 14: 1 sl st, * (1 tr, ch 1, 1 tr) into first ch-1 loop, ch 3, (1 tr, ch 1, 1 tr) into second ch-1 loop, ch 3, skip one ch-1 loop, (1 tr, ch 1, 1 tr) into fourth ch-1 loop, ch 3, (1 tr, ch 1, 1 tr) into last ch-1 loop, ch 7, (5 unfinished tr, 1 closing stitch) into tr between the two groups of tr in previous round, ch 7 *. Rep from * to * to end of round closing with 1 sl st into 4th starting ch.

Round 15: 1 sl st, * (1 tr, ch 1, 1 tr) into first ch-1 loop, ch 4, skip ch-3 loop of previous round, (1 tr, ch 1) 6 times into second ch-1 loop, ch 1, skip second ch-3 loop, (1 tr, ch 1) 6 times into third ch-1 loop, ch 3, skip last ch-3 loop, (1 tr, ch 1, 1 tr) into last ch-1 loop, ch 7, 1 sc into closing stitch of 5 tr in previous round, ch 7 *. Repeat from * to * to end of round closing with 1 sl st into 4th starting ch.

Round 16: 1 sl st, (1 tr, ch 3, 1 picot [= ch 3, 1 sl st into 3rd ch from hook], ch 3, 1 tr) into ch-1 loop, ch 1, (1 tr, ch 3, 1 picot, ch 3, 1 tr, ch 1) 6 times, working into the first, third and fifth ch-1 loops of both 6-tr groups of previous round, ch 1, (1 tr, ch 3, 1 picot, ch 3, 1 tr) into ch-1 loop, ch 5, 1 sl st into sc of previous round, ch 5 *. Rep from * to * to end of round closing with 1 sl st into 4th starting ch.

● *To finish:* press the centerpiece under a damp cloth with a hot iron, starching lightly if necessary.

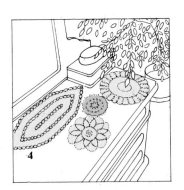

The centerpieces illustrated in color on page 87

Daisy motif centerpiece (4)
Color illustration on page 87

Standard: ☆☆☆

Gauge: Each ring measures 1.6 cm ($\frac{5}{8}$ in) in diameter.

Size: The centerpiece is 57 cm ($22\frac{1}{2}$ ins) long and 20.8 cm ($8\frac{1}{8}$ ins) wide.

Materials: 50 g (2 oz) crochet cotton no. 12 in white; size 10 steel crochet hook.

Stitches used: double crochet (see page 29); single crochet (see page 28).

Method

● The centerpiece consists of 184 rings and 128 daisy motifs joined together. The motifs are worked as follows.

● *Rings:* Instead of working a length of foundation ch as the basis for each ring, wind the yarn 4 times round a finger or a pencil. Holding the loops in position, slip them off and work in sc over all the strands, covering the ring closely with the stitches. It is a good idea to work the same number of stitches on each ring so that they will all be the same size. Finish off neatly and repeat until 184 rings have been made.

● *Daisies:* Each motif is made separately as follows. Make 8 ch and join with a sl st to form a ring.

Round 1: Ch 3, (1 dc, ch 2) 11 times into the ring. Close round with 1 sl st into 2nd starting ch.

Round 2: (1 sc, ch 3, 1 sc) into each ch-2 loop, closing round with 1 sl st into first sc.

● *To finish:* arrange the rings and daisies as shown in the chart and join them together in sl st. Lightly starch the centerpiece and press it under a damp cloth with a hot iron.

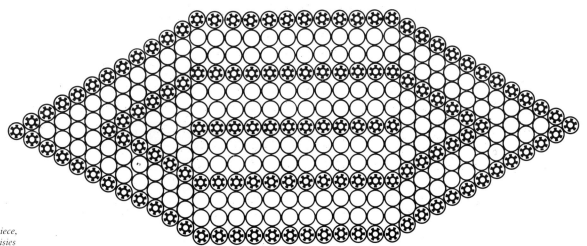

Chart for the Daisy motif centerpiece, consisting of 184 ring and 128 daisies

Checked rug (1)
Color illustration on page 88

Standard: ☆

Gauge: 26 stitches × 18 rows = 10 × 10 cm (4 × 4 ins).

Size: The rug measures 224 × 157 cm (86 × 62 ins).

Materials: 800 g (29 oz) beige, flecked sport yarn; 400 g (14½ oz) light beige, flecked sport yarn; 100 g (3½ oz) rust sport yarn; size F crochet hook.

Stitches used: Single crochet and slip stitch (see page 28).

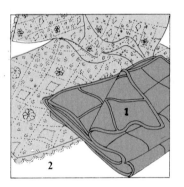

The articles illustrated in color on page 88

Method

● The rug consists of 90 rectangles each measuring 22 × 17 cm (8½ × 6¾ ins). They are worked separately and then sewn together.

● *To make the rectangles:* Make 35 ch and work as follows:

Row 1: Starting in 3rd ch from hook work * 1 sc, ch 1, skip 1 base stitch. Rep from * to *, ending row with 1 sc, ch 2, turn.

Row 2: * 1 sc into ch of previous row, ch 1 *. Rep from * to * to end of row, ending with 1 sc into first turning ch.

Repeat Row 2 until work measures 22 cm (8½ ins) in length. Finish off.

Work 20 rectangles in the lighter shade and 70 in the dark.

● *To make up:* With the rust-colored wool, sew together 10 of the lighter rectangles with whipstitching (see page 147) along the shorter sides to form a strip. Make another strip with the other 10 lighter rectangles.

Now join the darker rectangles in the same way to make 7 strips of 10 rectangles.

Whipstitch the 9 strips together with the 2 lighter strips on the outside and the 7 darker ones in the center.

With the rust-coloured wool, work in sc around the outer edge of the rug, working 3 sc into the same stitch at each corner.

Starting at a corner, work the edging into the sc as follows:

Round 1: * 1 sc, ch 6, skip 5 base stitches *. Rep from * to * along all four sides, closing with 1 sl st into sc of first corner.

Round 2: * 1 sc into sc of previous row, 7 sc into ch-6 loop *. Rep from * to * along all four sides, closing with 1 sl st into first sc. Finish off.

The rug does not need to be pressed.

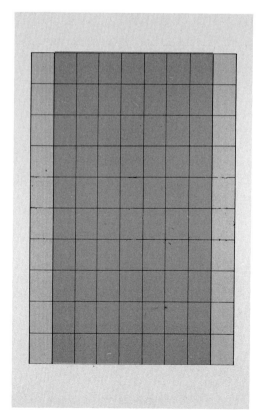

Chart for the Checked rug

Double-bed coverlet (2)
Color illustration on page 88

Standard: ☆☆☆

Gauge: 50 stitches × 22 rows = 10 × 10 cm (4 × 4 ins).

Size: The coverlet measures 260 × 280 cm (approx. 102 × 110 ins).

Materials: 1,800 g (4 lbs) crochet cotton no. 12 in white; size 9 steel crochet hook.

Stitches used: Single crochet (see page 28);

☐ space
⊠ block
◯ chain stitch
⌐ double crochet

The overall pattern of diamond motifs
for the Double-bed coverlet

double crochet, treble and double treble (see
page 29).

Method

● The main part of the coverlet is worked
back and forth, in one piece.
Make 1,200 ch and work 1 row in sc and
1 row in dc.
Begin following the chart and work 270 cm
(106 ins) in pattern, ending with 1 row in dc
and 1 row in sc.
● *To finish:* Work an edging along all four
sides of the completed rectangle in the
following way, starting from a corner:
Round 1: Work in sc, insuring that the stitches
are even and that there is a multiple of 4 sc on
each side, plus 3 sc worked into each corner.
Close round with 1 sl st into first sc.
Round 2: Ch 6, ∗ skip 1 sc, 1 dc, ch 3 ∗. Rep
from ∗ to ∗ all the way round, working 1 dc,
ch 3, 1 dc, ch 3 into corner stitch. Close round
with 1 sl st into 3rd starting ch.
Round 3: 1 sl st, ∗ 1 sc into center of ch-3 loop
of previous round, ch 2, 7 tr into center of next
ch-3 loop, ch 2 ∗. Rep from ∗ to ∗ all the way
round, working 9 tr into ch-loop at corners.
Close round with 1 sl st into first sc.

Round 4: Ch 1, * 1 sc into sc of previous round, ch 3, (1 tr, ch 1) into each tr of previous round, ch 2 *. Rep from * to * all the way round, working (1 tr, ch 1) into each of the 9 corner tr in previous round. Close round with 1 sl st into starting ch.

Round 5: 3 sl sts, ch 8, * (1 dtr, ch 3) into each tr of previous round *. Rep from * to * all the way round, working (1 dtr, ch 3) into each of the 9 corner tr in previous round. Close round with 1 sl st into 5th starting ch.

Round 6: (3 sc, 1 picot [= ch 3, 1 sl st into 3rd ch from hook]) into each ch-3 loop of previous round. Close round with 1 sl st into first sc. Finish off.

● *To finish:* press the coverlet under a damp cloth with a hot iron, or have it professionally pressed.

The garments illustrated in color on page 105

Red collar (1)
Color illustration on page 105

Standard: ☆☆

Gauge: The foundation chain for the first size measures 24 cm (9½ ins).

Size: The smallest size is for a child aged 6–8. The figures in brackets correspond to sizes for children aged 8–10 and 10–12.

Materials: 10(15–20) g/¼ (½–¾)oz crochet cotton no. 5; size 4 steel crochet hook.

Stitches used: Single crochet, slip stitch (see page 28); double crochet, treble (see page 29); crab stitch (see page 70).

Method
● The collar is worked back and forth.
   Make 79 (91–103) chains plus 3 turning chains.

Row 1: 1 dc into 4th ch from hook, * ch 4, skip 2 foundation ch, 2 dc into next ch *. Repeat from * to * to end of row. Ch 1, turn.

Row 2: * 1 sc into first of the 2-dc in previous row, ch 3, 1 sc into 2nd dc, 4 sc into ch-4 loop *. Rep from * to *, working (1 sc, ch 3, 1 sc), into last 2-dc.

Row 3: 1 sl st, * 1 sc into first ch-3 loop, * (3 tr, ch 3) 3 times into next ch-3 loop *. Rep from * to *, ending with 1 sc into last ch-3 loop.

Row 4: * 1 sc into sc, 3 sc into ch-3, 1 sc into first tr, 1 picot (= ch 3, 1 sl st into 3rd ch from hook) above 2nd tr, 1 sc into 3rd tr *. Rep from * to *, ending with 1 sc. Finish off.

● *To finish:* Complete neck edge by working one row in sc and one row in crab stitch.
   Insert hook into last stitch at one end of neck edge, make 50 ch and work a row of sc back to neck edge. Make a second tie to match at other end. Finish off both ends neatly.
   Press under a damp cloth with a hot iron. For a really crisp look, starch the collar lightly.

Chart for the red collar
○ chain stitch
⊤ double crochet
⅂ treble
● slip stitch
✕ single crochet
⌣ crab stitch
⚹ 1 picot = 3 chain stitches joined together by 1 slip stitch

Red skirt (2)

Color illustration on page 105

Standard: ☆

Gauge: 15 stitches × 11 rows = 10 × 10 cm (4 × 4 ins).

Size: The skirt is suitable for a 4-year-old girl; the figures in brackets refer to sizes for children aged 6 and 8.

Materials: 200(250–300)g/7(9–11)oz red sport yarn; size G crochet hook; waist elastic 2.5 cm (1 in) wide.

Stitches used: Single crochet (see page 28); double crochet (see page 29); crab stitch (see page 70).

Method
● The skirt is made in two identical pieces, joined by two side seams.

Make 50 (70–90) ch and work in sc for 3 cm (1¼ ins).

Work one row of sc, inserting hook into back loop only of each stitch in previous row, then work in sc for a further 3 cm (1¼ ins).

Fold the strip in half lengthwise along the row of raised sc and work 1 row in sc, inserting the hook into both edges to join the two pieces and form the waistband.

Work 1 increase row as follows: * 1 dc, 2 dc into next sc *. Rep from * to * to end of row. This will give the skirt a gathered effect.

Continue in dc, inserting the hook into the space between the dc of each previous row, for 30(35–40)cm/12(14–16)ins. Finish off.

● *To make up:* Join the two pieces with flat seams, leaving the waistband open at one side. Thread the elastic through, sew ends firmly together and finish waistband.

Work one row in sc and one row in crab st along the lower edge of the skirt.

Press side seams lightly under a damp cloth with a warm iron.

The garments illustrated in color on page 105

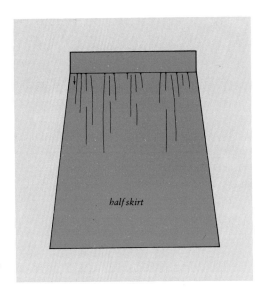

half skirt

Child's light blue beret (3)

Color illustration on page 105

Standard: ☆

Gauge: 32 stitches × 30 rounds = 10 × 10 cm (4 × 4 ins).

Size: The beret measures 22 cm (approx. 8½ ins) in diameter; head circumference is 44 cm (17½ ins).

Materials: 80 g (3 oz) crochet cotton no. 5 in light blue; a few grams (¼ oz or less) white crochet cotton no. 5; size 4 steel crochet hook.

Stitches used: Single crochet and slip stitch (see page 28); crab stitch (see page 70).

Method
● The beret is worked in the round (see page 30), without turning the work.

With blue cotton make 8 ch and close round with 1 sl st.

Work 16 sc into ring. Continue in rounds of sc, working evenly-spaced increases on each round to obtain a flat circle 22 cm (approx. 8½ ins) in diameter. The number of stitches on this final round should be a multiple of 6.

Now work 5 rounds without increasing in the blue cotton and 1 round without increasing in the white cotton.

The next 2 rounds are worked as follows:
Round 1: * 3 sc in white cotton, 3 sc in blue cotton *. Repeat from * to * to end of round.

Round 2: As Round 1, working blue on white and white on blue.

Continue in blue cotton, working 5 rounds in sc and decreasing 8 stitches in each round.

● *To finish:* Using white cotton, work 1 round in sc followed by an edging of crab stitch.

Press the beret under a damp cloth with a hot iron.

The garments illustrated in color on page 105

Child's white waistcoat (4)
Color illustration on page 105

Standard: ☆

Gauge: 18 stitches × 17 rows = 10 × 10 cm (4 × 4 ins).

Size: The waistcoat is for a child aged 5–6. The figures in brackets refer to sizes for children aged 7–8 and 9–10.

Materials: 250(300–350)g/9(11–13)oz of sport yarn in white; size G crochet hook.

Stitches used: Single crochet and half double crochet (see page 28); crab stitch (see page 70).

Method
● The waistcoat is worked back and forth. The waist ribbing and edgings are worked vertically.
● *Back:* Starting with the waist ribbing, make 10(15–20) ch and work in sc for 25(30–35) cm/10(12–13¾)ins, inserting hook into the

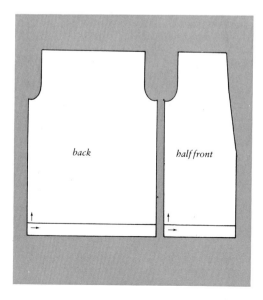

back loop only at the top of each stitch in the previous row. Finish off.

Along the length of the ribbing work 3 sc into each hole at the edge. Continue as follows:
Row 1: Sc to end of row.
Row 2: * 1 sc, 1 hdc * . Rep from * to * to end of row.

These two rows form the pattern. Rep until work measures 20(25–30) cm/8(10–12) ins.

For armhole shaping, decrease at each end of next 3 rows as follows: first row, decrease 3 stitches; 2nd row, decrease 2 stitches; 3rd row, decrease 1 stitch.

Continue in pattern as above for 10 (15–20) cm/4(6–8) ins.
● *Fronts:* make 10 (15–20) ch and work waist ribbing as for Back, working only half the length: 12.5(15–17.5) cm/5(6–7) ins.

Finish off and work along the long edge as for Back. Work in 2-row pattern as for Back for 11(13–15) cm/4¼ (5¼–6) ins.

For V-neck, continue in pattern, decreasing 1 stitch at beginning of alternate rows 5 times. When work measures the same as Back to armhole, decrease at armhole edge as for Back.

Complete Front to match Back. Fasten off.

Work a second Front in the same way, reversing shapings.

● *To make up:* Join side and shoulder seams with backstitch (see page 147).

Starting at corner of Right Front, work in sc all around neck opening, up Right Front, across back of neck and down Left Front. Work 2 further rows of sc.

Complete with 1 row in crab stitch. Finish off.

Work 1 row in sc and 1 row in crab stitch around each armhole.

Press the waistcoat lightly under a damp cloth with a cool iron.

Boy's tie (5)
Color illustration on page 105

Standard: ☆

Gauge: 32 stitches × 18 rows = 10 × 10 cm (4 × 4 ins).

Size: The tie is 115 cm (45¼ ins) long and 6cm (2½ ins) wide.

Materials: 30 g (1oz) crochet cotton no. 5 in dark blue; size C aluminum or size 1 steel crochet hook.

Stitches used: Single crochet (see page 28).

Method
- The tie is worked back and forth.

Make 21 ch and work in sc for 45 cm (18 ins). Decrease 1 stitch at the end of every row until 7 stitches remain.

Work in sc without decreasing for 25 cm (10 ins). This part goes under the collar.

Increase 1 stitch at beginning of every row until there are 21 stitches. Continue in sc for a further 45 cm (18 ins). Finish off.

- *To finish:* Turn in the long edges of the wide parts of the tie by about 1.5 cm ($\frac{5}{8}$ in) or until the edges touch in the center. With small stab stitches, sew the hems in position at each end and use a flat stitch to join the two hems.

Press the tie on the wrong side under a damp cloth with a hot iron.

Green jacket (6)
Color illustration on page 105

Standard: ☆

Gauge: 10 stitches × 11 rows = 10 × 10 cm (4 × 4 ins).

Size: The jacket is for a child aged 6–7. The figures in brackets refer to sizes for children aged 8–9 and 10–11.

Materials: 600 (650–700)g/21 (23–25) oz green tweedy sport yarn; size H crochet hook; 5 buttons.

Stitches used: Single crochet (see page 28); crab stitch (see page 70).

Method
- The jacket is worked back and forth. The Back and Fronts are worked in one piece as far as the armhole.

Make 72 (80–90) ch. Work in sc for 30 (34–38) cm/12 (13$\frac{1}{2}$–15) ins, making 5 vertical buttonholes (see page 137) 2 rows deep at equal intervals along edge of Left or Right Front, depending on whether the jacket is intended for a boy or a girl.

Now divide the work into three: the two side pieces will form the two Fronts and the central piece will form the Back. There should be 18 (20–23) stitches for the Left Front, 36 (40–46) stitches for the Back and 18 (20–23) stitches for the Right Front. The three parts are now worked separately:
- *Back:* For the armholes, decrease at each end of next 3 rows as follows: first row, 3 stitches; second row, 2 stitches, third row, 1 stitch.

Continue in sc for 12 (14–16) cm/5 (5$\frac{1}{2}$–6$\frac{1}{4}$) ins. Finish off.
- *Right Front:* Decrease at armhole edge as for Back.

Continue for 11 (13–15) cm/4$\frac{1}{2}$ (5$\frac{1}{4}$–6) ins and then decrease 2 stitches at neck edge.

Complete to match Back and finish off.
- *Left Front:* As Right Front, reversing shapings.
- *Sleeves:* Make 26 (30–34) ch and work in sc for 32 (36–40) cm/12$\frac{1}{2}$ (14–16) ins. Finish off.

The garments illustarted in color on page 105

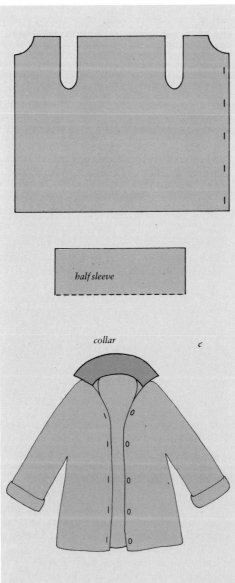

half sleeve

collar

• *To make up:* Join sleeve and shoulder seams. Insert sleeves into armholes and back-stitch them in place.

With right side facing, work 1 row in sc around neck edge. Continue in sc for 8 cm (3¾ ins) to form a collar.

Complete by working 1 row of crab stitch around the edges of the jacket, including the sleeves.

Sew on buttons to correspond to button-holes.

The jacket should not be pressed.

The garments illustrated in color on page 106

White stole (1)
Color illustration on page 106

Standard ☆☆

Gauge: 15 stitches × 12 rows = 10 × 10 cm (4 × 4 ins).

Size: The stole measures 200 × 58 cm (79 × 23 ins), including the fringe.

Materials: 350 g (12½ oz) 2-ply wool in white; size E aluminum or size 00 steel crochet hook.

Stitches used: Single crochet (see page 28); double crochet (see page 29).

Method
• The stole is worked back and forth.

Make 81 foundation ch and work as follows:

Row 1: Starting in 2nd ch from hook work 1 sc into each ch to end, ch 7, turn.

Row 2: Skip first 5 sc of previous row, * 4 dc into next sc, ch 4, skip 4 sc, 1 dc, ch 4, skip 4 sc *. Repeat from * to *, ending with ch 4, skip 4 sc, 1 dc into turning ch of previous row, ch 1 turn.

Row 3: 1 sc into first ch-4 loop of previous row, * (ch 4, 4 dc into next ch-4 loop) twice, ch 4, 1 sc into next ch-4 loop, 1 sc into single dc of previous row, 1 sc into next ch-4 loop *. Repeat from * to * ending with ch 4, 1 sc into ch-7 loop at end of row, 1 sc into 3rd turning ch, ch 1, turn.

Row 4: 1 sc into 2nd sc of previous row, 1 sc into first ch-4 loop, * ch 6, 4 dc into next ch-4 loop, ch 6, 1 sc into next ch-4 loop, 3 sc into 3-sc of previous row, 1 sc into next ch-4 loop *. Repeat from * to * ending with 1 sc into last ch-4 loop, 1 sc into last sc, 1 sc into turning ch of previous row, ch 1, turn.

Row 5: 1 sc into 2nd sc of previous row, * (ch 4, 4 dc into ch-6 loop) twice, ch 4, 3 sc into 3 central sc of 5-sc of previous row *. Repeat from * to * ending with 1 sc into last sc of previous row, 1 sc into turning ch, ch 7, turn.

Row 6: 4 dc into first ch-4 loop of previous row, * ch 4, 1 dc into next ch-4 loop, ch 4, 4 dc into next ch-4 loop, ch 4, 1 dc into central sc of 3-sc of previous row, ch 4, 4 dc into next ch-4 loop *. Repeat from * to * ending with 4 dc into last ch-4 loop, ch 4, 1 dc into turning ch of previous row, ch 3, turn.

Row 7: 1 dc into first ch-4 loop, ch 4, * 1 sc into next ch-4 loop, 1 sc into single dc of previous row, 1 sc into next ch-4 loop, ch 4, (4 dc into next ch-4 loop, ch 4) twice *. Repeat from * to * ending with ch 4, 1 dc into ch-7 loop of previous row, 1 dc into 3rd turning ch, ch 6, turn.

Row 8: * 1 sc into ch-4 loop, 3 sc into 3-sc of previous row, 1 sc into next ch-4 loop, ch 6, 4 dc into next ch-4 loop, ch 6 *. Repeat from * to * ending with ch 3, 1 dc into 3rd turning ch of previous row, ch 3, turn.

Row 9: 1 sc into first ch-4 loop, * ch 4, 3 sc into central 3 sc of 5-sc of previous row, (ch 4, 4 dc into next ch-4 loop) twice *. Repeat from * to * ending with ch 4, 1 dc into ch-6 loop, 1 dc into 3rd turning ch, ch 5, turn.

Row 10: * 4 dc into ch-4 loop, ch 4, 1 dc into central sc of 3-sc of previous row, ch 4, 4 dc into next ch-4 loop, ch 4, 1 dc into next ch-4 loop, ch 4 *. Repeat from * to * ending with 4 dc into last ch-4 loop, ch 2, 1 dc into 3rd turning ch of previous row, ch 1, turn.

Rows 3–10 form the pattern and are repeated until work measures 148 cm (58 ins). Work 1 row in sc.

• *To finish:* Work a border into the row of sc at each end of the stole as follows:

Row 1: Ch 3, 2 dc into first base stitch, * ch 3, skip 4 base stitches, (3 dc, ch 2, 3 dc) into next base stitch *. Repeat from * to * ending with ch 3, 3 dc into last base stitch, ch 3, turn.

Row 2: 1 dc into base of 3 turning ch, * ch 3, (2 dc, ch 2, 2 dc) into ch-2 loop of previous row *. Repeat from * to * ending with ch 3, 2 dc into 3rd turning ch of previous row, ch 3, turn.

Row 3: 1 dc into base of 3 turning ch, * ch 2, 1 sc into ch-3 loops of Rows 1 and 2, ch 2, (2 dc, ch 1, 2 dc) into ch-2 loop of previous row *. Repeat from * to * ending with ch 2, 2 dc into 3rd turning ch of previous row, ch 3, turn.

Row 4: 1 dc into base of 3 turning ch, * ch 3, (2 dc, ch 1, 2 dc) into ch-1 loop of previous row *. Repeat from * to * ending with ch 3,

2 dc into 3rd turning ch of previous row. Finish off.

Make a fringe (see page 140) 25 cm (10 ins) long at each end of the stole, making one knot into each ch-1 loop of final row.

The stole should not be pressed.

Navy blue dress (2)
Color illustration on page 106

Standard: ☆☆

Gauge: 22 stitches × 20 rows = 10 × 10 cm (4 × 4 ins).

Size: Women's size 38. The figures in brackets refer to sizes 36 and 34.

The garments illustrated in color on page 106

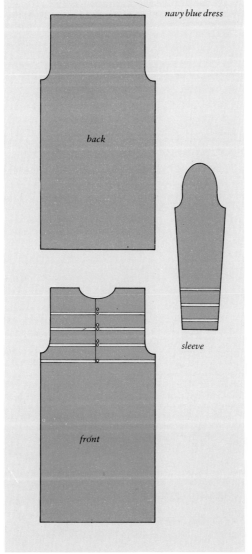

navy blue dress

back

front

sleeve

Materials: 800 (750–700)g/29 (27–25)oz 2-ply wool in dark blue; a few grams 2-ply wool in white; size D aluminum or size 1 steel crochet hook; 7 white buttons.

Stitches used: Single crochet (see page 28).

Method
• The dress is worked back and forth.
• *Back:* Make 120 (110–100) ch and work straight in sc for 70 (65–60) cm/27½ (25½–23½) ins.

For armhole shaping, decrease at each end of next 3 rows as follows: first row, decrease 4 stitches; second row, decrease 3 stitches; third row, decrease 2 stitches.

Continue without shaping for 23 (21–18) cm/9 (8¼–7) ins. Finish off.
• *Front:* Work exactly as for Back until Front measures 65 cm (25 ins).

The work is now divided into two and each half is continued separately, working 2 rows in white wool and 7 in blue.

Work a total of 4 bands of white, shaping armhole as for Back when work measures 70 (65–60) cm/27½ (25½–23½) ins. Continue straight for 20 (18–15) cm/8 (7–6) ins.

Shape neck by decreasing 5 stitches at neck edge and then continue until work measures the same as Back.

Finish off. Complete 2nd half in same way.
• *Sleeves:* make 46 (42–38) ch and work in sc for 3 cm (1¼ ins). Increasing 1 stitch at each end of every 5th row, work 2 rows in white wool and 7 rows in blue. Repeat this sequence 3 times.

Continue working in blue wool, still increasing 1 stitch at each end of every 5th row, for a further 32 (28–24) cm/12½ (11–9½) ins.

Shape top of sleeve by decreasing at each end of next 3 rows as follows: first row, decrease 4 stitches; 2nd row, decrease 3 stitches; 3rd row, decrease 2 stitches. Continue shaping by decreasing 1 stitch at each end of every row until 10 (8–6) stitches remain.

• *To make up:* Work 3 rows in sc along both edges of Front opening, making 7 horizontal buttonholes (see page 138) over 1 stitch, at regular intervals.

Join side, shoulder and sleeve seams with a flat stitch.

Insert sleeves into armholes and backstitch (see page 147) into position.

Starting 3 cm (1¼ ins) from right neck edge and ending the same distance from left neck edge, work in sc for 8 cm (3¼ ins) to form the collar. Complete by working 1 row in sc all around the edge of the collar.

Press the whole dress under a damp cloth with a cool iron.

Vest in loop stitch (3)
Color illustration on page 106

Standard: ☆

Gauge: 22 stitches × 22 rows = 10 × 10 cm (4 × 4 ins).

Size: Women's size 36–38. The figures in brackets refer to sizes 30–32.

Materials: 450 (400) g/1 lb (14 oz) random dyed sport yarn or crêpe; size E aluminum or size 00 steel crochet hook; leather thong 1 meter (40 ins) long.

Stitches used: Loop stitch (see page 49); single crochet (see page 28).

Method
- The vest is worked back and forth.

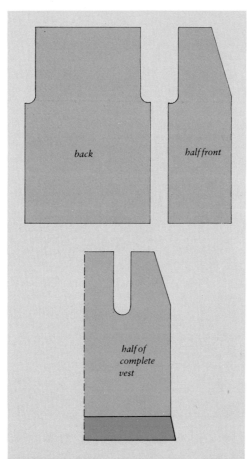

back

half front

half of complete vest

The garments illustrated in color on page 106

- *Back:* Make 90 (80) ch and work in loop stitch for 34 (32) cm/13½ (12½) ins.
  Shape armholes by decreasing 4 stitches at each end. Continue working in loop stitch for a further 24 (22) cm/9½ (8½) ins. Finish off.
- *Front:* make 50 (45) cm ch and work in loop stitch for 34 (32) cm/13½ (12½) ins.
  Shape armhole by decreasing 5 stitches at one edge and shape V-neck by decreasing 1 stitch at the other edge on alternate rows.
  When work measures the same as Back, finish off.
  Make a second Front in the same way, reversing the shapings.

- *To make up:* Join side and shoulder seams in backstitch (see page 147).
  Starting from bottom corner of Left Front, work 9 cm (3½ ins) in loop stitch along the lower edge, increasing 1 stitch at beginning and end of each row. Finish off.
  Work 1 row in sc down both Front edges.
  Cut the leather thong in half and knot one piece on each Front edge, just where the V-neck decreasing begins.
  The vest should never be pressed as this would flatten the loops.

Dress in natural wool (4)
Color illustration on page 106

Standard: ☆☆

Gauge: 24 stitches × 20 rows = 10 × 10 cm (4 × 4 ins).

Size: Women's size 36. The figures in brackets refer to sizes 34 and 32.

Materials: 800 (750–700) g/29 (27–25) oz natural wool in 4-ply; size E aluminum or size 00 steel crochet hook; 5 buttons.

Stitches used: Single crochet (see page 28).

Method
- The main part of the dress is worked back and forth in one piece, starting from the cuff of the left sleeve. The lower border is then worked in rounds.
  Make 75 (70–65) ch and work in sc for 50 (47–44) cm/19½ (18½–17½) ins; this is the length of the sleeve.
  Increase 140 (130–120) stitches at end of next two rows. Work in sc over all these stitches for 14 (13–12) cm/5½ (5¼–5) ins.
  To make neck opening, divide the work in

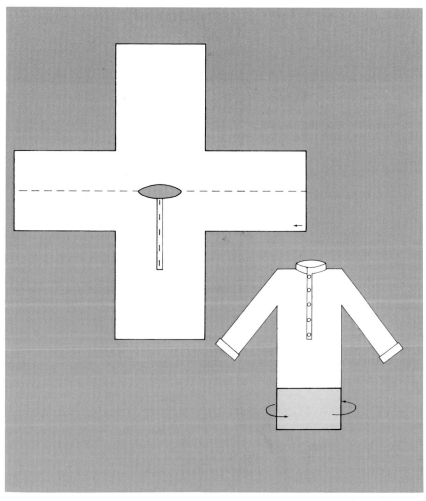

The garments illustrated in color on page 107

half and work Front and Back separately as follows. Work across Back for 16 cm. On the Front decrease 1 stitch at neck edge of every row, for 5 cm (2 ins). This completes the left front. To make the vertical opening, leave 37 (34–31) cm/14½ (13½–12¾) ins unworked and make the same length of chain. On the following row work in sc into ch and into remaining stitches. Continue across all stitches for 3 cm (1¼ ins). Make 4 evenly spaced horizontal buttonholes over 2 stitches (see page 138). Work 3 cm (1¼ ins) and then increase 1 stitch at neck edge of each row for 5 cm (2 ins). The Front should now measure the same as the Back.

On the following row work in all stitches of both Front and Back. Continue for 14 (13–12) cm/5½ (5¼–5) ins.

Decrease 140 (130–120) stitches at each end of next two rows and work right sleeve to match left. Finish off.

● *To make up:* on wrong side, sew the sides

together with backstitch (see page 147); fold the sleeves in half lengthwise and backstitch seam.

Along vertical opening of left front work in sc for 6 cm (2½ ins) and stitch it to the right front at the bottom with small stab stitches.

Now work in sc for 9 cm (3½ ins) all around neck opening, making 1 horizontal buttonhole over 2 stitches (see page 138) in line with those on the right front, after 4–5 cm (1¾ ins) have been worked. Finish off.

Around lower edge of dress work rounds of sc for 26 (24–22) cm/10¼ (9¼–8½) ins. Finish off.

Sew 4 buttons on button band of left front to correspond to the buttonholes on right front. Sew the 5th button on to the neckband to correspond to the buttonhole.

Press the seams lightly under a damp cloth with a warm iron.

Silver Lurex bag

Color illustration on page 107

Standard: ☆

Gauge: 20 stitches × 20 rounds = 10 × 10 cm (4 × 4 ins) in basketweave stitch.

Size: The bag is 20 cm (approx 8 ins) deep and 16 cm (6½ ins) wide; the round base is 10 cm (4 ins) in diameter.

Materials: 80 g (3 oz) silver Lurex; size F aluminum crochet hook.

Stitches used: Single crochet and slip stitch (see page 29); basketweave stitch (see page 44).

Method

● The bag is worked in the round (see page 30), without turning the work, beginning in the center of the round base.

Make 4 ch and join with a sl st to form a ring. Work in sc, increasing at regular intervals on each row to make a flat circle measuring 10 cm (4 ins) in diameter. The number of stitches on the last row should be a multiple of 4. Work one round without increasing in dc, inserting the hook into the back loop only of each stitch of previous row.

Change to basketweave stitch and continue without increasing. Basketweave stitch is worked in the round as follows:

Round 1: Ch 2, * 4 forward dc (counting ch-2 as first forward dc), 4 back dc *. Repeat from * to * closing round with 1 sl st into 2nd starting chain.

Round 2: As Round 1.

Round 3: As Round 1.

Round 4: Ch 2, *4 back dc (counting ch-2 as

The garments illustrated in color on page 107

first back dc), 4 forward dc *. Repeat from * to * closing round with 1 sl st into 2nd starting chain.
Round 5: As Round 4.
Round 6: As Round 4.
Repeat these 6 rounds for 16 cm (6¼ ins).
Work 5 rounds in sc and then 1 round as follows: * 3 sc, 1 picot (= ch 3, 1 sl st into 3rd ch from hook) *. Repeat from * to * to end of round. Finish off.

● *To finish:* Make a chain string (see page 141) 120 cm (approx. 47 ins) long and thread it through the last round of basketweave pattern, passing it in front of the back dc and behind the forward dc.
To close the bag pull the string tight and tie it into a bow. Now make a double chain (see page 141) as a shoulder strap and sew neatly to the bag.
The bag should not be pressed as this could damage the Lurex thread.

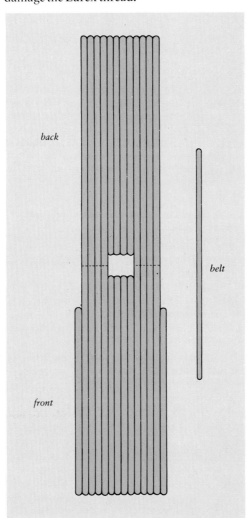

back

front

belt

Cocktail dress with silver Lurex thread
Color illustration on page 107

Standard: ☆☆

Gauge: The first medallion in each strip measures 3.5 cm (1⅜ ins) in diameter.

Size: Women's size 36–38. The figures in brackets refer to sizes 32–34.

Materials: 350 (300)g/12½ (11) oz 2-ply wool in light green and 50 g (2 oz) fine silver Lurex thread; size C aluminum or size 1 steel crochet hook.

Stitches used: Double crochet and treble (see page 29); single crochet and slip stitch (see page 28).

Method
● The dress is made of separate strips joined together. Each strip consists of semi-circular motifs and is worked as follows:
Round 1: Make 12 ch and join with a sl st to form a ring, ch 3.
Round 2: Work 19 dc into ring and close with a sl st in 3rd starting ch, ch 1.
Round 3: (1 sc into dc, 1 picot [= ch 3, 1 sl st into 3rd ch from hook], 1 sc into next dc) 10 times, ending with 1 sl st into starting ch.
Round 4: Make 8 ch, turn work, 1 sl st into sc after first picot, ch 4, turn.
Round 5: 11 tr into ch-8 loop, skip 1 picot of first motif, 1 sl st into sc, ch 1, turn.
Round 6: (1 sc into tr, 1 picot, 1 sc into next tr) 6 times, skip 1 picot of first motif, 1 sl st into sc. Rep from Round 4.
Make 2 strips 80 (75) cm/31½(29½) ins long, 8 strips 200 (190) cm/79 (75) ins long and 8 strips 95 (90) cm/37½ (35½) ins long.

● *To make up:* Join the strips in the order shown in the diagram.
Fold in half at the shoulders, indicated by the dotted line in the diagram, and sew the sides together using a flat seam for the length of shorter strips.
For the belt, work one strip 95 cm (37½ ins) long as for the dress.
As Lurex thread can easily be damaged by heat, it is advisable not to press the dress. If necessary, the seams can be lightly pressed under a damp cloth with a cool iron.

Raffia hat (3)

Color illustration on page 107

Standard: ☆☆

Gauge: 15 stitches × 6 rows = 10 × 10 cm (4 × 4 ins).

Size: Circumference of head 57 cm (22½ ins).

Materials: 70 g (2½ oz) pink raffia; 10 g (½ oz) crochet cotton no. 5 in pink; size H and size C aluminum or size 1 steel crochet hooks.

Stitches used: Double crochet (see page 29); single crochet and slip stitch (see page 28); crab stitch (see page 70).

Method

● The hat is worked in the round (see page 30), without turning the work. The ribbon is worked back and forth.

Using raffia and size H crochet hook, make 8 ch and join with a sl st to form a ring. Work 16 dc into ring, closing round with 1 sl st.

Work 4 rounds in dc, increasing evenly on each round to form a flat circle, with a multiple of 4 stitches. Work a further 3 rounds in dc without increasing.

Next round: * 2 dc, ch 2, skip 2 base stitches *. Repeat from * to *. This row forms the eyelet holes through which the crocheted ribbon is threaded.

Work a further 5 rounds in dc to form the brim, increasing at regular intervals on each round so that the brim lies flat.

● *To finish:* Work one round in sc and 1 round in crab stitch around the edge of the brim.

The ribbon is made in the pink cotton with the size C crochet hook. Make 5 ch and work in sc for 60 cm (24 ins). Finish off.

Press ribbon under a damp cloth with a hot iron and thread it through the eyelet holes in the crown of the hat. Cross ends over and stitch neatly to the brim with small stab stitches. The brim can be lightly pressed with a cool iron.

The garments illustrated in color on page 107

Pink sash (4)

Color illustration on page 107

Standard: ☆

Gauge: 13 stitches × 8 rows = 10 × 10 cm (4 × 4 ins).

Size: The sash measures 155 × 12 cm (61 × 5 ins) and the fringes are 20 cm (8 ins) long.

Materials: 100 g (4 oz) no. 5 crochet cotton in three shades of pink; size H aluminum crochet hook.

Stitches used: Treble (see page 29); single crochet (see page 28).

Method

● The sash is worked lengthwise and the cotton is used double, i.e. two threads are worked together.

Starting with the palest shade, make 201 ch.

Row 1: Starting in 7th ch from hook, * 1 tr, ch 1, skip one base ch *. Repeat from * to * to last base ch, 1 tr, ch 5, turn.

Row 2: * 1 tr into ch-1 loop of previous row, ch 1 *. Repeat from * to *, ending with 1 tr into ch-6 loop of previous row, ch 5, turn.

Now change to the medium shade and work 2 rows as Row 2, then work 2 rows in the deepest shade.

Continue in this way, changing shade every 2 rows, until sash measures 155 cm (61 ins).

● *To finish:* Using 1 strand of all three shades, work 1 row of sc along all four sides of sash.

Using the 3 shades together, make a simple fringe (see page 140) 20 cm (8 ins) long at each end of sash.

Press the sash under a damp cloth with a hot iron.

Yoke for a dress (5)

Color illustration on page 107

Standard: ☆☆☆

Gauge: 1 row worked in Irish net stitch measures 10 × 1.5 cm (4 × ⅝ in).

Size: The yoke is 7 cm (2¾ ins) deep and fits a size 34–36 dress.

Materials: 70 g (2½ oz) crochet cotton no. 12 in écru; size 10 aluminum crochet hook.

Stitches used: Single crochet and slip stitch (see page 28); double crochet and treble (see page 29).

Method

● The yoke is made in six pieces: two are stitched on to the bodice of the dress, two form

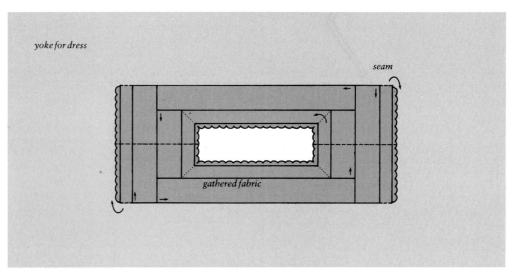

yoke for dress

seam

gathered fabric

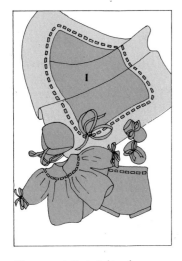

The garments illustrated in color on page 108

the shoulders and two form the sleeves. Each piece is worked back and forth in Irish net stitch. The length of each piece should be measured against the person for whom the dress is intended. Crochet lace is worked around the edges of the finished yoke.

Make 33 ch and work as follows:

Row 1: (1 sc, ch 3, 1 sc) into 9th ch from hook, * ch 5, skip 3 foundation ch, (1 sc, ch 3, 1 sc) into next ch *. Repeat from * to * to last 4 ch, ch 5, skip 3 ch, 1 sc into last ch, ch 5, turn.

Row 2: (1 sc, ch 3, 1 sc) into 3rd ch of ch-5 loop, ch 5 *. Repeat from * to * ending with 1 sc into turning ch, ch 5, turn.

Rep Row 2 until work reaches the required length. Finish off.

● *To make up:* Press each piece under a damp cloth with a hot iron.

Sew the pieces together with small, neat stitches, as shown in the diagram. To complete the yoke, work a lace border around neck and edges of sleeve as follows:

Round 1: * Ch 9, skip 8 base stitches, 3 unfin tr, yo, draw yarn through all 4 loops on hook, ch 1, skip 3 base stitches, 3 unfin tr, 1 closing stitch as before *. Rep from * to * to end of round.

Round 2: Ch 4, * (3 unfin tr, 1 closing stitch, 4 ch, 3 unfin tr, 1 closing stitch) into ch-1 loop, ch 4, 1 sc into 5th ch of ch-9 in previous round, ch 4. Rep from * to * to end of round.

Round 3: * 4 sl sts into ch-4 of previous round, ch 10 *. Rep from * to * to end of round.

Round 4: * Ch 5, (2 tr, ch 3, 2 tr) into loop below the 4 sl sts in previous round, ch 5, (2 tr, ch 3, 2 tr) into 5th ch of the ch-10 in previous round, ch 5. Rep from * to * to end of round.

Round 5: * Ch 5, 14 tr into first ch-3 loop between the tr, ch 5, 1 sc into 2nd of the ch-3 in

the following loop *. Rep from * to * to end of round.

Round 6: * 5 sl sts into the ch-5 of previous row, (1 tr into first of the 14 tr in previous row, ch 1, skip 1 base stitch, 1 picot) 7 times *. Rep from * to * to end of row.

The yoke is now ready to be applied to two rectangles of silk of the size required with embroidered chain stitch (see page 144), using the same crochet cotton. The dress is given further interest with a hemstitched tuck and hem on the skirt.

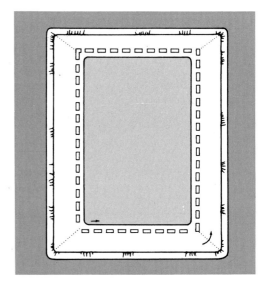

Pram rug in white and yellow (1)

Color illustration on page 108

Standard: ☆

Gauge: 16 stitches × 10 rows = 10 × 10 cm (4 × 4 ins).

Size: The rug measures 72 × 50 cm (approx. 28 × 20 ins).

Materials: 100 g (3½ oz) 1-ply mohair in yellow; 60 g (2 oz) 2-ply mohair in white; size E aluminum or size 00 steel and size G aluminum crochet hooks; 200 cm (2¼ yds) yellow satin ribbon.

Stitches used: Double crochet (see page 29); slip stitch (see page 28).

Method
● The center of the rug is worked back and forth while the border and edging are worked in the round.

Using yellow wool and size 00 crochet hook, make 103 ch and work as follows:

Row 1: Starting in 7th ch from hook, ∗ 2 dc into next ch, ch 1, skip 2 foundation ch ∗. Repeat from ∗ to ∗ ending with 1 dc in last foundation ch, ch 3, turn.

Row 2: 1 dc into first ch-1 loop, ∗ ch 1, 2 dc into next ch-1 loop ∗. Repeat from ∗ to ∗ ending with 2 dc into turning ch of previous row, ch 4, turn.

Row 3: ∗ 2 dc into ch-1 loop, ch 1 ∗. Repeat from ∗ to ∗ ending with 1 dc into 3rd turning ch of previous row.

Repeat Rows 2 and 3 until work measures 30 cm (12 ins).

Change to white wool and with the size G crochet hook work 7 rounds around all four edges of the yellow rectangle as above, closing each round with 1 sl st into 3rd starting ch. At each corner, work (2 dc, ch 2, 2 dc) into the same stitch.

● *To finish:* Work an edging in white wool with the size G crochet hook all around the rug as follows: 4 dc into each ch-1 loop, ch 1. Close round with 1 sl st into 3rd starting ch. Finish off. Thread the yellow ribbon under alternate pairs of double crochets in the second round worked in white wool and tie ends of ribbon in a bow.

The rug should not be pressed.

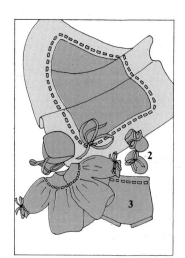

The garments illustrated in color on page 108

Baby's mitts (2)

Color illustration on page 108

Standard: ☆

Gauge: 16 stitches × 10 rows = 10 × 10 cm (4 × 4 ins).

Size: To fit a baby aged 0–1 month. The figures in brackets refer to sizes for 2 and 4 months.

Materials: 10 (15–20) g/¼(½–¾) oz 1-ply mohair in yellow; size E aluminum or size 00 steel crochet hook; 40 cm (16 ins) yellow satin ribbon.

Stitches used: Single crochet and slip stitch (see page 28); double crochet (see page 29); crab stitch (see page 70).

Method
● The mitts are worked in the round (see page 30), without turning the work.

Make 21 (36–42) ch and join with a sl st to form a ring.

Round 1: Work 1 sc into each base ch.

Rounds 2–5: Work in sc.

On following rounds replace first dc by ch 3 and close each round with 1 sl st in 3rd starting ch.

Round 6: ∗ 2 dc into 1 sc, ch 1, skip 2 sc ∗. Repeat from ∗ to ∗.

Round 7: 1 sl st, ∗ 2 dc into ch-1 loop, ch 1 ∗. Repeat from ∗ to ∗.

Repeat Round 7 for another 3 (4–5) rounds; now begin to decrease gradually on every round until 3 (4–5) stitches remain. Finish off and thread the end through last round to close the circle. Fasten off.

Make a second mitt in the same way.

● *To finish:* Complete wrist edges by working 1 round of crab stitch. Thread the ribbon through the first round of dc.

The mitts should not be pressed.

Baby's pants (3)

Color illustration on page 108

Standard: ☆

Gauge: 22 stitches × 13 rows = 10 × 10 cm (4 × 4 ins).

Size: To fit a baby aged 0–1 month. The figures in brackets refer to sizes for 2 and 4 months.

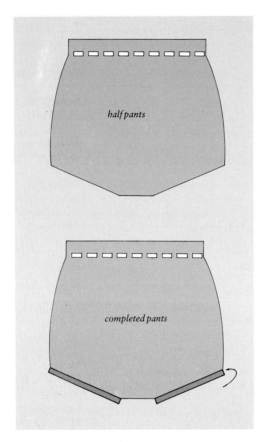

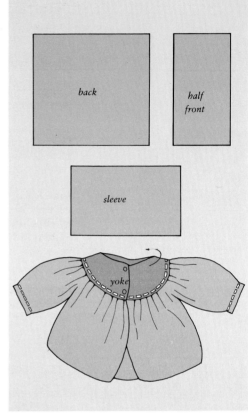

Materials: 30 (40–50) g/1 (1½–2) oz 1-ply mohair in yellow; size E aluminum or size 00 steel crochet hook; 90 cm (approx. 36 ins) yellow satin ribbon.

Stitches used: Single crochet (see page 28); double crochet (see page 29).

Method
● The pants are worked back and forth starting from the waist in two pieces.
● *Front:* Make 40 (50–60) ch and work in sc for 2 rows. Work 1 row in dc and then continue in sc for 13 (16–19) cm/5¼ (6¼–7½) ins. Still working in sc, decrease for the leg-shaping as follows: decrease 2 stitches at each end of each row 7 (9–10) times to leave 12 (14–20) stitches in the middle for the crotch. Finish off.
● *Back:* Work another piece exactly as Front.

● *To make up:* Join side seams and crotch with backstitch (see page 147). Now work around each leg as follows:
Round 1: Work in sc to give a multiple of 3 stitches.
Round 2: * 2 dc into 1 sc, ch 1, skip 2 sc *. Repeat from * to *, closing round with 1 sl st into first dc. Finish off.

Thread the yellow ribbon under pairs of double crochets of the dc row.
The pants should not be pressed.

Matinée jacket (4)
Color illustration on page 108

Standard: ☆☆

Gauge: 16 stitches × 10 rows = 10 × 10 cm (4 × 4 ins).

Size: To fit a baby aged 0–1 month. The figures in brackets refer to sizes for 2 and 4 months.

Materials: 30 (40–50) g/1 (1½–2) oz 1-ply mohair in yellow; size E aluminum or size 00 steel crochet hook; 70 cm (approx. 28 ins) yellow satin ribbon; 2 small yellow buttons; a length of embroidery cotton to work the buttonholes.

Stitches used: Double crochet (see page 29); single crochet (see page 28); crab stitch and twisted cord edging (see page 70).

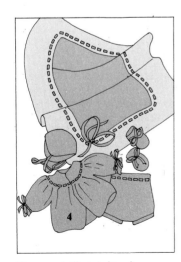

The garments illustrated in color on page 108

Method

- This matinée coat is worked back and forth in five separate pieces which are joined at the yoke and then worked as one piece.
- *Back:* Make 52 (64–73) ch and work as follows:

Row 1: Starting in 7th ch from hook, * 2 dc into next ch, ch 1, skip 2 foundation ch *. Repeat from * to * ending with 1 dc in last foundation ch, ch 3, turn.

Row 2: 1 dc into first ch-1 loop, * ch 1, 2 dc into next ch-1 loop *. Repeat from * to * ending with 2 dc into turning ch of previous row, ch 4, turn.

Row 3: * 2 dc into ch-1 loop, ch 1 *. Repeat from * to * ending with 1 dc into 3rd turning ch of previous row.

Repeat Rows 2 and 3 until work measures 15 cm (18–22) cm/6 (7–8½) ins. Finish off.

- *Fronts (2 alike):* Make 25 (31–34) ch and work as Back.
- *Sleeves (2 alike):* Make 31 (37–43) ch and work as Back for 15 (18–22) cm/6 (7–8½) ins.

Join side seams and sleeve seams for 10 (13–16) cm/4 (5¼–6¼) ins, starting from lower edge.

Now join the remaining 5 (5–6) cm/ 2 (2–2½) ins of Sleeves to the Fronts and Back.

- *Yoke:* Starting at Right Center Front, work 1 row in dc across Right Front, Right Sleeve, Back, Left Sleeve and Left Front.

Change to sc and work 5 (7–8) cm/ 2 (2¾–3¼) ins, decreasing at regular intervals on each row until 40 (50–60) stitches remain.

- *To finish:* Work 1 row in crab stitch around neck edge. Finish off.

Thread the ribbon through the single row of double crochets at beginning of yoke and through the second row at wrists.

Sew the buttons on to yoke on Left or Right Front, depending on whether the jacket is for a boy or girl.

Work two buttonholes to correspond on opposite Front, using a crocheted twisted cord edging or buttonhole stitch.

The jacket should not be pressed.

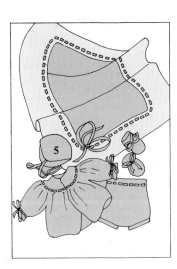

The garments illustrated in color on page 108

Bonnet (5)

Color illustration on page 108

Standard: ☆☆

Gauge: 16 stitches × 10 rows = 10 × 10 cm (4 × 4 ins).

The garments illustrated in color on page 109

Size: To fit a baby aged 0–1 month. The figures in brackets refer to sizes for 2 and 4 months.

Materials: 20 (30–40) g/¾ (1–1½) oz 1-ply mohair in yellow; size E aluminum or size 00 steel crochet hook; 40 cm (16 ins) yellow satin ribbon.

Stitches used: Single crochet (see page 28); double crochet (see page 29); crab stitch (see page 70).

Method

- The bonnet is worked back and forth.

Make 40 (49–61) ch and work in sc for 3.5 (4.5–5.5) cm/1¼ (1¾–2¼) ins. Continue as follows:

Row 1: Ch 4, * skip 2 sc, 2 dc into next sc, ch 1 *. Repeat from * to * ending with 1 dc into last sc, ch 3, turn.

Row 2: 1 dc into first ch-1 loop, * ch 1, 2 dc into next ch-1 loop *. Repeat from * to * ending with 2 dc into ch-4 loop, ch 4, turn.

Row 3: * 2 dc into ch-1 loop, ch 1 *. Repeat from * to * ending with ch 1, 1 dc into 3rd turning ch of previous row, ch 3, turn.

Repeat Rows 2 and 3 for 3.5 (4.5–5.5) cm/ 1¼ (1¾–2¼) ins. Continue, decreasing 1 group of 2-dc at the center of each row 5 (6–7) times.

- *To finish:* Sew up the opening at back of neck and work 2 rows in sc along lower edge of bonnet. Now work 1 row in sc and 1 row in crab stitch all around the edge of the bonnet.

Cut the ribbon in half and sew 1 piece neatly to each corner of lower edge to tie under baby's chin.

The bonnet should not be pressed.

Pink and white bootees (1)

Color illustration on page 109

Standard: ☆

Gauge: 28 stitches × 18 rows = 10 × 10 cm (4 × 4 ins).

Size: To fit a baby aged 0–1 months. The figures in brackets refer to sizes for 2 and 4 months.

Materials: 10 (15–20) g/¼ (½–¾) oz crochet cotton no. 5 in white; 10 (15–20) g/¼ (½– ¾) oz crochet cotton no. 5 in pink; size 4 steel crochet hook.

Stitches used: Single crochet, half double crochet and slip stitch (see page 28).

Method
● The bootees are worked in the round (see page 30) without turning the work, from the center of the sole.

Using white cotton, make 18 (23–26) ch. Work in sc, make 3 sc into last ch and work back along other side of length of ch, making 3 sc in first ch. Continue in this way until the sole is an oval measuring 9 (10–12) cm/ 3½ (4–5) ins long and 4 (5–6) cm/1½ (2–2½) ins wide.

Work next row in sc, working into back loop of each base stitch; this is the last row of the sole.

Work 4 rows straight. To form toe, mark central 3 stitches at one end of oval with contrasting thread and decrease 1 stitch at each side of them on each of next 6 (7–8) rounds. Work 2 rounds without decreasing. Using pink cotton, work one round as follows: * 1 hdc, ch 1, skip 1 base stitch; rep from * to last stitch, 1 hdc. This forms the eyelet holes for the ribbon.

Continue in dc with the pink cotton for 4 (5–6) cm/1½ (2–2½) ins. Finish off.

Make a second bootee in the same way.

● *To finish:* Using the pink cotton, make two simple plaited cords (see page 142) 30 cm (12 ins) long. Thread them through the eyelet holes and tie in a bow at center front. Turn the pink border outwards.

The garments illustrated in color on page 109

To mold the bootees into shape stuff them with cotton wool or tissue paper.

White bib with ribbons (2)
Color illustration on page 109

Standard: ☆☆

Gauge: 30 stitches × 20 rows = 10 × 10 cm (4 × 4 ins).

Size: The bib is 22 cm (approx. 8½ ins) deep and 19 cm (7½ ins) wide.

Materials: 40 g (1½ oz) no. 8 crochet cotton in white; size 4 steel crochet hook; 120 cm (48 ins) pale green satin baby ribbon.

Stitches used: Single crochet (see page 28); double crochet (see page 29).

Method
● Make 66 ch and work as follows:
Row 1: 10 sc, (3 sc into next stitch, 10 sc) 5 times to form 5 corners.

Continue in this way for a further 14 rows, working 3 sc into the 2nd sc of the 3-sc in the previous row.

Make a row of eyelet holes as follows: * 1 dc, ch 3, skip 3 sc *. Rep from * to * to last sc, 1 dc.

Work 1 row in sc along all 6 sides, working 3 sc into each corner. Break thread and continue working in sc on the 2 central sections only for 14 rows, increasing as before at the central corner.

Work another row of eyelet holes as above and 1 row in sc. Finish off.
● *To finish:* Work the following border round outside edge of bib (i.e. excluding neck edge): * 1 sc, ch 3, skip 2 sc, 1 sc *. Rep from * to * to last stitch, 1 sc. Finish off.

Thread the green ribbon through the two rows of eyelet holes and secure with small stitches on the wrong side of bib. Cut remaining length of ribbon in half and sew neatly to each end of neck-edge.

Press under a damp cloth with a hot iron.

Pink and white bib (3)
Color illustration on page 109

Standard: ☆☆

Gauge: 30 stitches × 20 rows in double crochet = 10 × 10 cm (4 × 4 ins).

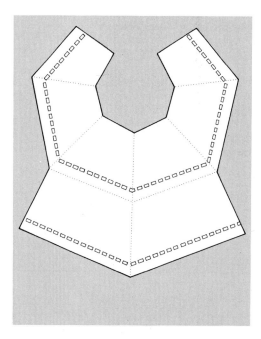

Size: The bib measures 22 cm (8½ ins) long and 16 cm (6¼ ins) wide.

Materials: 20 g (¾ oz) crochet cotton no. 5 in pink; 20 g (¾ oz) crochet cotton no. 5 in white; size C aluminum or size 1 steel crochet hook.

Stitches used: Single crochet and slip stitch (see page 28); double crochet (see page 29); crab stitch (see page 70).

Method
● The central part of this bib is worked as an oval (see page 30), from the right side.
Using pink cotton, make 30 ch.
Round 1: Starting in 2nd ch from hook work 28 sc into foundation ch, 3 sc into last ch, work 28 sc into the opposite side of the foundation ch, and 3 sc into last stitch. Close round with 1 sl st into starting ch.
Round 2: 28 sc, 2 sc into next stitch, 1 sc, 2 sc into next stitch, 28 sc along opposite side, 2 sc into next stitch, 1 sc, 2 sc into last stitch.
Continue in sc for a further 5 rounds, increasing at each end as in Round 2.
When the seven rounds have been completed, work 10 ch at each neck-edge corner to form neck opening. Starting at end of one length of ch-10, work in white crochet cotton as follows:
Row 1: Ch 1, * (1 sc, ch 1, 2 dc) into 1 base stitch, skip 2 stitches *. Repeat from * to * to last stitch of other length of ch-10, 1 sc, ch 3, turn.
Row 2: 1 dc into last dc of previous row, * (1 sc, ch 1, 2 dc) into ch-1 loop *. Repeat from * to * to last ch-1 loop, skip this loop, 1 sc into turning ch of previous row, ch 3, turn.
Rep Row 2 seven times. Finish off.

● *To finish:* Starting from one corner of neck opening, using pink crochet cotton work 1 row of edging as follows: * 1 sc, ch 3, 1 sl st into 3rd ch from hook, 1 sc into same base stitch *. Repeat from * to * around outside edge of bib. Finish off. With pink crochet cotton, work 1 row in sc and 1 row in crab st around neck edge. Finish off.
To make the ties, work 60 ch starting at one corner of neck-edge and then work 1 sc into each ch. Make a second tie in the same way.
Press the bib under a damp cloth with a hot iron.

The garments illustrated in color on page 109

Yellow and white bootees (4)
Color illustration on page 109

Standard: ☆☆

Gauge: 30 stitches × 20 rows = 10 × 10 cm (4 × 4 ins).

Size: To fit a baby aged 0–1 month. The figures in brackets refer to sizes for 2 and 4 months.

Materials: 10 (15–20) g/¼ (½–¾) oz crochet cotton no. 5 in white; a few grams of crochet cotton no. 5 in yellow; size 4 steel crochet hook.

Stitches used: Single crochet and slip stitch (see page 28).

Method
● The bootees are worked in the round (see page 30) without turning the work, starting from the top.
Using yellow crochet cotton, make 32 (36–40) ch and join with a sl st to form a ring. Work 1 sc into each foundation ch. Work 2 (3–4) rounds in sc.
Change to white crochet cotton and work a further 3.5 (4.5–5.5) cm/1½ (1¾–2¼) ins in sc.
Make eyelet holes in next round as follows: * 1 dc, ch 1, skip 1 base stitch *. Repeat from * to * to last stitch, 1 dc.
Work 1 round in sc. Now work back and forth on 16 (18–20) stitches for 5 (6–7) cm/ 2 (2–2¾) ins to form the upper part of the foot of the bootee.
Working in the round again, work along one of the sides of the upper part, continue across the heel, along the other side and over the toe. Continue in this way, decreasing one stitch on each side of the center of the toe for 2.5 (3.5–4.5) cm/1 (1½–1¾) ins to form the sides of the foot and the heel.
To make the sole, continue to work in the round, decreasing half the number of stitches on each round, i.e. work 1 sc, skip 1 sc, until 3 (4–4) stitches remain. Finish off, leaving a strand of yarn a few inches long. Thread yarn through remaining stitches on wrong side and draw together. Fasten off.
Work a second bootee in the same way.

● *To finish:* Make two twisted cords (see page 141) 30 cm (12 ins) long, thread them through the eyelet holes and tie in a bow.
To mold the bootees into shape, stuff them with cotton wool or tissue paper.

The articles illustrated in color on page 110

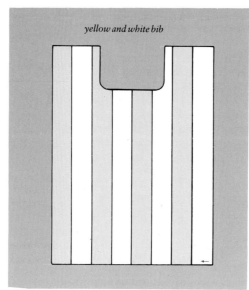

yellow and white bib

Yellow and white bib (5)

Color illustration on page 109

Standard: ☆

Gauge: 28 stitches × 22 rows = 10 × 10 cm (4 × 4 ins).

Size: The bib is 21.5 cm (8½ ins) deep and 16 cm (6¼ ins) wide.

Materials: 20 g (¾ oz) crochet cotton no. 5 in yellow; 20 g (¾ oz) crochet cotton no. 5 in white; size C aluminum crochet hook.

Stitches used: Half double crochet and single crochet (see page 28); crab stitch (see page 70).

Method
● The bib is worked back and forth, lengthways.

Using white crochet cotton, make 56 ch and work 4 rows in hdc. Change to yellow crochet cotton and work 4 rows.

With white crochet cotton work 2 rows, decreasing 13 stitches at end of second row to form one side of neck opening. Work a further 2 rows with the white crochet cotton, 4 rows with the yellow, 4 rows with white and 2 with yellow. Make 13 ch at the end of the row just worked to form the other side of the neck opening.

Work another 2 rows with the yellow crochet cotton, 4 rows with the white and 4 rows with the yellow.

● *To finish:* Using the yellow crochet cotton, work 1 row in sc and 1 row in crab st all around the bib, including the neck edge.

To make the ties, insert hook into corner of neck edge, work 70 ch and then work 1 sc into each foundation ch. Fasten off. Make a similar tie on opposite corner of neck.

Press the bib under a damp cloth with a hot iron.

White shawl with fringe (1)

Color illustration on page 110

Standard: ☆☆

Gauge: Two motifs of the shell pattern measure 7 × 2 cm (2¾ × ¾ ins).

Size: The shawl is triangular, measuring 205 cm (approx. 80 ins) across the top and 100 cm (approx. 40 ins) deep, including the fringes.

Materials: 50 g (2 oz) cashmere and silk mixture in white; size F aluminum crochet hook.

Stitches used: Double crochet (see page 29); single crochet and slip stitch (see page 28).

Method
● The shawl is worked back and forth from the tip of the triangle.

Make 11 ch.
Row 1: Starting in 7th ch from hook, work 6 dc into same ch, skip 3 ch, 1 dc into last ch, ch 1, turn.
Row 2: 1 sc into each dc of 6-dc group, ch 1, 1 sl st into top of turning ch of previous row, ch 3, turn.
Row 3: 5 dc into ch-1 loop, 1 dc between 3rd and 4th sc of 6-sc of previous row, 6 dc into turning ch-1 of previous row, ch 1, turn.
Row 4: * 1 sc into each dc of 6-dc group, ch 3 *. Repeat from * to * ending with ch 1, 1 sl st into 3rd turning ch of previous row, ch 3, turn.
Row 5: 5 dc into ch-1 loop, * 1 dc between 3rd and 4th sc of 6-sc of previous row, 6 dc into ch-3 loop *. Repeat from * to * ending with 6 dc into turning ch-1 of previous row, ch 1, turn.

Repeat Rows 4 and 5. The number of shell motifs made on every second row will automatically increase by 1. Continue until work measures 85 cm (33½ ins).

Work a border along 2 sloping sides of triangle as follows:

Row 1: Ch 6, ∗ 1 dc into ch-1 loop into which 6-dc was worked, ch 3 ∗. Repeat from ∗ to ∗ ending with 1 dc into last stitch and working (1 dc, ch 3) twice into point of shawl.

Row 2: Ch 6, ∗ 1 dc into ch-3 loop of previous row, ch 3 ∗. Repeat from ∗ to ∗ ending with 1 dc and working (1 dc, ch 3) twice into corner.

Repeat Row 2 four times, then work Row 1 across upper edge of shawl, including ends of side borders, missing 3 base stitches between each dc.

Repeat Row 2 twice across upper edge and then finish with 1 picot row as follows: ∗ ch 3, 1 sl st into 3rd ch from hook, 3 sl st into ch-3 of previous row ∗. Repeat from ∗ to ∗ ending with 1 picot and 1 sl st into last dc.

● *To finish:* Make a simple fringe (see page 140) 20 cm (8 ins) long, making 1 knot into each ch-3 loop along the two sloping sides of the shawl and 3 knots into loop at point.

The shawl should not be pressed.

The articles illustrated in color on page 110

Two-color cushion (2)

Color illustration on page 110

Standard: ☆☆

Tension: (Front) 20 stitches × 8 rows = 10 × 10 cm (4 × 4 ins); (Back) 20 stitches × 11 rows = 10 × 10 cm (4 × 4 ins).

Size: The cushion measures 30 × 35 cm (approx. 12 × 14 ins).

Materials: 80 g (3 oz) light blue silk; 40 g (1½ oz) dark blue silk; size F aluminum crochet hook; 1 zip-fastener 30 cm (12 ins) long in light blue; cushion pad.

Stitches used: Two-color wavy chevrons (see page 55); double crochet (see page 29); single crochet (see page 28).

Method
● *Front:* Using the light blue silk, make 56 ch and work in two-color wavy chevrons for 34 cm (13½ ins), alternating the light blue and the dark blue silk and ending with a light blue row. Finish off.
● *Back:* Using the light blue silk, make 56 ch and work in sc for 34 cm (13½ ins). Finish off.

● *To make up:* Join the two longer sides and one short side of the cushion on wrong side with a backstitch seam (see page 147). Insert zip.

Using the dark blue silk, work 1 row of sc along the three sewn-up edges, inserting the hook into Front and Back on each stitch. Still using the dark blue silk, work one row of sc along the Front edge and one row along the Back edge on each side of zip.

Press the cushion with a lukewarm iron and insert pad.

Red crochet hook case (3)

Color illustration on page 110

Standard: ☆

Tension: 20 stitches × 18 rows = 10 × 10 cm (4 × 4 ins).

Size: The crochet-hook case measures 15 × 7.5 cm (6 × 3 ins).

Materials: 30 g (1 oz) crochet cotton no. 8 in red, used double; size G aluminum crochet hook.

Stitches used: Single crochet (see page 28); double crochet (see page 29).

Method
● The crochet-hook case is worked in the round (see page 30) without turning the work, from the base upwards.

Make 12 ch. Work one row in sc, working 2 sc in the last ch, and work back in sc along the other side of the base chain, working 2 sc in the first ch.

Work 1 round in sc without increasing, inserting the hook into the back loop only of each stitch. Continue working in the round without increasing for 10 cm (4 ins).

Work 1 round as follows: ∗ 1 dc, ch 3, skip 3 base stitches ∗. Repeat from ∗ to ∗, closing round with 1 sl st. This forms the eyelet holes through which the ribbon is threaded. Work in sc for a further 4.5 cm (1¾ ins). Finish off.

● *To finish:* Make a chain 20 cm (8 ins) long and thread through eyelet holes. Knot ends securely.

The bag should not be pressed.

Colored slippers (4)

Color illustration on page 110

Standard: ☆☆

Gauge: 15 stitches × 12 rows = 10 × 10 cm (4 × 4 ins).

Size: To fit medium sizes. The figures in brackets refer to small sizes.

Materials: The slippers are made from odds and ends of wool in various colors; each pair requires 100 g (4 oz) altogether; size F aluminum crochet hook.

Stitches used: Single crochet (see page 28).

Method

● The slippers are worked in the round (see page 30), without turning the work, starting in the center of the sole.

The pattern does not include instructions for changing color since this depends on the yarns available.

Make 25 (20) ch and work in sc, working 3 sc into the last base ch, working back on the opposite side of the ch and working 3 sc into first ch. Continue in sc for 4.5 (4) cm/ $1\frac{3}{4}$ ($1\frac{1}{2}$) ins, increasing in the same way at both ends of the oval. Work 1 round in sc without increasing, inserting hook into back loop only of each stitch in previous round. Work a further 5 rounds in the same way, decreasing 1 stitch on each round at the center of one end of the oval to form the heel.

At the other end of the oval, work in rows of sc back and forth on the 18 (16) stitches on either side of the central stitch for 10 (8) cm/ 4 ($3\frac{1}{4}$) ins, joining the beginning and end of each row to the sides of the slippers with sl sts. This forms the upper part of the slipper.

Begin working in the round again, into all the stitches, for 5 (4) cm/2 ($1\frac{1}{2}$) ins. Finish off.

Work a second slipper to match.

● *To finish:* Work one row of sc around the front of the slipper, inserting the hook into the single crochet stitches already worked.

The slippers should not be pressed.

Sausage dog (5)

Color illustration on page 110

Standard: ☆☆

Gauge: 10 stitches × 5 rows in dc = 10 × 10 cm (4 × 4 ins).

Size: The dog is 65 cm ($25\frac{1}{2}$ ins) long, including its tail and tongue.

Materials: 100 g (4 oz) sport yarn in yellow; 50 g (2 oz) sport yarn in brown; a few grams sport yarn in red; sizes F and H aluminum crochet hooks; 2 buttons; stuffing.

Stitches used: Double crochet (see page 29); single crochet and slip stitch (see page 28).

The articles illustrated in color on page 110

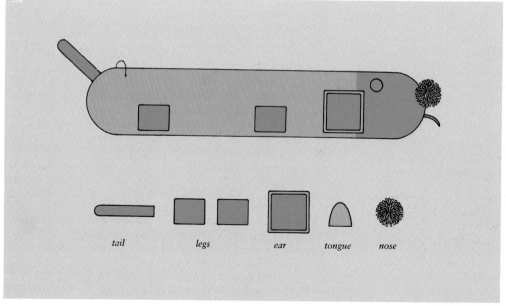

tail   legs   ear   tongue   nose

Method
- The body of the dog is worked in the round (see page 30), without turning the work. The ears, legs, nose, tongue and tail are worked separately and sewn on to the body.

Using yellow wool and size H crochet hook, make 16 ch and join with a sl st to form a ring. Work 1 round in dc, increasing 4 stitches at regular intervals in the round.

Continue in dc, inserting the crochet hook into the space between double crochets in the previous round and increasing 4 stitches every 2 rounds, until work measures 38 cm (15 ins).

Change to brown wool for the head and continue in dc, without increasing, for 6 cm ($2\frac{1}{2}$ ins).

Work a further 6 cm ($2\frac{1}{2}$ ins), decreasing on every round so that only 10 stitches remain. Finish off, leaving a short length of yarn to close the ring.
- *Tail:* Using brown wool and the size H crochet hook, make 12 ch and join with a sl st to form a ring.

Work in sc for 7 cm ($2\frac{3}{4}$ ins) and then decrease evenly over 3 cm ($1\frac{1}{4}$ ins) so that 4 stitches remain. Finish off, leaving a short length of yarn to close the ring.
- *Legs:* Using brown wool and size H crochet hook, make 6 ch and work 4 rows in dc. Finish off.

Make 3 more legs in the same way.
- *Ears:* Using brown wool and a size H crochet hook, make 10 ch and work 9 cm ($3\frac{1}{4}$ ins) in dc. Finish off.

Using yellow wool, work 1 row of sc around the edge of the ear.

Make another ear in the same way.
- *Tongue:* Using red wool and size F crochet hook, make 2 ch and work in sc for 4 rows, increasing 1 stitch at each end of every row. Finish off.
- *Nose:* Using yellow wool, make a pompon (see page 141) using a disc 5 cm (2 ins) in diameter.

- *To make up:* Push the stuffing into the body through the 16-ch opening. Using yellow wool and size H crochet hook, work 2 rounds of dc into this ring and then continue in dc, decreasing gradually until 5 stitches remain. Finish off, leaving a short length of yarn to close the ring.

Sew the ears to the body where the brown and yellow sections meet. Sew the tongue and nose securely to the brown part and 2 legs on each side of the yellow body. Sew the tail to the top of the rounded end. Sew the buttons into position on the brown part.

The articles illustrated in color on page 110

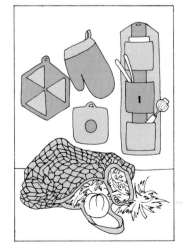

The articles illustrated in color on page 127

Knitting needle case (6)
Color illustration on page 110

Standard: ☆

Gauge: 18 stitches × 26 rows = 10 × 10 cm (4 × 4 ins).

Size: The knitting needle case measures 50 cm (approx. 20 ins) in length.

Materials: 40 g ($1\frac{1}{2}$ oz) crochet cotton no. 5 in dark blue; 20 g ($\frac{3}{4}$ oz) crochet cotton no. 5 in red; 10 g ($\frac{1}{4}$ oz) crochet cotton no. 5 in white; size D aluminum or size 1 steel crochet hook; a stiff cardboard tube with base.

Stitches used: Single crochet and slip stitch (see page 28); double crochet (see page 29).

Method
- The tube is worked in the round (see page 30), without turning the work.

Using the red cotton, make 5 ch and join with a sl st to form a ring. Work 10 sc into the ring.

Continue working in sc, increasing at regular intervals on each round to form a flat circle with a diameter of 4.5 cm ($1\frac{3}{4}$ ins).

Change to dark blue cotton and work 1 row in sc, inserting hook into back loop only of each stitch in previous row. Continue in sc for 11 cm ($4\frac{1}{2}$ ins) without increasing.

Continue in the same way, alternating the colors as follows: 2 cm ($\frac{3}{4}$ in) in red cotton; 1 cm ($\frac{3}{8}$ in) in dark blue cotton; 1.5 cm ($\frac{5}{8}$ in) in white cotton; 1 cm ($\frac{3}{8}$ in) in dark blue cotton; 1.5 cm ($\frac{5}{8}$ in) in white cotton; 1 cm ($\frac{3}{8}$ in) in dark blue cotton; 1.5 cm ($\frac{5}{8}$ in) in white cotton; 4 cm ($1\frac{1}{2}$ ins) in red cotton; 1.5 cm ($\frac{5}{8}$ in) in white cotton; 1 cm ($\frac{3}{8}$ in) in dark blue cotton; 1.5 cm ($\frac{5}{8}$ in) in white cotton; 1 cm ($\frac{3}{8}$ in) in dark blue cotton; 1.5 cm ($\frac{5}{8}$ in) in white cotton; 1 cm ($\frac{3}{8}$ in) in dark blue cotton; 2 cm ($\frac{3}{4}$ in) in red cotton; 11 cm ($4\frac{1}{4}$ ins) in dark blue cotton.

Still using dark blue cotton, work 1 row in dc and 4 cm ($1\frac{1}{2}$ ins) in sc.

- *To finish:* Insert the stiff cardboard tube into the crocheted cylinder.

Using dark blue crochet cotton, work 30 cm (12 ins) of twisted cording (see page 141) and thread it through the round of double crochet.

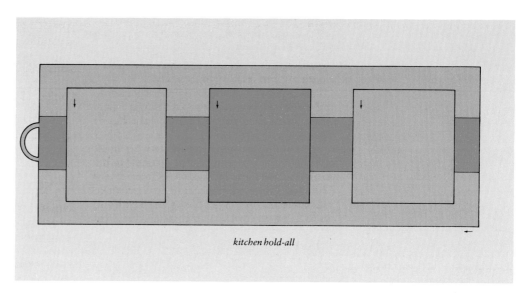

kitchen hold-all

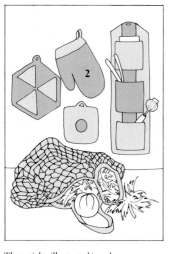

The articles illustrated in color on page 127

Kitchen hold-all (1)

Color illustration on page 127

Standard: ☆

Tension: 14 stitches × 8 rows = 10 × 10 cm (4 × 4 ins).

Size: The hold-all measures 44 cm (approx. 17 ins) long and 15 cm (6 ins) wide.

Materials: 40 g (1½ oz) blue linen yarn; 60 g (2 oz) gray linen yarn; size G aluminum crochet hook.

Stitches used: Double crochet (see page 29); single crochet (see page 28); crab stitch (see page 70).

Method
- The hold-all is worked back and forth lengthwise.
  Using the gray yarn double, make 42 ch and work in dc for 3 rows. Change to blue yarn, use double and work a further 4 rows in dc. Rejoin the two strands of gray and work another 3 rows. Finish off.
- *Pockets:* All three pockets are worked separately using yarn double. Make two in gray and one in blue, working as follows: Make 14 ch and work 9 rows in dc. Finish off.
- *To make up:* Sew three sides of each pocket to the strip, positioning them as shown in the photograph on p.127.
  Using gray yarn double, work 1 row of sc around the strip, making a ch-4 loop (see page 138) in the center at the top of the strip.
  Using 1 strand of gray yarn and 1 strand of blue yarn, work 1 row of crab stitch around the strip. Work 1 row in crab stitch along the top edge of each pocket, using the same color yarn as the pocket itself.
  Press the strip and pockets under a damp cloth with a hot iron.

Oven glove (2)

Color illustration on page 127

Standard: ☆☆

Gauge: 16 stitches × 16 rows = 10 × 10 cm (4 × 4 ins).

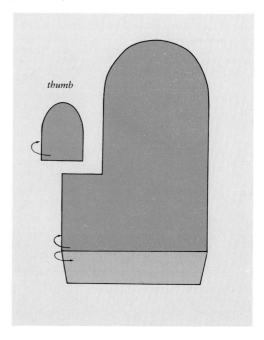

thumb

Size: The glove is 21 cm (8¼ ins) long and 13 cm (just over 5 ins) wide.

Materials: 50 g (2 oz) blue linen yarn; 10 g (¼ oz) gray linen yarn; size G aluminum crochet hook.

Stitches used: Single crochet and slip stitch (see page 28); crab stitch (see page 70).

Method
• The glove is worked in the round (see page 30), without turning the work.

Using the blue yarn double, make 40 ch and join with a sl st to form a ring. Work 1 sc into each base ch and then continue straight in sc for 6 cm (2½ ins). Leave 10 stitches unworked as the basis for the thumb.

Continue working in the round on the remaining 30 stitches for 8 cm (3¼ ins). Work a further 3 cm (1¼ ins) in sc decreasing the number of stitches on each round by half, by missing one base stitch every two stitches, so that only 5 stitches remain. Finish off.

Return to the 10 stitches left unworked and make the thumb by working in rounds of sc for 5 cm (2 ins). Now decrease by missing one base stitch every two stitches, as above, until 3 stitches remain. Finish off.

• *To finish:* Close top of thumb and main part of glove with small stitches and finish off on wrong side of work.

Using one strand of gray and one of blue, work 5 rows in sc and 1 row in crab stitch. On the opposite corner to the thumb, work a ch-4 loop (see page 138).

Iron the glove lightly under a damp cloth, taking care not to flatten it too much.

Pan-holder (3)
Color illustration on page 127

Standard: ☆

Gauge: 16 stitches × 16 rows = 10 × 10 cm (4 × 4 ins).

Size: The pan-holder measures 12 × 12 cm (5 × 5 ins).

Materials: 10 g (¼ oz) gray linen yarn; 10 g (¼ oz) blue linen yarn; size G aluminum crochet hook.

Stitches used: Single crochet and slip stitch (see page 28); crab stitch (see page 70).

Method
• The pan-holder is worked in the round (see page 30), without turning the work.

Using 1 strand of gray and one of blue, make 4 ch and join with a sl st to form a ring.
Round 1: 3 sc into each of the 4 base ch.

Work 12 rounds in sc, working 3 sc into each corner.

• *To finish:* Work one round of crab stitch around the edge and make a ch-6 loop (see page 138) in the center of one side.

The central rosette is made as follows, using two strands of blue yarn: Make 4 ch and join with a sl st to form a ring.
Round 1: Ch 1, 11 sc into ring, complete round with 1 sl st into first ch.
Round 2: Inserting hook into front loop only of sc in previous round, work (1 sc, ch 4, 1 sc) into each sc. Complete round with 1 sl st.
Round 3: Inserting hook into back loop only of sc in previous round, work (1 sc, ch 6, 1 sc) into each sc. Finish off.

Sew rosette to center of pot-holder and finish off on wrong side of work.

Press the pot-holder under a damp cloth with a hot iron but without flattening the rosette.

Saucepan mat (4)
Color illustration on page 127

Standard: ☆

Gauge: 16 stitches × 16 rows = 10 × 10 cm (4 × 4 ins).

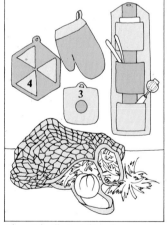

The articles illustrated in color on page 127

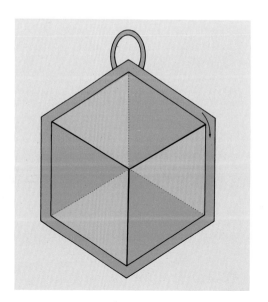

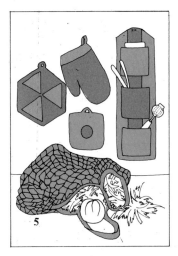

The articles illustrated in color on page 127

Size: The mat is 20 cm (8 ins) in diameter.

Materials: 10 g (¼ oz) gray linen yarn; 15 g (½ oz) blue linen yarn; size G aluminum crochet hook.

Stitches used: Single crochet (see page 28); crab stitch (see page 70).

Method
● The mat consists of 3 diamond-shaped medallions joined together as shown in the diagram.

Follow instructions for making the diamond-shaped medallion on page 59, using the yarn double and starting with the gray yarn. On Row 15, at the half-way point, change to blue yarn.

● *To finish:* Sew the sections together with small, neat stitches.

Work 1 row of sc in blue around mat, working 2 sc into one base stitch at each corner of the hexagon. Finally, work 1 row in crab stitch all round mat. Work a ch-6 loop (see page 138) at one of the corners.

Press the mat under a damp cloth with a hot iron, taking care not to flatten the crab-stitch edging.

Mesh shopping bag (5)
Color illustration on page 127

Standard: ☆☆

Gauge: 20 × 20 meshes = 10 × 10 cm (4 × 4 ins).

Size: Before being made up the mesh measures 70 × 70 cm (27½ × 27½ ins).

Materials: 40 g (1½ oz) unbleached dishcloth cotton; size E aluminum or size 00 steel crochet hook; 150 cm (approx 60 ins) string.

Stitches used: Double crochet (see page 29).

Method
● The bag is made as a square of crocheted netting, worked back and forth.

Make 178 ch and work as follows:
Row 1: Ch 7, ✳ skip 4 base stitches, 2 dc, ch 4 ✳. Repeat from ✳ to ✳ to last stitch, 1 dc, ch 4, turn.
Row 2: Skip 1 base stitch, ✳ 2 dc, ch 4, skip 4 base stitches ✳. Repeat from ✳ to ✳ to last 2 stitches, ch 1, skip 1 base stitch, 1 dc.

Repeat these two rows until work reaches required size.

● *To make up:* Work 1 row of dc around all 4 sides, working 3 dc into each corner loop.

Fold the dc edging over and stitch neatly into place. Thread the string through the hem thus formed and gather 2 sides opposite each other. Gather only the center of the other two sides, as shown in diagram. Fasten the gathering in place with a few stitches. Now cover the hem closely with dc, closing the stitches below the border.

To make the handles, sew the ends of a piece of string 25 cm (10 ins) long to each of the two gathered sides. Cover both pieces of string closely with a row of dc, closing the stitches below the border.

The bag does not require pressing.

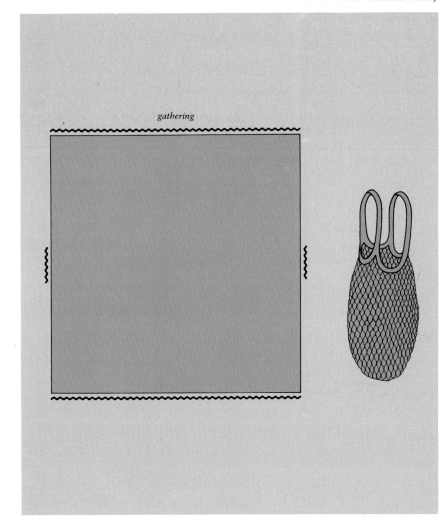

gathering

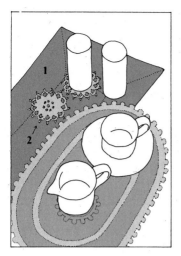

The articles illustrated in color on page 128

Blue table mat (1)

Color illustration on page 128

Standard: ☆☆

Gauge: 18 stitches × 12 rows = 10 × 10 cm (4 × 4 ins).

Size: The table mat measures 45 × 32 cm (18 × 12½ ins).

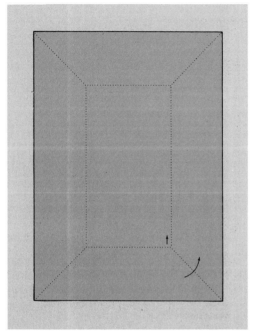

Materials: 100 g (4 oz) crochet cotton no. 8 in dark blue; size F aluminum crochet hook.

Stitches used: Single crochet (see page 28); crab stitch (see page 70).

Method
● The table mat is made in two stages: a rectangle is worked back and forth and then edged with a border worked in the round (see page 30).
   Using the cotton double, make 22 ch and work in sc for 28.5 cm (11¼ ins). Finish off.
   Still using 2 strands of the cotton, starting from one corner, work 1 round in sc, working 3 sc into each of the 4 corner stitches. Continue in sc working the 3 corner sc into the 2nd of the 3 corner sc of the previous round. When border measures 9 cm (3½ ins) finish off.

● *To finish:* Work 1 row in crab stitch along all 4 sides. Finish off.
   Press the mat under a damp cloth with a hot iron.

Yellow coaster (2)

Color illustration on page 128

Standard: ☆☆

Gauge: At the end of the first round the ring measures 2.3 cm ($\frac{7}{8}$ in) in diameter.

Size: The coaster measures 10 cm (4 ins) in diameter.

Materials: For 6 coasters you will require 40 g (1½ oz) crochet cotton no. 12 in yellow; size 6 steel crochet hook.

Stitches used: Slip stitch and single crochet (see page 28); double crochet and treble (see page 29).

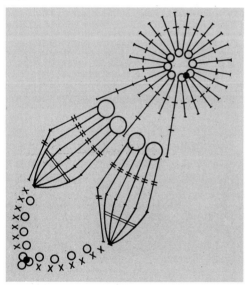

Chart for the yellow coaster
○ chain stitch
⼦ treble
● slip stitch
× single crochet
⚯ 1 picot = 3 chain stitches joined by 1
     slip stitch

Method
● The coaster is worked in the round (see page 30).
   Make 8 ch and join with a sl st to form ring. Work the beginning of each round by replacing first dc with ch 3 and first tr with ch 4. Close each round with 1 sl st into top of starting ch.
Round 1: 24 dc worked into the ring.

131

Round 2: (1 dc, ch 2, skip 1 dc) 12 times, closing round with 1 sl st.
Round 3: 6 tr into each ch-2 loop of previous round, closing round with 1 sl st.
Round 4: (1 dc into first dc of previous round, 1 unfin dc into each of next 5 dc, yo, draw yarn through all 5 loops on hook, ch 8) 12 times, closing round with 1 sl st.
Round 5: (7 sc, 1 picot [= ch 3, 1 sl st into 3rd ch from hook], 7 sc) into each ch-8 loop, closing with 1 sl st. Finish off.

● *To finish:* Press the coaster with a hot iron.

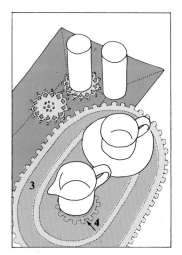

The articles illustrated in color on page 128

Red and white table mat (3)

Color illustration on page 128

Standard: ☆

Gauge: 15 stitches × 6 rows = 10 × 10 cm (4 × 4 ins).

Size: The table mat measures 43 × 29 cm (17 × 11½ ins).

Materials: 40 g (1½ oz) red raffia; 20 g (¾ oz) white raffia; size H aluminum crochet hook.

Stitches used: Double crochet (see page 29); single crochet and slip stitch (see page 28).

Method
● The table mat is worked in the round (see page 30), without turning the work.
    Using the red raffia, make 20 ch. Work 1 dc into each ch and 3 dc into last ch. Work back along other side of foundation ch, working 3 dc at end of round. Continue in dc, increasing as in first round at each end of the oval, for another 4 rounds, closing each one with 1 sl st.
    Using white raffia, work 2 rounds in sc, increasing in the same way at each end of oval. Close both rounds with 1 sl st.
    Rejoin red raffia and work 2 rows in dc, closing each round with 1 sl st.

● *To finish:* Using the white raffia, work an edging as follows: 1 sc, * 1 picot (= ch 3, 1 sl st into 3rd ch from hook), skip 1 base stitch, 2 sc *. Repeat from * to * to end of round, ending with 1 sc. Finish off.
    If you think that the mat needs pressing, use a cool iron.

Red and white coaster (4)

Color illustration on page 128

Standard: ☆

Gauge: At the end of the first round the ring measures 1.3 cm (½ in) in diameter.

Size: The coaster has a diameter of 11 cm (4½ ins), including the edging.

Materials: For 6 coasters you will require 100 g (4 oz) white raffia and 20 g (¾ oz) red raffia; size H aluminum crochet hook.

Stitches used: Single crochet and slip stitch (see page 28).

Method
● The coaster is worked in the round (see page 30).
    Using the white raffia, make 5 ch and join with a sl st to form a ring. Work in sc, increasing at regular intervals on each round to form a flat circle measuring 8 cm (3¼ ins) in diameter. Close with 1 sl st. Finish off.

● *To finish:* Using the red raffia, work an edging as follows: 2 sc, * 1 picot (= ch 3, 1 sl st into 3rd ch from hook), 2 sc *. Repeat from * to * to end of round, closing with 1 sl st into first sc. Finish off.
    The coaster can be pressed with a cool iron.

More useful information

Working in several colors

Attractive multicolor patterns can easily be worked in crochet by introducing one or more new yarns in a different color, either in the course of a row or at the beginning of a row. Multicolor patterns are usually worked in simple stitches such as single crochet or double crochet.

The technique of working in a new yarn in the middle of a row is also useful when you come to the end of a ball of yarn and have to start another.

Adding a second color

When working in single crochet, the end of the new yarn can either be worked in before the

Joining a new thread or second color

1. Working over the end of the new thread before it is required. The last single crochet in the first color is closed with the second color.
2. Closing the last single crochet in the first color with the second color and working in the end afterwards.
3. 4. 5. Joining a new thread when working in double crochet.

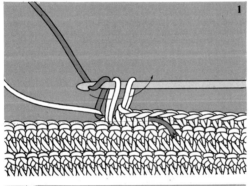

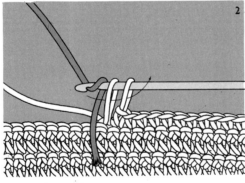

first stitch is worked in the second color or afterwards. To join the second color before it is required, lay the end along the top of the previous row and work a few stitches over it as shown in Fig 1. Close the last single crochet in the first color by drawing the new yarn through the 2 loops on the hook. Alternatively, close the last stitch in the first color with the new yarn, leaving a short loose end; lay this end along the top of the previous row and work a few stitches over it as if it were part of the previous row.

When working in double crochet, join the second color as follows: lay the new yarn along the top of the previous row and work a

few stitches over it. At the point where the second color is required, work 1 dc in this manner: yo with first color, insert hook into top of previous row, yo with both colors, draw both through, yo with second color only and complete as a normal dc.

If the first color is not to be used again it can be fastened in a similar way: cut the thread leaving a short end, lay this along the top of the

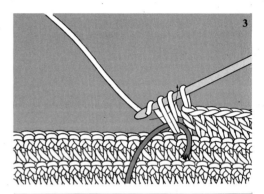

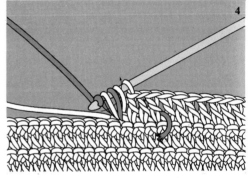

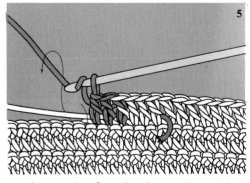

previous row and work a few stitches over it. Equally, if the colors are to be alternated on the same row, the first color can be worked in until it is required.

Alternating colors

Colors can be alternated in several ways to produce different patterns.

Horizontal stripes are worked by changing color at the beginning of a row. This is done by working the turning chain at the end of the previous row with the second color. The first color is left at the side of the work. If working back and forth in rows the stripes have to

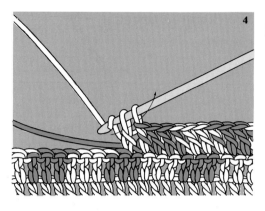

last stitch in the first color with the second color. If there is only one stripe in each color, the yarn is left hanging at the back of the work after the block of stitches has been worked so that it is in the correct place on the following row.

Checked patterns are worked by alternating blocks of color on each row, working in the yarn not in use as described above. On every row or every alternate row contrasting blocks are worked over each other.

Non-geometric colorwork patterns are usually worked from a chart similar to a filet crochet chart; in this case each square corresponds to one stitch in a given color.

Alternating colors

1. 2. Working in single crochet over the first color so that it is ready to be brought back into use.
3. 4. Working in double crochet over the first color so that it is ready to be brought back into use.

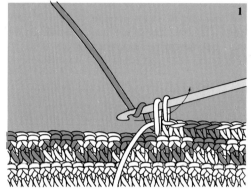

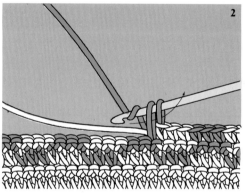

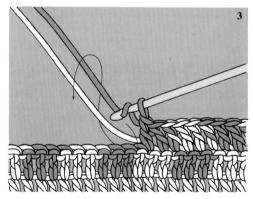

consist of an even number of rows. If working in the round the yarn left at the beginning of a round can be reintroduced on any subsequent round.

Vertical stripes are worked by alternating two or more colors on each row, always working a block of stitches in one color over the block of stitches in the same color on the previous row. As described above, when changing from one color to another, close the

136

Finishing touches for garments

Whether you are designing your own garment or are following a printed pattern, it is important to know how to work details such as buttonholes, buttons and pockets, since these can add interest to a plain garment and a professional finish to your work.

Buttonholes

Buttonholes can be worked horizontally or vertically. Their size depends on the size of the buttons. When they have been worked by one of the methods described below, they can be finished by working around them in buttonhole stitch using a matching cotton or finer yarn. If the garment was worked in worsted or sport yarn, it is often possible to split it and use a single strand for finishing the buttonhole.

Vertical buttonhole in single crochet. This is made by dividing the work in two and working each side separately. At the point where you wish to start a buttonhole, turn and work back and forth across these stitches until the buttonhole is the required length, ending at buttonhole edge (Fig 5). Now work in slip stitch down the edge of the buttonhole to the last complete row. On the remaining stitches of the row, work back and forth to match the other side, again ending at the buttonhole edge. The buttonhole is completed by working across all the stitches of the row (Fig 6).

Vertical buttonhole in double crochet. Since each row of double crochet is quite deep, when working vertical buttonholes choose buttons that correspond to the depth of two or three rows.

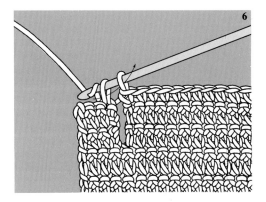

To make a buttonhole over two rows, work to the required point, turn and work back, ending at the outside edge of the work. Put a safety pin through loop, remove hook and leave yarn at edge of work. Take a new ball of yarn and work 2 rows across the unworked stitches of the last complete row. Break off the new thread and work over all the stitches with the original thread to close the buttonhole (Figs 7 and 8).

Horizontal buttonholes. At the point where a buttonhole is required, work three or four stitches at the beginning of the row. Now work a few chain stitches – the number will depend upon the thickness of the yarn and the size of

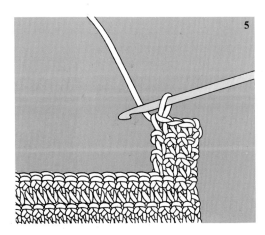

Making buttonholes

5. 6. a vertical buttonhole in single crochet
7. 8. a vertical buttonhole in double crochet

the buttons. Skip the same number of stitches in the previous row (Fig 1) and work normally for the rest of the row. In the following row, work into the chain stitches as though they were ordinary base stitches.

Button-loops. Loops are even simpler to make than buttonholes since they are worked into the edge of the finished garment.

Work in slip stitch to the point at which you wish the loop to start. Make a length of chain which will accommodate the button, skip the

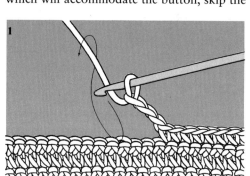

same number of base stitches and continue in slip stitch until you reach the point at which the next loop is to start (Fig 2).

Buttonholes in Afghan crochet. Vertical buttonholes in Afghan crochet are made exactly as those in ordinary crochet.

Horizontal buttonholes, however, are made as follows: on an (A) row work to the point where a buttonhole is required and wind the

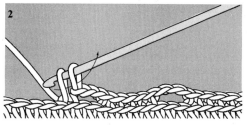

yarn round the hook two or more times depending on the length of buttonhole to be made (Fig 3). Skip the same number of base stitches and complete the row in the usual way. On the return row, work each of the loops off the hook, one by one, in the normal way (Fig 4).

Pockets

Patch pockets worked in contrasting yarn can produce a bold decorative effect, while inset pockets give a tailored look to a garment.

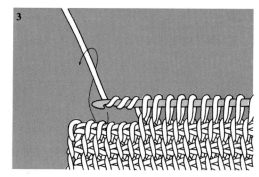

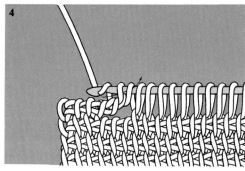

Patch pockets. These are the simplest type of pocket since they are worked separately and added to the completed garment, making it easy to decide upon their size and position. Make a crochet square either in the same stitch as the body of the garment or in the stitch used for edgings, baste in position and sew with neat stab stitches.

Inset pockets. These may be worked horizontally or vertically while crocheting the body of the work.

Horizontal inset pocket. Work the front of the garment to the point where you require the pocket opening. Decide the width and position of the opening, work to beginning and work pocket border (usually in the same stitch as is used to finish the other edges of the garment). Break thread. Make a foundation chain the same length as the pocket opening, work a

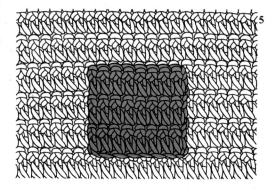

square in your main pattern stitch ending with a right side row. Place pocket lining behind pocket opening and continue across front, working into remaining stitches of row where you made the pocket border. On the following row work across all stitches of front, including stitches of pocket lining.

When the garment is finished, neatly stitch the three edges of the pocket lining to the wrong side.

6. an inset pocket

Making crocheted buttons

7. flat buttons
8. spherical button

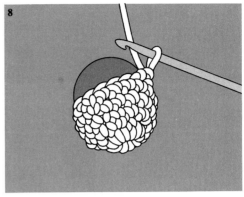

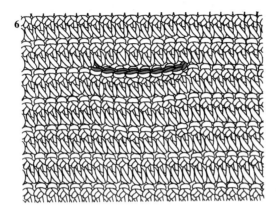

Vertical inset pocket. Work the front of the garment to the point where you require the pocket opening to begin. Divide the work and work back and forth across the side which will form the front of the pocket until the pocket opening is the required depth. Break thread. Return to where you divided the work, make a foundation chain corresponding to the required width of the pocket lining. Work across all stitches until the second side matches the first. On the following row work across all stitches, working into both front of pocket and pocket lining where they overlap. When the garment is finished, sew the remaining two sides of the pocket lining to the back of the work.

Crocheted buttons

Crocheted buttons made in the same yarn as the garment add a perfectly coordinated, individualistic touch. Both flat and spherical buttons can be covered in crochet.

To make flat buttons you will require some small rings, such as plastic curtain rings, slightly smaller than the required size of the finished button. Work into the ring in single crochet, completing the round with a slip stitch. Now turn the stitches just made into the center of the ring and stitch them firmly into place with the same thread. A further round of single crochet can be worked into the ring if this will not make the button too bulky (Fig 7).

To cover a spherical button you can either buy a special center or use a ball of cottonwool or stuffing material. In slip stitch, work in the round, increasing progressively until the center fits in the crochet cover and then gradually decrease so that the button is completely covered (Fig 8). Alternatively, if using stuffing, work in a similar way without inserting the center until there is an opening just large enough for the button to be filled with stuffing. Shape the button into a ball and work the closing stitches.

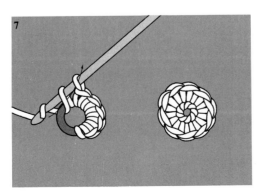

Decorative touches

This section describes how to make finishing touches such as tassels, fringes and cords. Many of these have already been referred to in the pattern section. They are both useful and decorative, adding interest to an otherwise plain garment.

Another way of enlivening a plain piece of crochet is to embroider it. A variety of stitches and patterns can be worked. The addition of beads or sequins to a piece of crochet can also be used to good effect.

Tassels

You will need a rectangular piece of cardboard the same length as the tassel you wish to make. Wind the yarn round and round the cardboard; each complete turn represents two strands of the finished tassel. Break the yarn when the tassel is the required thickness. With a darning-needle thread the end of yarn through all the loops at one end of the cardboard and fasten tightly with a knot. Remove the cardboard, wind the yarn round all the loops, just below the knot and fasten off. Cut through loops at the other end of the tassel and trim (Fig 1).

Tassels can be used to decorate berets, scarves, etc.

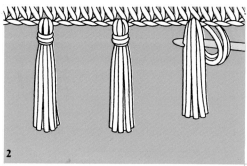

1. *making tassels*
2. *making a simple fringe*
3. 4. *making a knotted fringe*

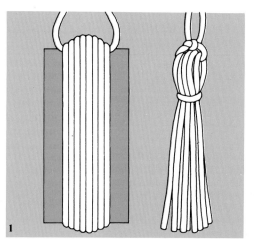

Fringes

To make a simple fringe cut the yarn into lengths twice the required length of the fringe.

Divide them into groups of three or four strands, depending on the thickness of the yarn and the required fullness of the fringe, and fold them in half. Draw the folded loops of one group through the edge of the border with a crochet hook, then hook the ends through this loop. Pull gently to tighten the knot. Repeat at regular intervals along the edge on the right side of the work. Finally trim the fringe with sharp scissors to make it even, laying the fringe flat on a table.

Knotted or lattice fringes are made in the same way but the strands should be cut longer than the required length of the fringe. When all the yarn has been knotted into the border, take half the strands of one group and half of the next group and make a knot a short distance down from the first knot. Now knot the remaining strands of the second group to half the strands of the next group and so on to end of fringe. As many rows of knots may be worked as you wish, alternating the knots and spaces left by the previous line (Figs 3 and 4).

Fringes can be used to complete scarves, stoles, shawls, bedspreads, table covers and curtains.

Pompons

You will need two circles of cardboard, about 2 cm ($\frac{3}{4}$ in) larger in diameter than the desired size of the pompon. Make a hole in the center of both discs equivalent to approximately a quarter of the diameter. With a long length of yarn threaded double into a blunt needle, cover the whole disc evenly, taking the needle through the hole and bringing the yarn round and through the hole again. Continue in this way until the hole in the center is almost closed (Fig 5).

With very sharp scissors, cut around the outer edge of the circles, inserting the point between the two layers of cardboard (Fig 6). Tie a double length of yarn tightly round the center, between the discs, and knot securely (Fig 7). Cut through each disc and remove them. Trim the resulting ball to make it as even and round as possible.

Pompons make an ideal finish for children's and adults' berets; they can also be sewn on to the ends of drawstrings on children's clothes.

Cords

Cords are particularly useful as drawstrings on children's clothes.

There are numerous ways of making cords.

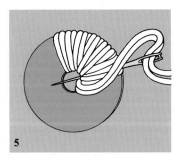

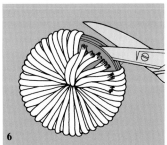

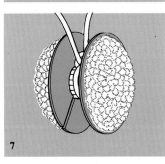

5. 6. 7. making a pompon by winding yarn over two cardboard discs
8. chain-stitch cord using two threads
9. chain-stitch cord using four threads
10. round cord

A few of the more common ones are described below and can be made in one or more colors.

Crocheted cords. Two-color cords can be crocheted by working a length of single chain and alternating the colors as follows. Place the threads from two different colored balls over the forefinger of the left hand and work alternate chain stitches with each color (Fig 8). If a thicker cord is required, four threads can be used instead of two, working with two at a time (Fig 9).

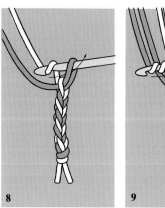 

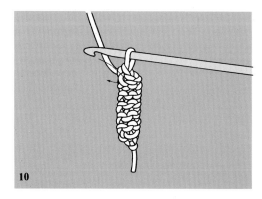

Round cords suitable for belts, curtain cords, etc., can be made in various thicknesses by working 5 or more chain stitches, closing the ring with a slip stitch and then working a slip stitch into each stitch (Fig 10) until the required length is reached. This type of cord can also be worked in several colors.

Twisted cord. Take a length of yarn about four times the length of cord required. Fold in half and fasten the folded end to a firm surface such as an ironing board, with a pin. Holding the other end of the two threads between thumb and forefinger twist them tightly until they begin to curl. Join the end you are holding to the folded end and allow the cord to twist

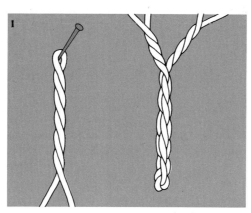

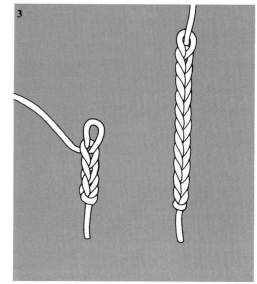

together of its own accord (Fig 1). Fasten both ends by knotting or by stitching if you intend to add a tassel or pompon.

Looped cord. Take a length of yarn eight times the length of cord required and fold it in half. At the fold make a slip knot with the forefinger of the right hand and a loop with the forefinger of the left hand (Fig 2). Slip the left loop into the right loop from front to back, pick up the loop again with the right forefinger and tighten it by pulling the left thread. Now make another loop on the left forefinger and slip it into the right loop (again from front to back). Pick up the loop with the left forefinger and tighten it by pulling the right thread.

Continue in the same way, alternating the loops from right to left, and always making a new loop on the thread that has just been tightened (Fig 3).

Simple braided cord. Take three lengths of yarn about twice the length of cord required. Knot the strands together at one end and fasten to a firm surface with a pin. Braid in the usual way and secure as described for Twisted cord (Fig 4).

Double braided cord. Take four lengths of yarn twice the length of the cord required. Knot all four strands together at one end and

fasten to a firm surface with a pin. Starting from the left we shall call them A, B, C and D. Pass A under B and C under D. Pass B over C and under D. * Pass D under C and over B. Pass B over C and under A. Pass A under C and over D. Pass D over C and under B. Pass B under C and over A. Pass A over C and under D *. Repeat from * to * for length of cord and fasten ends with a knot.

Embroidery on crochet

Embroidery can look very effective when worked on a plain crocheted background. A round-ended tapestry needle is ideal for this type of work and it is usual to use the same type of thread as for the article itself in either the same or a contrasting color.

Simple designs tend to be the most effective and any of the classic embroidery stitches can

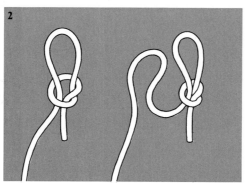

be used. The stitches described in this section are those most commonly used to work simple decorative motifs on crocheted articles.

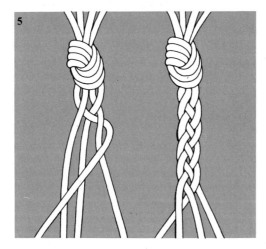

Knot stitch motifs. Knot stitch motifs are highly decorative and can be worked with contrasting yarns which stand out against crocheted backgrounds. A pattern of small flowers, worked as follows, is one of the most popular designs. Bring the needle from the wrong side to the right side of the work where the center of the flower will be; pull the thread through. Put the needle back through the work very close to the center and bring it out where the tip of the first petal will be. Wind the thread several times around the needle, then insert the needle at the central point again, bringing it out where the tip of the second petal will be; wind the thread around again, pass the needle through the center and so on, until all the petals have been worked.

Finish off the thread on the wrong side of the work, at the center of the flower, with several small stitches.

Running-stitch. Running-stitch can be worked on double crochet or on a mesh of filet crochet. Unless you want a textured effect, use the same type of thread as for the article itself. The stitch is worked from right to left, passing the needle under alternate trebles or vertical mesh stitches as though darning (Fig 7).

Overcast stitch on double crochet. This produces a corded effect and can be worked in several colors. The stitch is worked as follows: bring the needle through from the back to the front of the work at the base of the first double crochet that you wish to cover. Take several overcasting stitches around the double crochet bar, as shown in Fig 1, pulling the thread tightly on each stitch. Having covered the first

stitch from bottom to top, work in a similar way over the next stitch starting from the top and working downwards.

Embroidered chain stitch. Rows of chain stitch are usually worked as a border on a piece of crochet worked in a close-textured stitch such

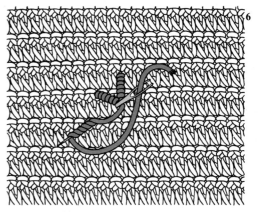

as single crochet. Embroidered chain stitch is worked as follows. Bring the needle through to the right side of the work. Holding the thread under the left thumb, take a vertical stitch, inserting the needle exactly where the thread was brought from the back of the work and bringing it out on the right side 1 row below. Keeping the loop under the needle, draw the thread through. Again holding the thread in position with the left thumb, insert the needle

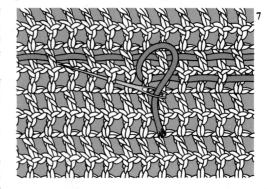

into the center of the loop formed by the previous stitch and bring it out on the right side, 1 row below, drawing the thread through.

Continue in this way, taking care to keep the stitches of uniform length and perfectly in line (Fig 2). Rows of small, even stitches will be formed at the back of the work.

Cross-stitch. Cross-stitch in contrasting colors can be used to emphasize a striped pattern if it is worked between bands of one background

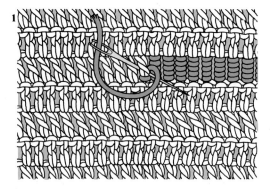

Beads and sequins

Attractive effects can be achieved by incorporating beads or sequins into crochet garments. Evening-wear is an obvious candidate for sparkling sequined motifs. The addition of these trimmings is not difficult but a certain amount of time and patience is required for the preliminary stage of threading the beads or sequins on to each ball of yarn. The yarn therefore has to be rewound into balls before the work can begin.

color and another or it can be used to create decorative motifs on a single-color background. Cross-stitch may be vertical or horizontal but whichever way it is worked, the stitches must be uniform.

Vertical cross-stitch is usually worked downwards and each stitch in the row is completed before the next is started. Bring the thread through to the front of the work. Insert the needle from top to bottom so that the thread makes a sloping stitch from left to right and then insert the needle so that a second sloping stitch from right to left is made over the first. This completes one cross-stitch (Fig 3). Vertical cross-stitch can also be worked upwards; the same method is used except that the first sloping stitch is worked from right to left and the second from left to right.

Horizontal cross-stitch is worked in two stages consisting of one row of half-stitches and a return row of half-stitches sloping in the other direction. The first row is worked from left to right, inserting the needle from top to bottom to make the stitches slope from left to

Threading beads or sequins on to the yarn. Take a length of sewing thread and insert both ends through the eye of a fine needle. Pass the end of the working yarn through the loop of sewing thread and fold it over, as shown in Fig 5. By threading the beads and sequins on to the needle they will thus slide easily on to the working yarn.

The number of beads or sequins required in the pattern should all be threaded on to the yarn before you begin to crochet to avoid

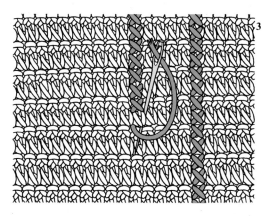

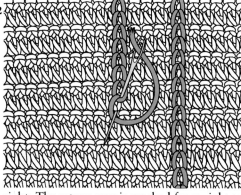

right. The return row is worked from right to left, inserting the needle from top to bottom to make the stitches slope from right to left, thus completing the crosses (Fig 4).

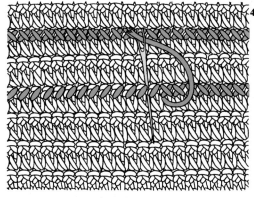

having to break the yarn in order to thread the next bead on to it. When working parts of the pattern where the beads are not required, simply work normally in your chosen stitch, slipping the beads or sequins along the yarn.

Incorporating beads or sequins into the work.
If you are working in single crochet, proceed as follows: Insert crochet hook into top of stitch in previous row, yarn over and draw loop through; slide the bead or sequin up to the stitch being worked, yarn over and draw loop through both stitches on hook so that the bead or sequin is anchored above the stitch of the previous row (Fig 6).

If you are working in double crochet, proceed as follows: Yarn over, insert hook into stitch in previous row, yarn over, draw loop through; slide the bead or sequin up to the stitch being worked, yarn over and draw through two loops, yarn over and draw through the last two loops on hook (Fig 7).

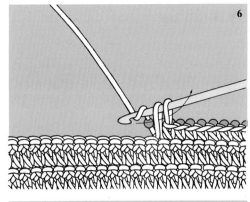

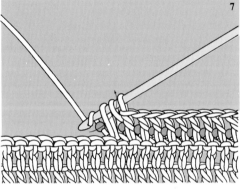

Crocheting with beads and sequins

5. threading beads on to the thread
6. incorporating beads into single crochet
7. incorporating beads into double crochet

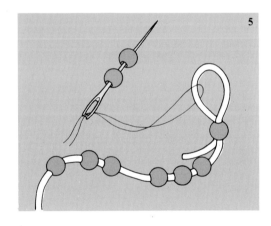

Making up

Making up includes all the finishing that has to be done when a piece of crochet has been completed. In the case of tablecloths and centerpieces this usually only involves blocking and pressing, whereas in the case of garments it is more complicated since the separate pieces have to be pressed and joined, and finishing touches such as zippers, buttons or patch pockets may have to be added.

Since it is the blocking and pressing of a piece of crochet that determines its final size and shape, it is often possible to correct any minor irregularities in the work at this stage.

The importance of making up should not be underestimated, since it can make or mar the final result. It should therefore be carried out with the same care and attention you would use when dressmaking.

Pressing pieces of crochet

Before pressing a piece of crochet it should be pinned into shape, wrong side up, on a padded, flat surface large enough to accommodate the whole piece of crochet. This is known as blocking. Check the garment measurements with a tape measure to ensure that they correspond to those given in the pattern, holding or gently stretching an edge if it is slightly too long or too short.

The type of yarn and stitches used should be taken into account when pressing a piece of crochet. Yarns such as cotton and linen should be pressed with a hot iron, wool should be steamed under a damp cloth, while synthetics require a cool iron or should not be pressed at all. Instructions for the pressing of a particular yarn are generally given on the label and should be followed scrupulously.

Certain types of crochet stitches, for example raised stitches and open work crochet, require special care. Avoid applying pressure on the raised parts of a pattern and press only the flat parts very carefully, using the point of the iron. Particularly delicate pieces of crochet, made with a fine thread in a very open design, should be starched or stiffened (see page 156) before being pressed. This will make them more hard-wearing, give them more body and help them keep their shape better.

Whether a damp cloth is used or not, only light pressure should be applied when pressing crochet: allow the iron to rest for a moment in one place on the piece and then lift it up but never move it as when ironing.

After pressing, each piece should be allowed to cool before the pins are removed. If a damp cloth has been used, this should now be dry.

Crocheted articles made in yarns that must not be pressed can be pinned into shape and left for some time under a damp cloth until completely dry.

Sewing pieces of crochet together

When making a garment or an article such as a rug or tablecloth made up of individual medallions the pieces should be sewn together by one of the methods described on page 147 once they have been pressed.

When making up garments it is advisable to sew the shoulders together first, followed by the sides and the sleeves. It is important that long seams should be matched row for row. Next, mark the center of the top of both sleeves

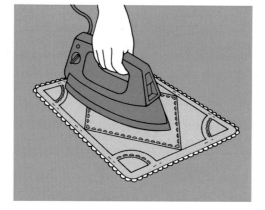

The final stage in the making of a crocheted garment is pressing and sewing up the separate pieces. Right: the correct way to press a piece of crochet.

and pin to shoulder seam; set each sleeve into position in the armholes, pinning and basting before backstitching.

Medallions are joined by pinning them right sides together, and sewing or crocheting them together with one of the stitches described below. Depending on the effect you wish to achieve the join can be invisible or it can be worked in a contrasting color. For example a very dark or black thread could be used to join the brightly colored medallions of a "patchwork" bedcover.

Backstitching. This is by far the most common method of sewing pieces of crochet together and gives one of the strongest seams. It is particularly suitable for the shoulder, sleeve and side seams of a garment. A blunt-ended needle should be used to avoid splitting the thread. If a blunt-ended needle is not available, use an ordinary needle and sew with the eye rather than the point.

Backstitch is worked as follows: Place the two pieces to be sewn right sides together, making sure that the ends meet perfectly; pin both ends together. Start sewing from the right, inserting the needle from front to back and then from back to front in the next stitch to the left. Pass the needle from front to back again at the point where you began, and bring it out two stitches to the left. Subsequent stitches are made from front to back at the end of the preceding stitch and from back to front through the next stitch to the left. Fasten off the thread.

While sewing the thread should not be pulled so that the stitches are tight, as this can pull the piece of crochet out of shape.

Sewing the pieces together
Right: backstitching
Far right: above, overcasting; below, a woven seam.

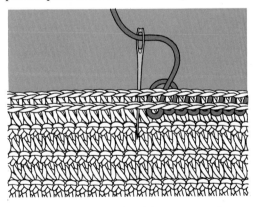

On the wrong side this seam makes a straight line; if done well it is very strong and is invisible on the right side of the work.

Backstitch can also be used to reduce the size of the pieces of a garment at the seams, if they are too big. To hold the crocheted fabric, work

the seam not more than 1 cm ($\frac{1}{2}$ in) away from the edge and pull the stitches tighter than when sewing an ordinary seam.

Overcasting or whipstitching. This is especially suitable for borders, relief stitches, and thick, bulky yarns.

Place the two pieces to be sewn right sides together with ends matching; pin both ends together. Work in a close overcast stitch without pulling the stitches too tight, as follows: Insert the needle at the back of the work and bring it through to the front. Work from right to left and make sure the two pieces match exactly.

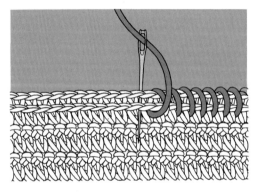

This seam is strong and will not lose its shape; on the wrong side it creates a corded effect.

Woven seam. This type of seam is particularly suitable for joining pieces crocheted in very fine yarns and for baby clothes. Proceed as follows: Lay the pieces to be joined side-by-side on a flat surface, wrong side up, matching rows where possible. Keeping the thread fairly loose, insert the needle into the first stitch farthest from you on the right, bringing it out through the matching stitch on the left. Work as shown in the illustration.

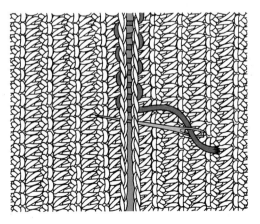

Joining pieces of crochet with a crochet hook

A crochet hook can be used instead of a needle to join pieces of crochet. The following are two of the most common methods.

Seam in single crochet. Put the two pieces to be joined with right sides together, insert the crochet hook from the front through edge stitches of both pieces, yarn over and draw yarn through, work 1 sc, insert hook into next stitch and work another sc. Continue in this way to end of seam. Cut thread and finish off neatly on wrong side of work.

Seam in slip stitch. This seam can either be worked on the outside, holding the pieces to be joined wrong sides together, if you wish to make a feature of it, or it can be worked as an invisible seam on the inside, holding the pieces to be joined right side together.

The seam is worked as follows: Insert the crochet hook from the front through edge stitches of both pieces, yarn over, draw yarn through and draw through loop on hook to complete slip stitch. Continue in this way to end of seam. Cut thread and finish off.

Joining the pieces with a crochet hook Right: above, a seam worked in single crochet; below, a seam worked in slip stitch.

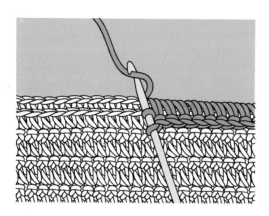

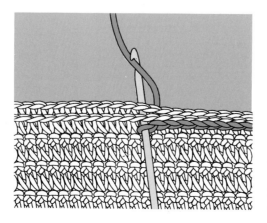

Putting in a zipper

One of the most convenient methods of fastening crocheted garments is a zipper. This is frequently used instead of loops or buttons, particularly on skirts, but also on sweaters, cardigans and jackets. Zippers which are closed at one end are used for skirts, the neck openings of sweaters etc; open-ended zippers which have a clasp at the bottom are used for jackets and cardigans.

A normal dressmaker's zipper is suitable for most types of crocheted garment. The heavier, stronger zippers (usually the ones that open at the bottom) are used for garments worked in thick yarn and for sportswear. Carefully measure the length of the opening and when you have decided on the type of zipper to use and found the color to match the garment, insure that the zipper is the same length as the opening (only the metal part of the zipper counts, not the extra tape at the bottom). If the zipper is too short the seam will pucker, if it is too long the edges of the opening will stretch.

A zipper is inserted as follows: Fit the zipper into the opening on the wrong side of the work and pin it into place on the right side. The teeth

148

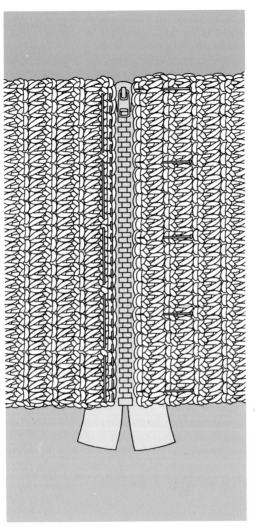

up the other side in the same way as the first.

To finish off on the wrong side, fold the tops of the tape back and stitch them to the edge of the work so that they do not get in the way of the zipper. Using appropriately colored thread, overcast (see page 147) around the edge including the folded ends. The zipper must open and close with ease. If the zipper catches it may be because the stitches have been worked too near the teeth.

How to sew on reinforcing tape

To strengthen the edges of cardigans and jackets, particularly where there are buttons and buttonholes, a grosgrain ribbon can be stitched on the inside.

Turn the ends of the grosgrain in and pin the ribbon along the length of the inside edge, taking care that no ribbon can be seen from the outside, and insuring that you do not distort the tension of the crochet.

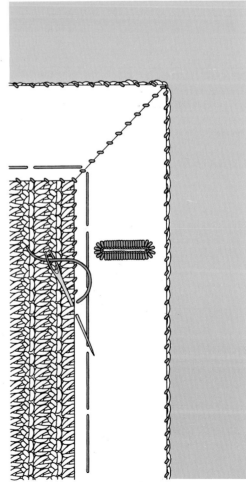

of the zipper should be just level with the edges of the opening; when the zipper is closed the edges should meet exactly. Baste on the right side of the work and remove the pins; open the zipper and stitch it in using an embroidery needle and thread the same color as the tape. With the thread on the wrong side of the work at the top right-hand corner stitch as close to the crocheted edge as possible in the following way: Pull the thread through the work, then pull it through to the back again slightly to the right, then forward again about 5mm ($\frac{1}{4}$ in) to the left of the preceding stitch, then through to the back and so on.

The stitches will be invisible on the right side of the work because the fine thread disappears into the crocheted fabric. On the wrong side long stitches similar to machine stitching will be visible on the tape.

When one side has been stitched, if the zipper is closed at the bottom, fasten the tape at the base with a couple of stitches, then sew

Stitch the ribbon in place with the appropriate colored thread using the same stitch as that described for inserting zippers. Having stitched all around the outside edge, mark the buttonholes with pins corresponding to the holes in the crochet; if no buttonholes have yet been made, position them at regular intervals. Make a slit in the ribbon and stitch around with buttonhole stitch as follows: Pass the needle from front to back just below the edge of the buttonhole, coming out on the wrong side; pass the needle through from front to back once again, passing the thread under the tip of the needle from left to right, and tighten the thread gently, so that the stitches lie flat.

If the grosgrain has to go around a corner, first sew the outer edge, then fold the ribbon at an angle and fasten it before stitching the inside edge.

Patching

A popular way of reinforcing the areas that get the most wear (elbows, knees etc.) or of hiding a hole is to sew on patches. Leather or suede patches can be purchased; decorative fabric patches can be made at home, to match the garment or to contrast with it. Bought patches come in various sizes, for children or adults, and they generally have little holes punched

around the edge to make sewing them on easier.

A patch is applied as follows: Pin it on to the garment, putting pins through the center as well as around the edge; take care neither to stretch it, nor to put it on too loosely. With a needle and thread of the right color begin sewing on the right side with the same stitch as used for sewing in zippers (see page 149), stitching through every hole to form a continuous line of stitching round the patch. If the patch is made of fabric use the following method: Fold in a border of 5 mm (¼ in) on the inside and baste. Pin the patch in place and stitch it on with buttonhole stitch (see above). If patching elbows, the second patch should be sewn on in the same way as the first, care being taken to make it perfectly symmetrical.

Inserting elastic with herringbone stitch

A convenient way of finishing the waist of a skirt is to stitch elastic on the inside. The elastic should be at least 2 cm (1 in) wide. It is inserted as follows: Establish the desired waist measurement of the skirt and cut the elastic to that length, allowing 2 cm (1 in) extra for the seam. Overlap the two ends and overcast them (see page 147).

Divide the elastic into five equal parts, marking each one with a pin. Turn the skirt inside out and divide the waist into five equal parts. Matching pins, baste the elastic into place and remove the pins.

Work around the waist in herringbone stitch as follows: Using a wool needle and the yarn used for the skirt secure the yarn above the elastic at a side seam. Working from left to right, bring the thread diagonally down across the elastic and take a horizontal stitch from

Patching

Right: above, applying a leather or suede patch; below, applying a fabric patch. Far right: finishing a waistband with elastic by working a herringbone casing so that the elastic moves freely.

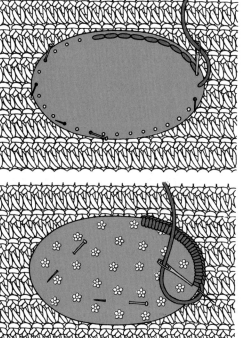

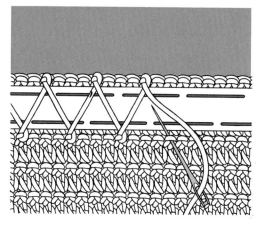

right to left below the lower edge of the elastic through two stitches of the garment but not through the elastic. Continue in the same way moving diagonally from top to bottom and bottom to top right around the waist; the elastic is thus able to move freely inside the herringbone stitch. Alternatively it can be fastened to the skirt by taking in a bit of the edge of the elastic on each horizontal stitch.

Making loops for belts

When a crocheted garment has a separate belt it is a good idea to make loops on the side seams of the garment.

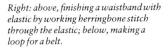

Right: above, finishing a waistband with elastic by working herringbone stitch through the elastic; below, making a loop for a belt.

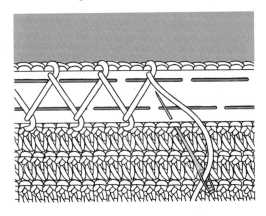

Loops for belts can be crocheted, using the same stitch as for the garment, and then sewn on, or they can be sewn with matching thread directly on to the garment. Stitched loops are made in the following way: Secure the thread at the back of the work where the belt is to be and bring the needle through to the front. Make four or five loose vertical stitches, slightly longer than the width of the belt. Beginning at one end cover these stitches closely with buttonhole stitch (see page 150).

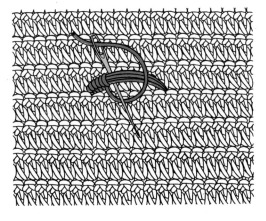

Household linen and furnishings

The patterns section of this book gives several examples of how crochet can be used for decorative household items such as tablecloths, bedspreads or curtains. Obviously skill, patience and time are necessary to make such large articles which may seem daunting to any but the most experienced crocheter. Bear in mind, however, that although the designs are often complicated, those consisting of separate medallions are relatively simple to work, and indeed to make up for yourself.

This section gives guidelines on how to take measurements for household linen and furnishings which will be useful for readers who wish to design their own patterns or adapt an existing one. It thus complements the section on pages 21–24 which explains how to adapt a garment pattern.

1. *taking the measurements for a circular tablecloth*
2. *taking measurements for a rectangular tablecloth*
3. *taking the measurements for a bedspread*

1

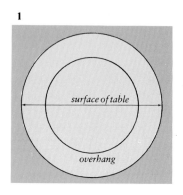

2

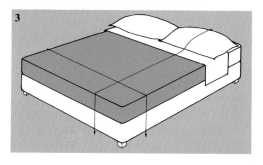

Taking measurements for a round tablecloth

If you wish to make a round tablecloth to fit a specific table, the most important thing to decide is how much the cloth should hang down over the edge of the table. The overhang may be only a few inches deep or the cloth may be floor length. The diameter of the finished tablecloth will be the diameter of the table top plus twice the depth of the overhang (Fig 1).

Having established the overall size of the cloth, work out how many pattern repeats are necessary by making a sample of the motif to be repeated. If the pattern consists of equal-sized motifs, you need only work 1 motif and measure its diameter. If, however, it is made up of concentric circles of different motifs, you must establish the width of each circle by working one of each different motif and measuring each diameter.

Once you know how many motifs are needed to make the desired size of tablecloth, you can work out how much yarn you will need by seeing how many motifs you can make with 1 ball and then dividing this into the total

3

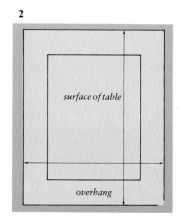

number of motifs to give you the total number of balls.

Taking measurements for a square or rectangular cloth

Exactly the same procedure is carried out as for a round tablecloth. The length of the finished cloth will be the length of the table for which it is intended plus twice the depth of the overhang; the width will be the width of the table plus twice the depth of the overhang.

Because square tablecloths tend to be made up of strips consisting of an equal number of motifs, rather than of concentric circles as in the case of round tablecloths, it is easier to calculate the number required.

Mattress	Measurements in centimeters	Measurements in inches
Single bed	90 × 190	35 × 75
Large single bed	100 × 200	40 × 79
Double bed	150 × 200	59 × 79
Large double bed	180 × 200	71 × 79

If you are not making a cloth to fit a specific table, you can of course join the motifs together, starting at one corner, as you work them and simply continue for as long as you wish or until you run out of yarn.

Taking measurements for a bedspread

Most crocheted bedspreads are not fitted but are rectangular throw-overs that must be large enough to cover the bed and fall to within one or two inches of the floor on three sides.

Either measure an existing bedspread which is the correct size or the bed itself, including the bedding which the bedspread will cover.

If the bedspread is to be tucked under the pillow, an extra 30 cm (12 ins) or so should be added to the length. If neither of these options is possible or if the bedspread is not being made for a particular bed, the table above gives approximate sizes for standard mattresses.

The overhang must then be added to these measurements. Since this varies a great deal depending on the type of bed and mattress, it is wise to check the exact measurement.

Taking measurements for curtains

Crocheted curtains are most effective when worked in filet crochet or another openwork stitch. They make an attractive alternative to net curtains since they let in the light while adding privacy to a room. An example is given on page 85, but since you will need to adapt any curtain pattern to fit a specific window, some guidelines are given below on how to calculate the width and length of curtains.

The length of any curtain is determined by several factors: the type of window for which the curtains are intended, the style of curtain and the type of curtain rod.

Figures 4, 5, 6 and 7 show the main styles of curtains. Curtains which fall below the sill or

full-length curtains are better made in fabric than in crochet. Half curtains, which usually hang from a rod placed half-way up the window, are only suitable for inward-opening windows, or sash windows if the lower part is never opened. Sill-length curtains should fall to within about 2 cm ($\frac{3}{4}$ in) of the window-sill. Half curtains normally fall to within 2 cm ($\frac{3}{4}$ in) of the window frame.

When measuring the length of curtains bear in mind that if they are to hang from a conventional metal or plastic rod with runners, this is designed to be hidden by the fabric, so you must measure from the top of the rod; if they are to hang from a decorative rod with rings, measure from immediately below the rings.

Openwork crocheted curtains are often hung from a brass rod or wire inserted under alternate stitches or through a hem at the top of the curtains, especially if they are not intended to be opened or closed. If this is the case, the curtains need not be gathered and the width is therefore easy to calculate: each curtain should be made a few inches wider than the curtain rod so that it hangs well and is not taut. If there is a pair of curtains, calculate the width on the basis of half the length of the rod.

Curtains which are designed to be opened and closed should be one and a half times the length of the rod if worked in a very thick yarn, or two-three times the length of the rod if thinner and lighter.

Styles of curtains

4. sill-length curtains
5. curtains below the sill
6. full-length curtains
7. half-curtains

Some useful tips

It is a truism to say that practice makes perfect, but this is definitely the case with crochet. Hopefully this book has provided a sound basis for anyone wishing to learn to crochet, but as you gain experience you will discover "tricks of the trade" which will improve your work. It is difficult to pass on this type of practical experience through a text-book, but this section gives some hints and suggestions which the author has found useful.

• When you have decided the type and color of yarn that you need for whatever you want to make, buy one or two extra balls or skeins. These will prove useful if the article becomes worn or is torn, or in the case of a dress or skirt, if fashion dictates longer skirks, the garment's life can be extended. It would be almost impossible to find the same dye number, at a later date, even if the same type of yarn were still available. Always remember to wash the spare yarn when the garment is washed to allow for slight fading.

• When crocheting, it is best to work with the thread from the center of the ball of yarn. It is easy to find the end if the ball is not wound too tightly: Press your forefinger and thumb into the middle of the ball and draw out some of the yarn. Locate the end, untangle the yarn if necessary and start work. You will find that you do not have to stop crocheting to unwind the yarn and the ball will not roll about on the floor. The same effect is achieved by using a wool-holder as described on page 11.

• When working an inset pocket in a garment that is worked in a thick yarn, it is a good idea to work the pocket lining in a finer yarn and with a finer crochet hook than is used for the main garment. Obviously a few extra stitches will have to be worked when making the foundation chain to ensure that the width of the lining is equal to the width of the opening. Work in the finer yarn to within about 2 cm ($\frac{3}{4}$ in) of the top of the pocket lining, change to the thicker yarn and hook and decrease the extra stitches on each side. The advantage of making the lining in a thinner yarn is that the pocket will lie flatter and be less bulky.

• The finish of buttonholes can be greatly improved by working a border of buttonhole stitch around each one, using matching embroidery thread.

• An attractive way of lengthening children's clothes when they become outgrown is to work a crochet border around the cuffs and along the hem with some extra yarn. Alternatively, if you are an experienced crocheter, you can invert the pattern and work a garment from the top downwards so that a few extra rows can be added at the bottom at a future date, unravelling and reworking the border if there is one.

• Avoid making too many joins in the same piece of crochet. The method for working in a new thread is described on page 135. On no account should you use a knot.

• If you wish to work out whether you have enough yarn to finish a particular piece, the length of yarn required for each row will be approximately 2–4 times the length of the row in centimeters, depending on the stitch being worked.

• Crochet garments worked in cotton in a close-textured stitch stretch less than those worked in wool in a loose, open-work stitch, but since any crocheted garment tends to lose its shape where it is tightest it is advisable to line skirts and to line trousers to knee-level. When cutting out a lining bear in mind that it must be wider than the garment for which it is intended so that the crocheted fabric is not taut and can retain its elasticity, and that it should be a little shorter than the garment so that it does not show below the hem. For example, the lining for a crocheted skirt should be 3–4 cm (1¼–1½ ins) shorter than the skirt itself.

• Another way to help a crocheted garment keep its shape is to sew a piece of tape into the shoulder seams and the neck of jackets and coats. A loop can then be sewn on to the neck-tape so that the garment can be hung up, but this should be avoided as much as possible. Crocheted garments should always be stored flat to prevent stretching.

• Another piece of useful advice, when the application of buttons or the insertion of a zip presents a problem, is to use one of the "touch-and-close" types of tape instead. These tapes have the added advantage of not being damaged by washing or dry-cleaning.

Washing crocheted articles

Crocheted articles should be washed carefully by hand, not by machine, following the washing instructions given on the ball band of the yarn. An explanation of the international symbols used is given below. If there are no washing instructions on the label or if you want to wash an old piece of crochet, the following guidelines will be useful.

When washing colored cottons for the first time, a color-fast test should always be made. This is done as follows: Immerse a piece of the yarn used to make the article in hot water, fold it in a piece of white cloth and squeeze well; if any color remains on the cloth, the article will either have to be dry-cleaned or very carefully washed in cold water. If no color is left on the cloth, the article can be washed in hot water, squeezed to remove as much water as possible and then laid flat on a sheet or towel to dry. Linen can be treated in the same way, providing that it is shrink resistant. If you are in doubt about this, it is better to have the article dry-cleaned.

Delicate articles made in wool should be washed by hand in lukewarm water with a neutral soap or special detergent for delicate items. Immerse the article for a minute or two

 How the article should be washed

 Whether the article can be bleached

 Whether the article can be ironed

 Whether the article should be dry-cleaned

in the suds, remove and rinse, also in lukewarm water, until all trace of soap or detergent has gone. The best method of drying woolen articles is to wrap them in a thick towel, as this will absorb a great deal of water, spread them out into shape on a flat surface, and leave to dry.

Articles crocheted in a synthetic yarn must be washed according to the composition of the yarn. Nylon, polyester or rayon can be washed in lukewarm water with neutral soap and hung up to dry. With all other synthetics it is better to have the garment dry-cleaned.

Caring for delicate crochet-work

Delicate crochet-work, such as centerpieces, crochet lace and insertions, requires special treatment.

Centerpieces, crochet lace and insertions worked in fairly thick yarn can be immersed in lukewarm water and neutral soapflakes but do not rub or wring them. Rinse well, first in lukewarm water and then in cold.

Some cottons can be lightly bleached to remove the more obstinate marks. It is advisable, however, to test the yarn for its bleach tolerance as follows: Immerse a piece of the yarn used to make the article in diluted bleach, fold the yarn in a piece of white cloth, squeeze well and check that no color is left on the cloth. If this is the case, the whole garment can be bleached using a solution of 1 dessertspoonful of bleach to 1 liter (2 pints) of cold water, leaving it to soak for a few minutes, and then rinsing it in cold water.

Small articles edged with very delicate crochet lace should be treated as follows: half fill a bottle with sand or water and wrap it in a clean white cloth. With a needle and thread attach the item to be washed with a few stitches and then cover the whole bottle with a piece of muslin or white linen, securing it firmly with a few stitches. Immerse the bottle in cold water with some neutral soap, bring to the boil and allow to boil for one hour. Repeat if any marks are particularly obstinate. When the article is clean, rinse well in cold water before detaching it from the bottle.

If the crochet lace is very old and fragile, leave it to soak in best quality olive oil for 24 hours before washing to restore some elasticity to the yarn. After washing and rinsing, centerpieces, lace and insertions should be spread out into shape and left to dry on a flat surface.

To ensure that cotton articles retain their crispness and shape it is a good idea to starch or stiffen them slightly before pressing. The best type of starch is made from pure wheat, but many different kinds are available commercially which are quick and easy to prepare, so it is best to follow the manufacturer's instructions. Dip the article several times into the prepared starch, then leave it wrapped in a cloth for an hour before pressing it. If the item to be starched is particularly fragile, dab the starch solution on gently. There is also the even simpler alternative of spraying the piece of crochet with spray-starch before pressing. This will give a slightly softer finish than traditional starch.

An old-fashioned but effective substitute for starch is a sugar and water solution. Make a syrup with plenty of sugar; when all the sugar has dissolved, leave to cool and immerse the article in the solution until it is saturated. Spread out into shape on a flat surface as described below and leave to dry.

As when making up crocheted garments, centerpieces of crochet lace need to be blocked before being pressed. Since they can easily be distorted, you should first make an accurate drawing of the geometrical shape of the piece, using a ruler, compass and set-square if necessary, on a large sheet of paper. Attach the sheet of paper to a wooden board on your ironing board and pin the wet piece of crochet out to fit the outline, with rustproof pins,

insuring that every point or picot on the outer edge is held in place. Now leave it to dry. When the article is completely dry, remove the pins and press carefully with a medium-hot iron. The finished result should be crisp, with all the intricacies of the delicate work clearly visible.

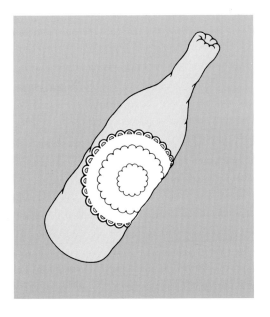

Far right: how to wash a small, delicate centerpiece

156

Glossary

Asterisk. An important symbol used in crochet patterns indicating the pattern repeat. The instructions between two asterisks are repeated over the main part of a row or round. The instructions outside the asterisks indicate how to begin and end a row or round.

Chain loop. One or more chain stitches joining two motifs in open-work crochet. The instruction "work... into the ch-... loop" means that the crochet hook is to be inserted in the space below the chain stitches when working the stitches indicated.

Decrease. This indicates that the number of stitches worked during a row or round is to be reduced by skipping a given number of stitches.

Draw yarn through. One of the basic steps performed when working any crochet stitch. It consists of bringing the crochet hook with the yarn looped around it back through one or more stitches already on the hook, leaving one loop on the hook ready to work the next stitch.

Eyelet holes. A row of openwork crochet through which a ribbon or cord may be threaded to gather or decorate a garment.

Foundation chain. A length of chain into which the stitches of the first row or round are worked.

Gauge. The gauge of a piece of crochet depends on how tightly you hold the yarn as you crochet, the thickness of the yarn and the size of the crochet hook. The gauge determines the texture and elasticity of a piece of crochet and it also affects the size of the finished work. It is important to establish your individual gauge by working a sample to see how the measurements of the finished garment will be affected. It is easier to use a smaller or larger crochet hook if necessary than to try to change the way in which you hold the yarn.

Increase. This indicates that a certain number of stitches are to be added during the working of a row or round to enlarge the work.

Medallion. A geometrical shape worked in crochet. Several medallions are often joined together to produce a patchwork effect or to make large articles such as rugs, bedcovers etc. A medallion is usually worked in the round, starting from the center.

Motif. A group or combination of stitches forming a distinctive shape that is repeated as part of the complete pattern.

Parentheses. Instructions within parentheses are to be repeated the number of times stated. Parentheses are often used in conjunction with asterisks to indicate a group of stitches repeated within the main pattern repeat.

Picot. Small decorative loop consisting of three or more chain stitches joined by working a slip stitch into the first chain.

Ring. The foundation chain for crochet worked in the round, made by working a length of chain and working 1 slip stitch into the first chain stitch.

Round. The equivalent of a row when working over a foundation chain joined into a ring. Rounds are worked continuously from right to left without turning the work. Each round is closed with a slip stitch into the top of the starting chain.

Row. Crochet can either be worked back and forth in rows or round and round. A row consists of all the stitches worked from right to left before turning the work.

Sample. A small piece of crochet made before starting the main work to check that your own gauge (the number of stitches and rows to one centimeter or inch) corresponds to that used in the pattern. A sample also enables you to check the amount of yarn you will require.

Standard. The patterns given in this book are graded according to the degree of expertise required by the crocheter. The simplest patterns are indicated by 1 star and the most complicated by 3 stars.

Starting chain. The equivalent of turning chain when working in the round.

Turning chain. The chain stitches worked at the beginning of a row to bring the hook level with the height of the next stitch. The turning chain of one row count as the first stitch of the next.

Yarn over (yo). One of the basic steps performed when working any crochet stitch. It consists of passing the crochet hook under the thread held over the left forefinger from front to back.

Index